AF252096

DIVINE LOVE
The Art of the Nativity

DIVINE LOVE
The Art of the Nativity

SARAH DRUMMOND

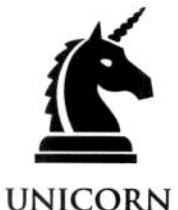

UNICORN

Published in 2021 by Unicorn, an imprint
of Unicorn Publishing Group LLP
5 Newburgh Street
London
W1F 7RG
www.unicornpublishing.org

ISBN 978-1-913491-86-4
10 9 8 7 6 5 4 3 2 1

Designed by Anna Hopwood/AH Design
Printed by Finetone Ltd

CONTENTS

INTRODUCTION

ALL FORMS OF LOVE EMANATE FROM THE DIVINE. All religions, all traditions, from every period and every culture tell us in innumerable and unfathomable ways that God is Love. In the Christian tradition, the supreme expression of Divine Love is the birth of Christ. 'For God so loved the world that He gave His only begotten Son, that whosoever believeth in Him, should not perish but have everlasting life' (John 3:16).

The feast of Christmas is embedded in our earliest childhood memories: a crescendo of excitement leads up to the day following twenty-six days of preparation (austere and/or a glut of spending and cooking), the daily ritual of opening a window in the Advent Calendar. A tree laden with decorations, log fires, stockings hung at the end of the bed. Lights, presents, family gatherings: a time for celebration and feasting. Despite the secularisation of this sacred event, the magic of Christmas still resonates.

The birth of Christ lies at the heart of the Christian mystery. The Second Person of the Trinity appears on earth, born of the Virgin Mary, of God the Father, through the power of the Holy Spirit, born in order to redeem mankind. From a tender age we recognise Nativity images – the newborn Christ Child in a manger, Mary, Joseph, the ox and the ass, the shepherds, the Magi, the angels, the star. We are so familiar with the scene that we are in danger of failing to see, to wonder, to question and to ponder. Blind to allegory and symbol ('because there was no room for them in the inn') we forego the sense of the sacred. We forget that all Nativity scenes refer to rebirth in the spiritual sense and that the function of religion is to reveal higher mysteries. St Augustine's words resound: 'What does it avail me that this birth is always happening, if it does not happen in me?

The Christmas holiday is celebrated all over the world, and not only in Christendom.

The birth of Christ was originally celebrated on 6 January in conjunction with the feast of the Adoration of the Magi – the Epiphany

– and, significantly, the Baptism of Christ (in the river Jordan), considered as the 'pneumatic birth' of Jesus Christ. According to some scholars, the earliest known celebration of the feast was probably in Egypt, where it replaced a festival of Isis (another virgin birth). Here the Dionysiac miracle of changing water into wine was celebrated at the same time, which perhaps explains why Christ's first miracle at the wedding feast at Cana, changing water into wine, was included in the same feast on 6 January.

Christmas does not appear in the list of festivals given by the early Christian writers Irenaeus (*c*. 120 – *c*. 200) and Tertullian (*c*. 155–220), while Origen (*c*. 185 – *c*. 254) found fault with pagans for celebrating birthdays. However, the *Chronograph* of 354, compiled at the request of a wealthy Roman Christian, records that a Christmas celebration took place in Rome on 25 December in the year 336 (during the reign of the Emperor Constantine the Great). At some point in the middle of the fourth century the date of the feast to celebrate the Birth of the Saviour – effectively the date of Christ's birthday – was changed in Rome under Pope Liberius from 6 January to 25 December.

The date 25 December marked the winter solstice in the Julian calendar then in use. It is also of course precisely nine months after the vernal equinox, 25 March, the feast of the Annunciation. It was also when the Romans held festivities in honour of Sol Invictus, the sun god. The choice of the date inspired St Augustine (354–430) to include this in his Christmas sermon: 'Hence it is that He was born on the day which is the shortest of our earthly reckoning and from which subsequent days begin to increase in length … He, therefore, who bent low and lifted us up chose the shortest day, yet the one whence light begins to increase.'

The event of the Nativity is told in only two of the canonical Gospels: Matthew immediately follows the Birth of Christ by the description of the 'wise men from the east'. A fuller account is found in Luke (1:2–20), starting with the decree from Caesar Augustus, ending with the visit of the shepherds. The earliest and best known of the many apocryphal gospels, the *Protoevangelium Jacobi* (Gospel of James, *c*. 150), widely disseminated and popular throughout all areas of Christendom, acted as a much loved and much used source of inspiration for the Christian faithful as well as for artists and craftsmen. The events of the Nativity were expanded and embroidered in the re-telling. This oral tradition and transmission is a reminder that people did not read: they relied on the spoken word, on storytelling, and on images. 'Illiterate men can contemplate on the lines of a picture what they cannot learn by means of the written word', as Gregory the Great (540–604, Pope 590–604), famously said.

Sacred images, like words, are essentially a description of something other. Since the earliest times, there was an understanding that the literal events of scripture conceal a hidden, deeply mysterious meaning that could reveal spiritual realities that are imperceptible in the ordinary way. The painter-craftsman is concerned with portraying the events told of the Nativity, and the image is a doorway, a threshold, and a symbolic language that we can learn to decipher. The artist offers us a glimpse into another realm, provided we leave the literal and the anecdotal, and recall that hidden beyond this allegorical representation lies a sacred mystery. For the artist-creator of a Nativity scene the greatest challenge is to evoke the divinity as well as the humanity of the Christ Child.

Neither theology nor iconography remains static. Christianity's circumstances changed. In Eastern Christendom Nativity icons continued (then as now) to hold close to a pattern which includes all the elements of the Birth of Christ, using imagery from an ancient tradition to describe the place and the event that often refer to the inner world of man, rather than to external life – and the mystery is encountered in the present moment. In the Christian West from around the twelfth century onwards the iconography continued to evolve, and works of devotion and reflection, notably the thirteenth-century *Legenda aurea (Golden Legend)* and the mid-fourteenth-century *Meditationes Vitae Christi (Meditations on the Life of Christ)*, exerted a powerful influence.

Over the course of many years I have been looking at and reflecting on hundreds of images – paintings, illuminated manuscripts, mosaics, frescoes, stained glass, sculpture, metalwork, ivories – concerning the different aspects of the Nativity. Numerous questions continue to arise, some of which I have tried to examine and explore. Yet the inexhaustible mystery deepens.

What is the origin of the iconography that we see in images of the Nativity? What is the meaning that lies behind it? Why are the ox and the ass (almost) always present? Why is Joseph so often depicted as sitting apart, alone and isolated? Who are the women bathing the Child? Why is the Christ Child sometimes shown lying on the ground? What is the significance of the shepherds? Why do the Magi sometimes wear crowns? Why was the Adoration of the Magi considered vital to the earliest Christians as they began to explore ways and symbols to express the essence of their beliefs? How did the artist and craftsman face the summons of suggesting both Christ's divine nature and His human nature?

Chapter I follows the decree ordered by Caesar Augustus for a census (a rarely depicted event). Joseph's anguished doubts concerning Mary who is with child, and the revelation from the angel, are considered. Then the journey to Bethlehem, Mary sitting on the ass, sometimes accompanied by Joseph's son (whom we find in the *Protoevangelium Jacobi*).

Chapter II focuses on the ox and the ass: these beasts of burden appear in almost every carved, sculpted and painted Nativity scene from the start (in the earliest examples they are shown long before Mary accompanies her Son), and this is so despite the fact that the ox is never mentioned in Luke or Matthew. According to the prophets, the mythical beasts represent opposites, now united. Silently guarding and attending, they seem to be totally concentrated with protecting this precious new Life.

Chapter III looks at the symbolism of the cave, a secretive dark place, synonymous with both ignorance and hidden treasure. Mentioned by Luke, and in the apocryphal gospels, noted by pilgrims to Bethlehem from the earliest days of Christianity, the cave is always visible in Orthodox Nativity icons, but less often in Western Nativity scenes, where it gradually gives way to stables and huts shown in recognisably Europeanised settings.

The manger is examined in Chapter IV, first presented by Luke: 'And she brought forth her firstborn son, and wrapped him up in swaddling clothes, and laid him in a manger; because there was no room for them in the inn.' Artists soon explored ways to suggest the Eucharistic connotations and the sacrifice of the Mass, linking the manger-altar of Christ's birth with His death: the Saviour to be born and to die in order to redeem man from sin.

Then the midwives are discussed in Chapter V. Never mentioned by Luke or Matthew, they form an important episode in the telling of the Nativity in the *Protoevangelium*, not only to assist at the birth but to illustrate the Divine nature of the Virgin birth, through disbelief and miraculous healing. The midwives are often depicted cleansing the Christ Child, the bath a visual reminder of a baptismal font, an emphasis on purification.

Chapter VI explores the theme and the role of the shepherds: in some of the images of the Nativity on very early fourth-century sculpted sarcophagi a youthful shepherd appears beside the crib. We see shepherds paying homage, awake to the celestial influence, led to the manger in the stable or cave by the light of the angel. The Annunciation to the Shepherds often shares the Nativity scene, shown up a hill in the distant background. It is also a subject which is treated on its own.

Birgitta's vision of the Nativity is explained and explored in Chapter VII. Known in English as St Bridget of Sweden, the fourteenth-century mystic and founder of a religious order made a pilgrimage to Bethlehem, where she experienced a vision of the Nativity. The details of her witnessing the Virgin giving birth and placing the newborn Christ Child on the ground presented a revolutionary way to reflect on the scene. With astonishing speed artists all over Christian Europe were soon depicting this new iconography.

Chapter VIII reveals how Mary was first shown at the Nativity on fourth-century sarcophagi scenes with the Christ Child seated on her lap as the Magi approach in adoration. Mary appears in all her roles – as

Mother of Christ, as representing the Church, and as intercessor – and she always embodies spiritual force, exalted to the cosmic level. The Virgin is seen to be sensitive to the deepest meaning of motherhood and childhood. She personifies watchfulness, conscious of the mystery of the Incarnation.

Chapter IX takes the role of Joseph and questions his disbelief, his revelations and dreams, his difficulties and doubts. Yet he is shown steadfastly in the scene, quiet, humble, often supportive and attentive. Sometimes dressed in yellow robes, a colour representing the royal house of David, Joseph is also repeatedly shown in Nativity scenes as an isolated figure, pondering and puzzling.

Chapter X focuses on the role of the Magi, their search, the splendour and exoticism of the wise men from the east – probably the favourite Nativity episode for artists, offering a visual feast. The display of outer glory expresses sharp contrast to the poverty and simplicity of the Birth of Christ the Saviour Redeemer.

Like the Magi and the shepherds, our journey is fundamentally a search for truth. Along the way we meet false trails, dragons and difficulties, we take wrong turnings, suffer a sense of both loss and confusion. But this yearning for Divine Love that lies at the heart of the Nativity leads us on…

Not in entire forgetfulness
And not in utter nakedness
But trailing clouds of glory do we come
From God who is our home.*

Our yearning, our longing to experience this love, indeed to live this unconditional love, lies at the core of our being. Our human sense of separateness and isolation expresses our fundamental human need (often unrecognised and unacknowledged) to be reunited with the Source. In this light, the Nativity evokes the re-birth, offered to all humanity, of the spirit.

* William Wordsworth, *Intimations of Immortality* (1807).

THE GOSPEL OF MATTHEW
CHAPTER 2:1–12

WHEN JESUS THEREFORE WAS BORN IN BETHLEHEM of Juda, in the days of King Herod, behold, there came wise men from the east to Jerusalem,

Saying: Where is he that is born King of the Jews? For we have seen his star in the east and are come to adore him.

And King Herod hearing this was troubled, and all Jerusalem with him.

And assembling together all the chief priests and the scribes of the people, he inquired of them where Christ should be born.

But they said to him: In Bethlehem of Juda. For so it is written by the prophet:

And thou Bethlehem the land of Juda are not the least among the princes of Juda; for out of thee shall come forth the captain that shall rule my people Israel.

Then Herod, privately calling the wise men, learned diligently of them the time of the star which appeared to them;

And sending them into Bethlehem said: Go and diligently inquire after the child, and when you have found him bring me word again, that I also may come and adore him.

Who having heard the King went their way; and, behold, the star which they had seen in the east went before them until it came and stood over where the child was.

And seeing the star they rejoiced with exceeding great joy.

And entering into the house they found the child with Mary his mother. And falling down, they adored him. And, opening their treasures, they offered him gifts: gold, frankincense, and myrrh.

And having received an answer in sleep that they should not return to Herod, they went back another way into their country.

THE GOSPEL OF LUKE
CHAPTER 2:1–19

AND IT CAME TO PASS THAT IN THOSE DAYS there went out a decree from Caesar Augustus that the whole world should be enrolled. This enrolling was first made by Cyrinus, the governor of Syria.
And all went to be enrolled, every one into his own city.
And Joseph also went up from Galilee, out of the city of Nazareth, into Judea, to the city of David, which is called Bethlehem: because he was of the house and family of David.
To be enrolled with Mary his espoused wife, who was with child.
And it came to pass that when they were there her days were accomplished that she should be delivered.
And she brought forth her firstborn son and wrapped him up in swaddling clothes and laid him in a manger; because there was no room for them in the inn.
And there were in the same country shepherds watching and keeping the night-watches over their flock.
And, behold, an angel of the Lord stood by them and the brightness of God shone round about them; and they feared with a great fear.
And the angel said to them: Fear not; for, behold, I bring you good tidings of great joy that shall be to all the people.
For this day is born to you a Saviour, who is Christ the Lord, in the city of David.
And this shall be a sign unto you: You shall find the infant wrapped in swaddling clothes and laid in a manger.
And suddenly there was with the angel a multitude of the heavenly army, praising God and saying:
Glory to God in the highest; and on earth peace to men of good will.
And it came to pass, after the angels departed from them into heaven, the shepherds said to one another: Let us go over to Bethlehem and let us see this word that is come to pass, which the Lord hath showed to us.
And they came with haste; and they found Mary and Joseph, and the infant lying in the manger. And seeing, they understood of the word that had been spoken to them concerning this child.
And all that heard wondered; and at those things that were told them by the shepherds.
But Mary kept all these words, pondering them in her heart.
And the shepherds returned, glorifying and praising God for all the things they had heard and seen, as it was told unto them.

From the Douay-Rheims Bible, New Testament, 1582

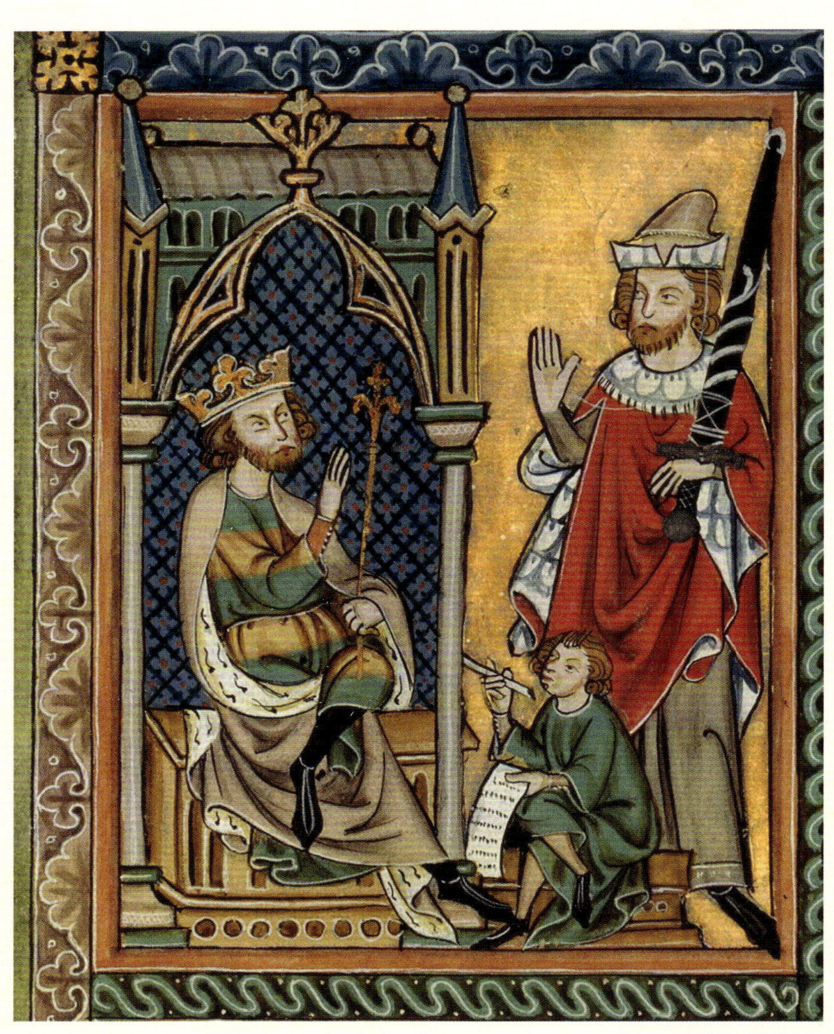

I JOSEPH'S DOUBT, HIS DREAM, THE JOURNEY TO BETHLEHEM

ALL VERSIONS OF THE GOSPELS (canonical and apocryphal) tell us that Jesus was born at Bethlehem. Luke begins his telling of the Nativity like this:

And it came to pass in those days, that there went out a decree from Caesar Augustus, that all the world should be taxed. And this taxing was first made when Cyrenius was Governor of Syria. And Joseph also went up from Galilee, out of the city of Nazareth, into Judea, unto the city of David, which is called Bethlehem (because he was of the house and lineage of David), to be taxed with Mary, his espoused wife who was great with child. (Luke 2:1–5).

In the *Plenarium* of Otto the Mild (a collection of sacred texts assembled *c.* 1330) the enthroned and crowned Caesar Augustus gives orders for the decree, and instructs the Governor, shown assertively holding his sword and accompanied by his scribe, to carry out the census [FIG. 1A]. We are then shown Joseph (wearing a Jewish hat) and Mary, sitting on a donkey, setting off for Bethlehem [FIG. 1B].

The fourteenth-century mosaics in the narthex of the Church of the Holy Saviour in Chora in Istanbul (also known as the Kariye Camii) show the event of the decree [FIG. 2]:[i] Cyrenius, Governor of Syria, wearing the impressive Roman headdress of the period and holding a scroll, symbol of authority, supervises the enrolment decreed by Caesar Augustus. Mary stands in front of a tower-like building, holding her mantle as though protectively shielding her unborn child, and Joseph (who is barefoot) stands behind her, accompanied by his sons (see below). In the centre a scribe unfurls the scroll on which he writes the names, overseen by a finely dressed guard who grasps a sheathed sword. Above, the inscription reads (in Greek, here translated): 'Mother of God … because he was of the house and lineage of David … to be taxed with Mary his espoused wife, being great with child.'

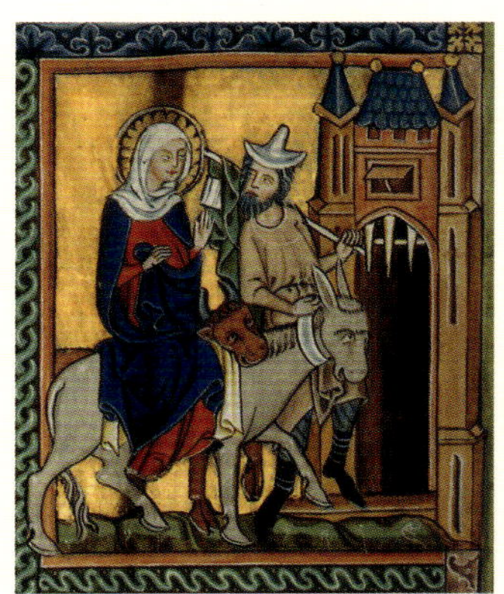

FIG. 1B. *(above) Scene from the same miniature in the* Plenarium *of Otto the Mild. Joseph leads the donkey carrying Mary towards the town gate of Bethlehem; the ox lays its head on the donkey's back.*

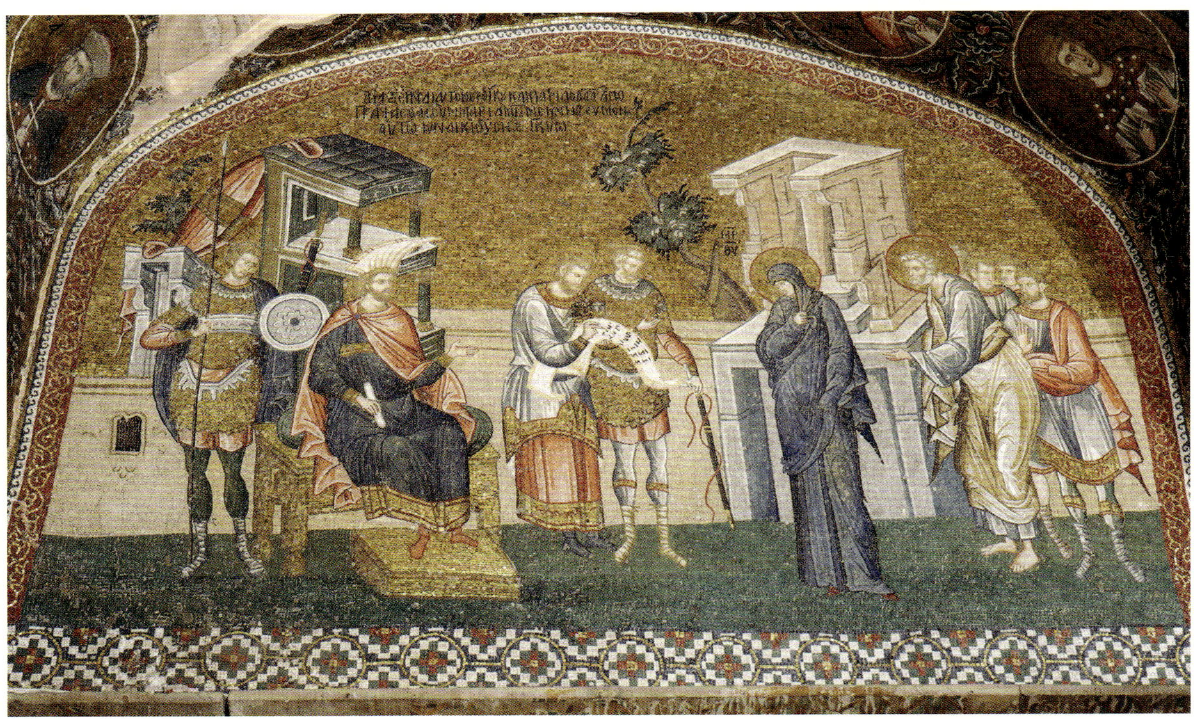

FIG. 2. *Mosaic in the Church of the Holy Saviour in Chora, Istanbul, c. 1315–21: Cyrenius, Governor of Syria, is supervising the enrolment. A scribe in the centre holds a scroll; Mary stands, shielding herself with her blue mantle; behind her are Joseph, barefoot, and his sons.*

Matthew records that Joseph was disturbed by Mary's pregnancy, the cause of which he did not know, and that he intended to 'put her away privily' (Matthew 1:19). But an angel tells him in a dream that the Virgin would give birth to a Son who would bring blessings (Matthew is referring to Isaiah 7:14).[ii] In another Chora mosaic [FIG. 3] Joseph lies on a kind of bed; the angel descends from above, his robes fluttering. In the background we see figures of two women, one, the Virgin, shielding herself with a blue cloak, the other perhaps her attendant. The inscription above in Greek reads in translation: 'Behold, the angel of the Lord appeared unto him in a dream, saying, Joseph, thou son of David, fear not to take unto thee Mary thy wife: for that which is conceived in her is of the Holy Ghost.'

Images depicting Joseph's true understanding of the origin of Christ's conception are rare. But two examples illustrate the truth dawning on him, perhaps a reflection of renewed interest in St Joseph at the time these works were made. In a panel of around 1400 by a painter of the Upper or Central Rhine whose name is unknown,

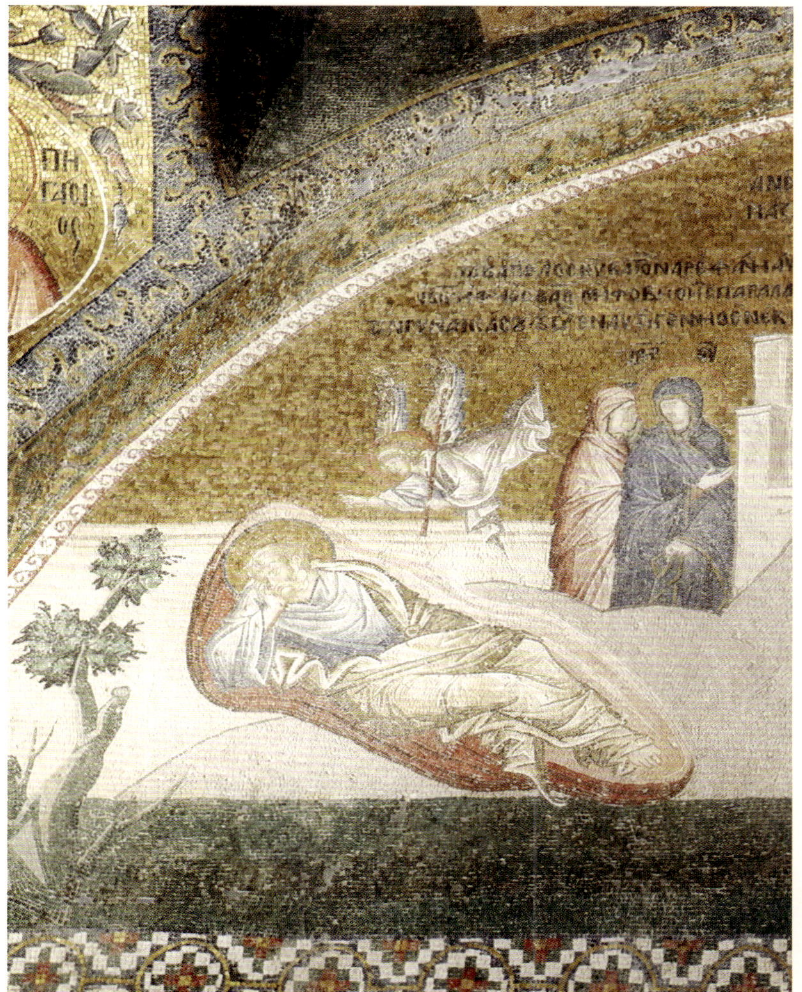

FIG. 3. *(left) Mosaic in the Church of the Holy Saviour in Chora, Istanbul, c. 1315–21: Joseph's dream and the angel's revelation. The angel of the Lord flies down to the sleeping Joseph. In the background the Virgin, in blue, is seen with another figure.*

FIG. 4. *(below) Joseph recognises Mary as the Mother of God, in a scene envisioned by the Master of Erfurt, c. 1400, oil on panel, 25 x 19 cm, Gemäldegalerie, Staatliche Museen, Berlin. As Mary sits spinning, the luminous Christ Child in her womb is revealed to Joseph who looks in awe through the side of Mary's carved wooden chair.*

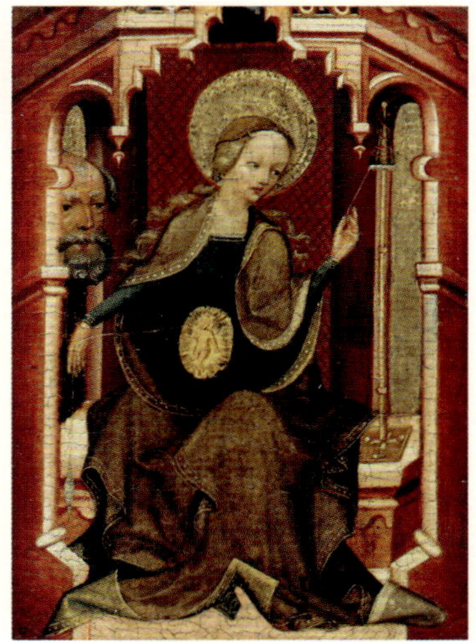

Joseph's doubts concerning Mary are dispelled [FIG. 4]. We see Mary seated on an elaborate ecclesiastically canopied chair attentively working with her spindle, and Joseph's head (distinctly large) thrust through the open side of Mary's seat as he gazes with an expression of awe at the illumined Infant depicted in Mary's womb. In another panel painted around 1410–20 by an Upper Rhenish Master Joseph's doubts concerning Mary are dispelled in a vision [see Chapter IX, FIG. 1]. The pregnant Mary sits with her needlework and Joseph stands at his work table, where he is suddenly visited by an angel

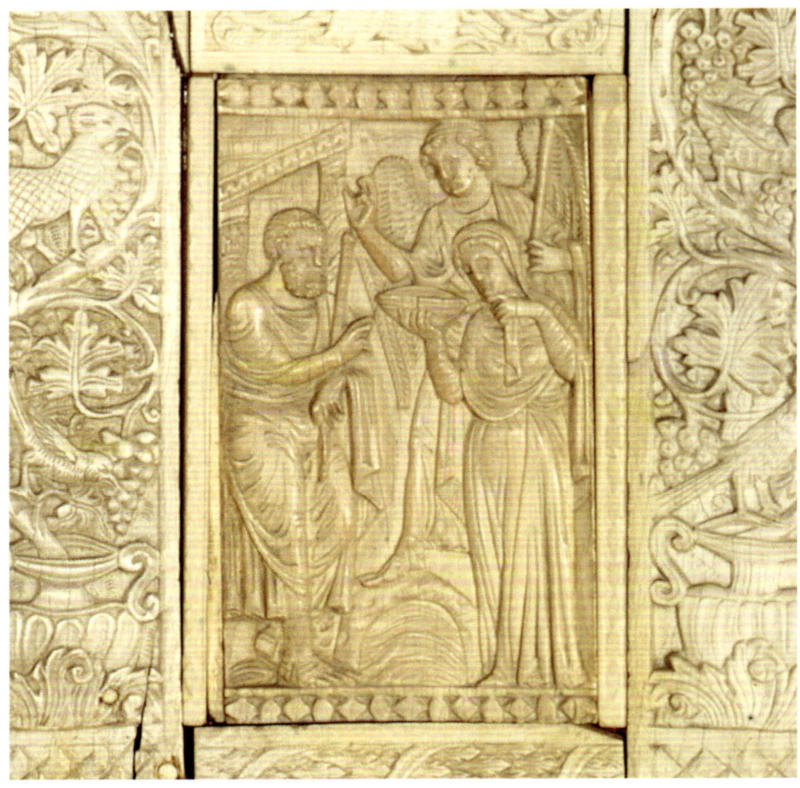

FIG. 5. *Panel of Archbishop Maximian's Throne, made in Ravenna or Constantinople, c. 545–53, ivory, 21 x 11.3 cm, Archiepiscopal Museum, Ravenna. The ordeal by water: Mary drinks poisoned water from the gourd, according to the event described in the Protoevangelium Jacobi. Joseph looks on, overseen by an angel.*

who instructs him in the Mystery.

Following the revelation of the dream, Joseph takes Mary into his care. According to the mid-second-century *Protoevangelium Jacobi* (Gospel of James) and to the eighth-century Gospel of Pseudo-Matthew – both apocryphal Infancy Gospels[iii] – the priests of the Temple where Mary had dwelt and worked call her to account: the trial by water follows, where both Mary and Joseph must drink bitter water to test their guilt or innocence.[iv] This event is rarely depicted, though it occurs in several rock-cut churches in Cappadocia; a mid-sixth-century ivory carving on Archbishop Maximian's Throne shows Mary drinking from a gourd, her face expressing the unpleasant taste of the liquid [FIG. 5].

And so the journey begins. Matthew and Luke tell us nothing about the journey to Bethlehem, and the event is not often depicted in Western Christendom, except in images and cycles under Byzantine influence.[v] Joseph's dream is seen in conjunction with the journey to

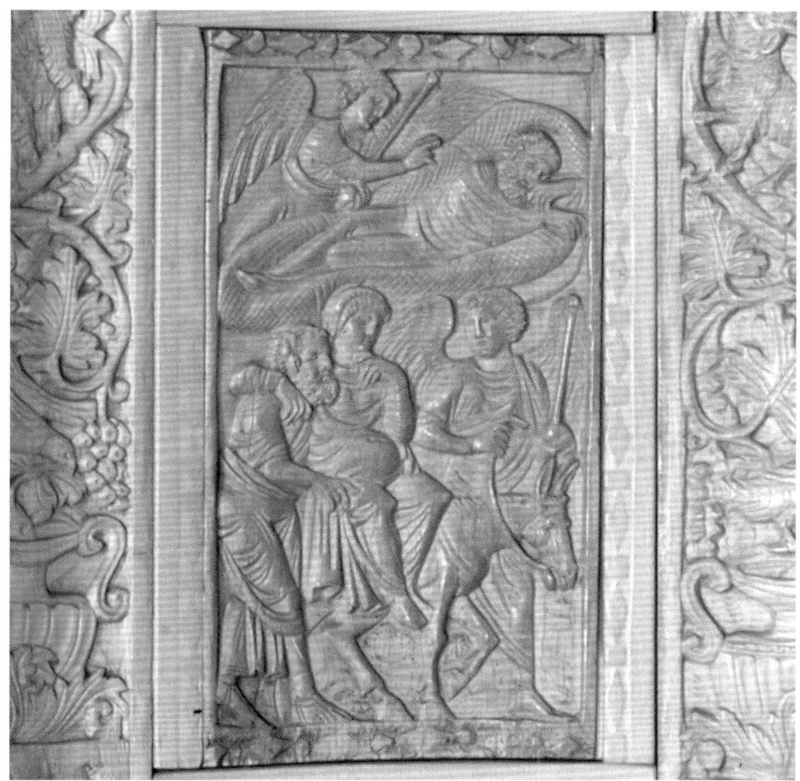

FIG 6. *Another panel of Archbishop Maximian's Throne: above is Joseph's dream; below, the journey to Bethlehem – the pregnant Virgin sitting on the ass, leaning on Joseph, led by an angel.*

Bethlehem in another panel of Maximian's Throne [FIG. 6]. At the top Joseph lies asleep, his head on his arm, one leg folded, his robes swathed about him, and an angel appears at his side. Below, Mary sits thoughtfully on the ass, her arm around Joseph's neck, the little group led by an angel. Remarkably, this small ivory shows the Virgin to be distinctly pregnant, with a rounded belly.

Details of the journey to Bethlehem are elaborated in the *Protoevangelium Jacobi* and in the *Meditationes Vitae Christi*, the latter written *c.* 1336–64 by a Franciscan for a Poor Clare nun.[vi] We learn from the *Protoevangelium* that Joseph took his son by his first marriage, who 'walked in front', leading the ass ridden by Mary. Joseph's son was later identified with the apostle James, and scholarly argument continues concerning the question of the 'Lord's brethren', referred to in both the canonical and the apocryphal gospels.[vii] Other manuscripts suggest that the widower Joseph was father of several sons, and occasionally we see several youths accompanying Mary and Joseph to Bethlehem [FIG. 2]. The *Legenda aurea*, compiled *c.* 1260 by Jacobus de Voragine,[viii] following in the canonical footsteps, declares that Joseph took an ass for Mary to sit on, and embroiders the story by adding to the entourage a young ox 'which Joseph intended to sell to help pay their taxes and provide their keep'. The *Meditationes Vitae Christi* reflect on the difficulties of the journey. 'Wishing to obey the command, Joseph started on his way with the Lady, taking with him an ox and an ass, since the Lady was pregnant ... And thus they went like poor merchants of beasts...' An image in the fourteenth-century *Plenarium* of Otto the Mild shows Mary sitting on the ass, accompanied by a benign ox whose head rests on the donkey's back, and led by Joseph, arriving at the gated entrance to the city [FIG. 1B].

Theologians and Church Fathers may well have disapproved of and discouraged these imaginative folkloric accounts, but the popularity of the legends was immensely widespread and long-lived, and continued to flourish in the wake of numerous translations and the invention of printing. The colourful and intimate details exerted considerable influence on artists over the centuries for both their symbolic and their allegorical evocations, as well as for their down-to-earth practicality, enabling prayerful devotion and reminding the faithful to relate particular aspects to their own lives in the present moment.

Pieter Bruegel the Elder's famous and enigmatic work painted in 1566, *The Census at Bethlehem* [FIG. 7], combines the journey with the taxation.[ix] Bruegel sets the event in the present, but the literal understanding of time is suspended. Contemporaries would have identified with figures and actions as the artist explores the human condition, physically and psychologically, both grim and comic, with extraordinary economy and understanding of body language. It is evening; the sun, in a pale and wintry low sky, will soon be setting. It is cold. We see children throwing snowballs and blowing up a pig's bladder to make a football; a man slaughters a pig and his wife collects the blood; others are just gawping. Ale is delivered in great barrels, chickens peck at the hardened ground. Here a man relieves himself against a wall, there a man shuts himself in, closing the shutters, withdrawing from the turmoil. The tax collector wears a fur-lined coat, and disorderly groups arrive to pay their taxes. Peasants pay with money or goods. We see them drinking and warming themselves. In the background at the left is the church,

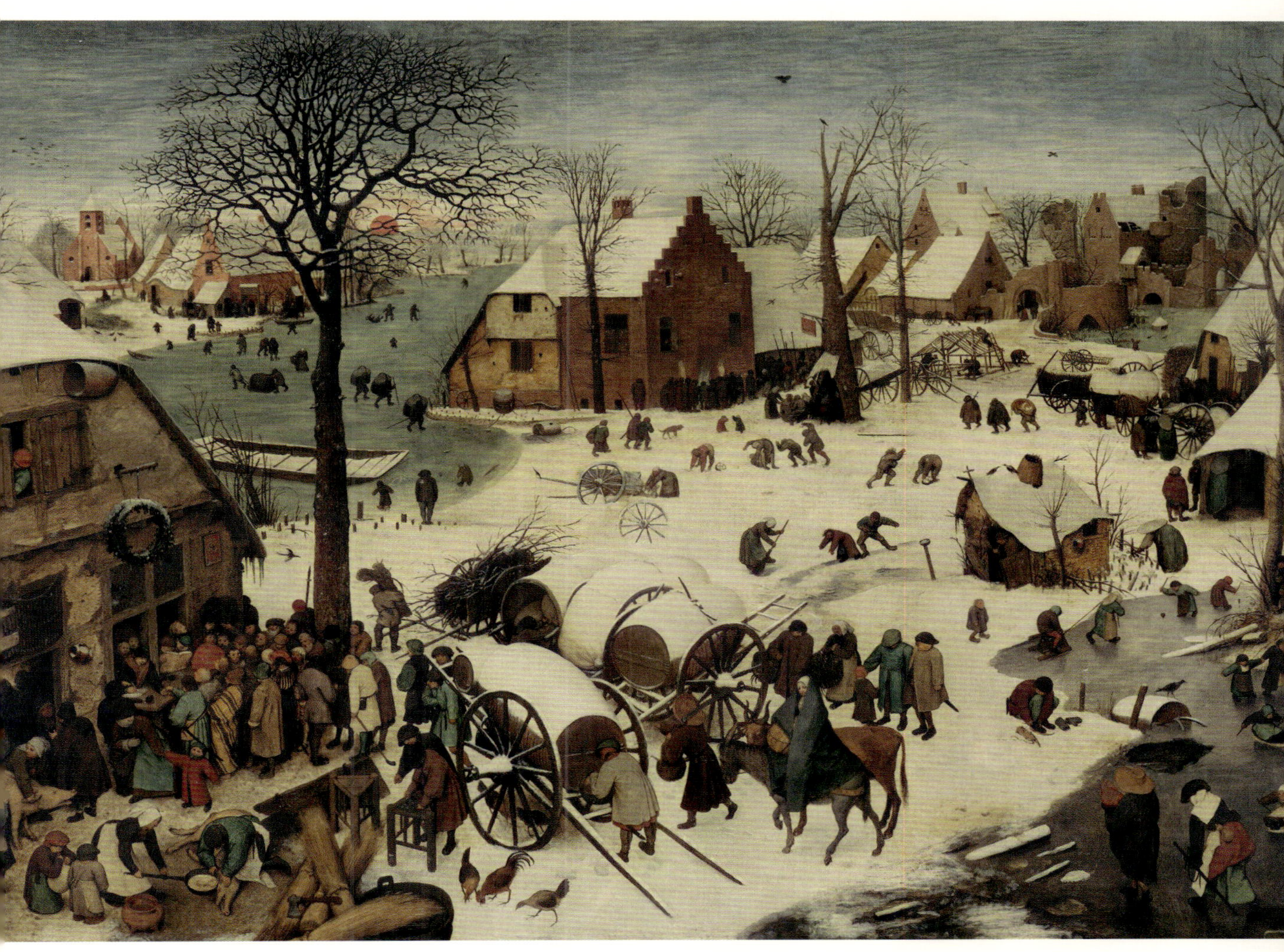

insignificantly far distant. On the other side is the castle – normally synonymous with protection, security, strength, but now in its ruined state partly in use as a farmhouse, a symbol of emptiness, of lack of leadership through man's greed and folly.[x]

Amid the hurly-burly force of the pictorial realism of the scene invisible elements are evoked: the cosmic dimension, the centre of the solar system. We see wheels – a constant theme for Bruegel – symbolic of the wheel of fortune, of the turning of time, of life's journey. At

FIG. 7. *Pieter Bruegel the Elder, The Census at Bethlehem, 1566, oil on panel, 115 x 163.5 cm, Musées royaux des Beaux-Arts de Belgique, Brussels. The subject of the journey is combined with the taxation, and set in Bruegel's own day. The holy family is in the centre of the painting, un-noticed.*

the centre of the painting, almost invisible, almost insignificant, a family group arrives: a man leading an ox, and a young woman riding a donkey. In stark contrast to the noisy busyness of the scene, Mary personifies stillness, silence, her condition symbolised by the rounded basket in front of her. Mary, through whom God appears on Earth, suggests the higher invisible Reality, through which humanity can relate to the Divine.

The scene is set in the ever present, a reminder of words in Christmas Sermon 1 by Meister Eckhart (1260–*c.* 1328): 'Here, in time, we are celebrating the eternal birth which God the Father bore and bears unceasingly in eternity.'

i Scholars have long debated the dates of various censuses in a search for historical veracity.

ii This is the first of three dreams: in the second, the angel warns Joseph to flee to Egypt; in the third dream Joseph is told that it is safe to return.

iii The *Protoevangelium Jacobi* is no doubt a compilation of many oral stories and legends, widely circulated and much loved all over Christendom. The Gospel of the Pseudo-Matthew is heavily indebted to the *Protoevangelium Jacobi*. See M.R. James, *The Apocryphal New Testament* (Oxford: Clarendon Press, 1924), and David R. Cartlidge and J. Keith Elliott, *Art and the Christian Apocrypha* (London and New York: Routledge, 2001).

iv This apocryphal legend is probably based on Numbers 5:11ff., although there it concerns a woman taken in adultery. The passage in the *Protoevangelium* reads: 'And the high priest said: "I will give you the water of the conviction of the Lord to drink and it will make manifest your sins before your eyes."'

v For instance in mosaics in San Marco, Venice, and in wall paintings in Castelseprio, northern Italy.

vi Once ascribed to the Pseudo-Bonaventura, this vastly popular manuscript was widely copied and circulated, and subsequently translated into many languages (over two hundred manuscripts still survive). With repeated exhortations to meditate on all the events narrated, it has been called a handbook of contemplation and includes long homilies on the gentle Franciscan virtues. See Isa Ragusa and Rosalie B. Green, transl. and ed., *Meditations on the Life of Christ* (Princeton, NJ: Princeton University Press, 1961), and Sarah McNamer, 'The Debate on the Origins of the *Meditationes Vitae Christi*', in *Archivium Franciscanum Historicum*, vol. 111, nos 1–2 (June 2018), pp. 65–112.

vii Joseph's son, referred to as James in some accounts, was possibly one of the two apostles called James (one the son of Zebedee), and possibly later a bishop of Jerusalem, and came to be called James the Just. See Project Canterbury: www.anglicanhistory.org>usa>mahan.james.

viii This collection of folk stories and legends became a medieval bestseller, translated from the Latin into numerous languages, and first printed in 1496.

ix For a detailed analysis of Bruegel's work see Richard Temple, *Peter Bruegel the Elder and Esoteric Tradition* (PhD, Prince's School of Traditional Arts, University of Wales, 2007).

x It has been suggested that this may be a reference to the oppressive military occupation of the Netherlands by Spanish forces at the time.

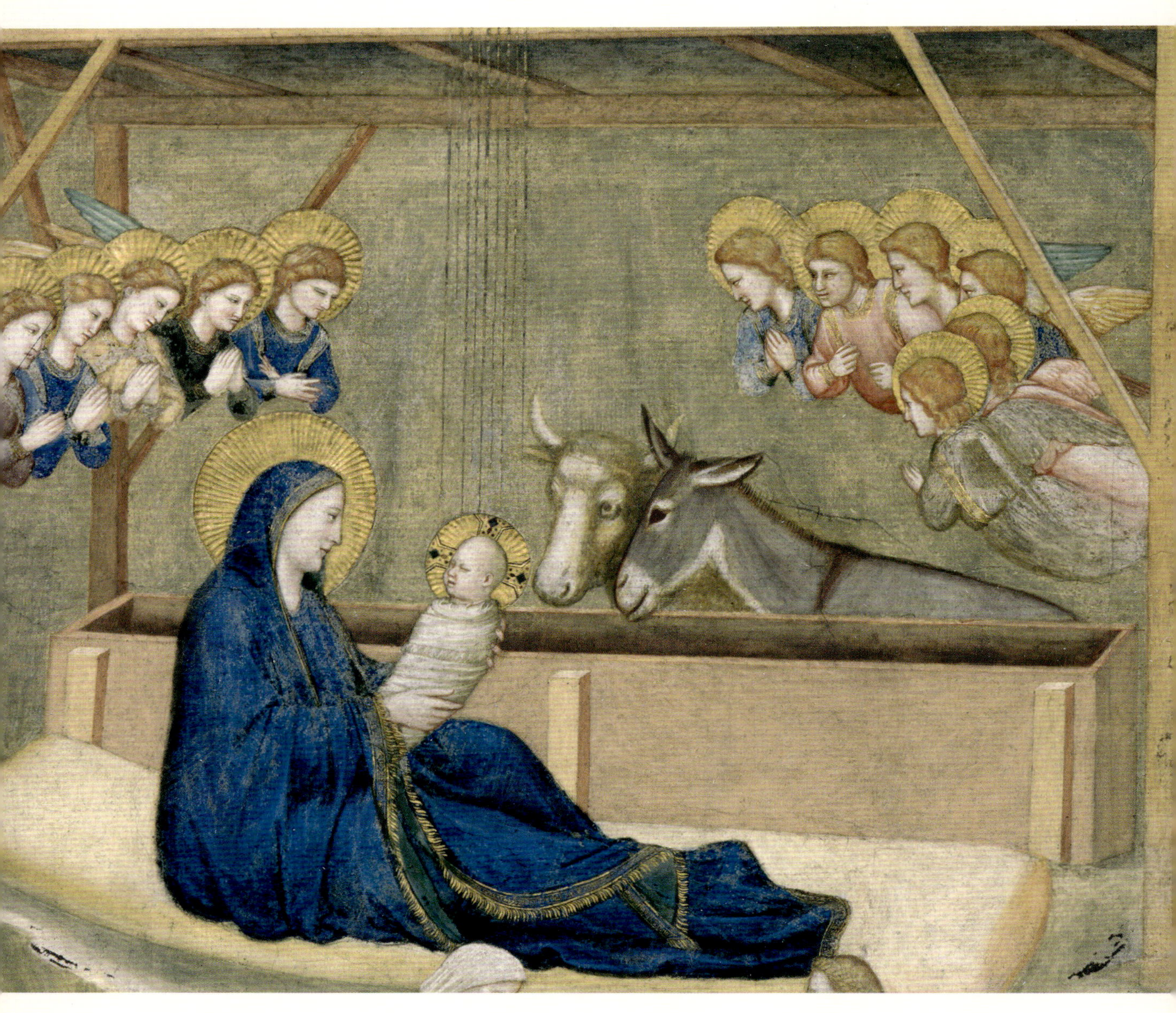

II THE OX AND THE ASS

FROM THE BEGINNING THE OX AND THE ASS are almost always present in scenes of Christ's Nativity.[i] These attendant beasts of burden, silent witnesses, appear as mythological foster parents. The earliest known images of the Nativity appear on sarcophagi of the fourth century. In the pediment on the lid of one of them we see the Christ Child lying in the manger, wrapped in swaddling clothes, overseen by the accompanying ox and ass [FIG. 1]. The sarcophagus is now incorporated in the pulpit of Sant'Ambrogio in Milan.

Yet the ox and ass are not mentioned in the Gospels of Matthew and Luke (the only two canonical Gospels to tell the story of the Nativity), though Luke (2:7) reports that Mary wrapped her son in swaddling clothes and 'laid him in a manger, because there was no room for them in the inn' – and certainly a manger suggests animals. Occasionally the figure of a shepherd is also included in these ancient carvings. On the cover of the sarcophagus of Marcus Claudianus (*c.* 330–35) a shepherd is shown pondering as he leans on his staff, while the ox and ass seem to breathe warmly on to the Christ Child below them [FIG. 2].

These ancient images depicting the ox and the ass watching over Christ's crib are sometimes linked with a scene showing the Adoration of the Magi, who pay homage to the Christ Child as he sits enthroned on the Virgin's lap. The juxtaposition of the two

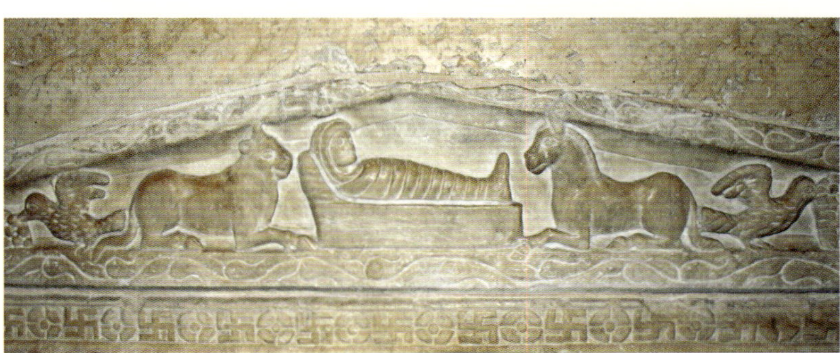

FIG. 1. *(right) The Christ Child flanked by the ox and the ass, on a pediment of the sarcophagus of Stilicho, end of the fourth century, incorporated in the Romanesque pulpit of Sant'Ambrogio, Milan.*

FIG. 4 DETAIL. *(left) From Giotto and workshop, fresco of the Nativity, c. 1310. See page 27.*

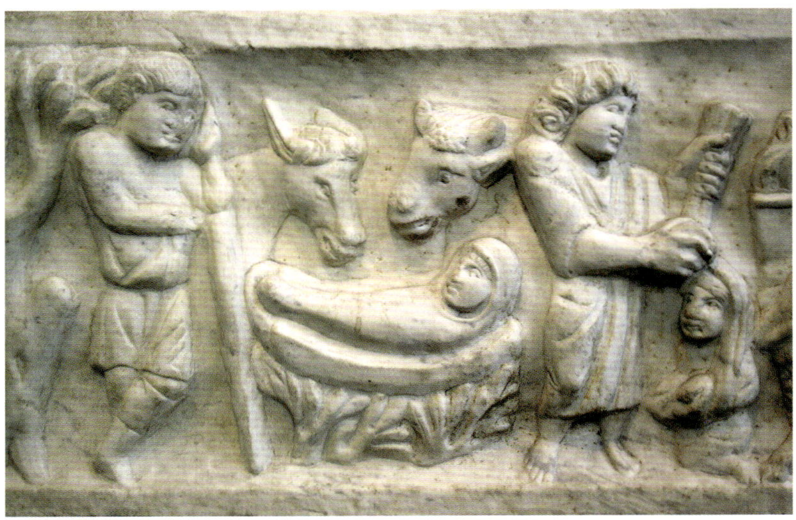

FIG. 2. *Detail of the sarcophagus of Marcus Claudianus, c. 330–35, Palazzo Massimo alle Terme, Rome. The swaddled Christ Child lies in the manger, overseen by the ox and the ass, while a shepherd stands nearby.*

events acts as a vibrant reminder that the feast of the Epiphany – the manifestation of Christ to the Gentiles, represented by the Magi – on 6 January originally encompassed the feast of the Nativity (moved to 25 December *c.* 350). We see the very close proximity and essential role of the ox and the ass in an early ninth-century ivory carving, the bottom strip of a diptych [FIG. 3]. Here they guard the tightly bound Infant, while Mary and Joseph are shown on one side, the Annunciation to the Shepherds on the other.

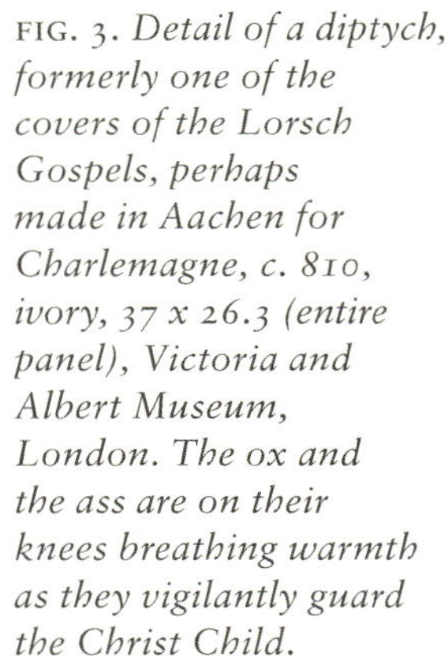

FIG. 3. *Detail of a diptych, formerly one of the covers of the Lorsch Gospels, perhaps made in Aachen for Charlemagne, c. 810, ivory, 37 x 26.3 (entire panel), Victoria and Albert Museum, London. The ox and the ass are on their knees breathing warmth as they vigilantly guard the Christ Child.*

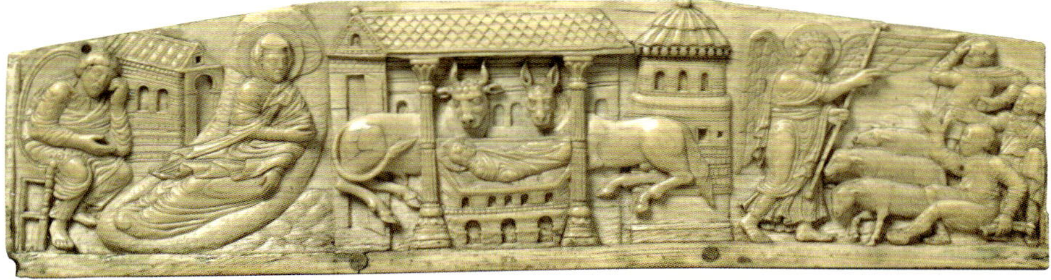

The manger-crib itself appears in a variety of forms – box-like, or made of brick, wood, stone, or wattled basketwork (evoking associations with the finding of Moses). The ox and ass may be depicted at either end of the manger, or standing together, or behind the crib in arched openings. Perhaps they represent our own animal instincts. They are there, sometimes breathing warmth, sometimes

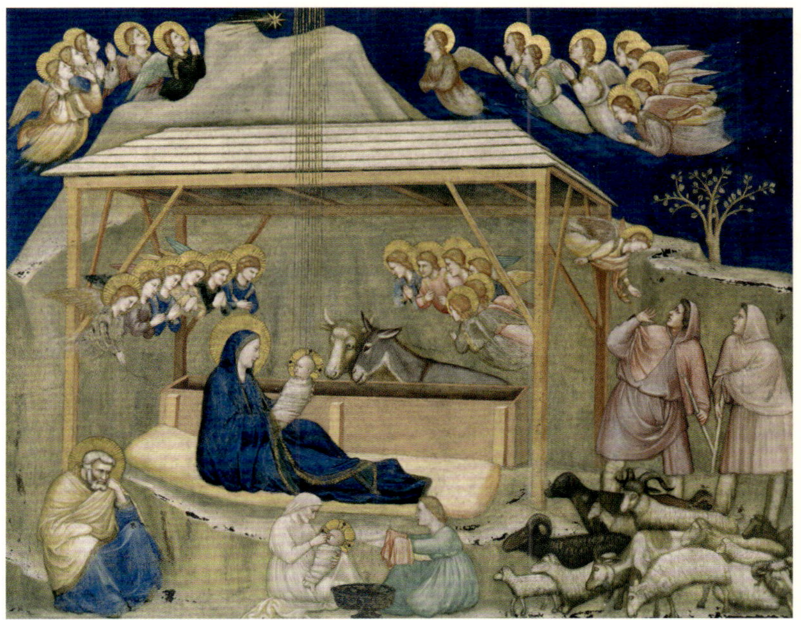

FIG. 4. *Giotto and workshop, fresco of the Nativity in the Lower Church at Assisi, c. 1310. The Virgin lifts the Infant Christ up to the watching ox and ass; light pours down from the celestial realm, flanked by ranks of angels. To the right is the Annunciation to the Shepherds; in the foreground, the midwives bathe the Christ Child; to the left, Joseph sits apart.*

eating straw or hay, often watching and vigilant, for example, in Giotto's fresco in Assisi [FIG. 4].

We are so accustomed to seeing the ox and the ass in Nativity scenes that we almost fail to wonder: why are the ox and the ass deemed to be vital to the event? What is their significance? What is the origin of this iconography? Why were these beasts so deeply embedded in the psyche of Christians from the beginning?

We know that at the time when the sarcophagi were made, at the tail end of the Roman empire, the Christian faithful – still very much a small minority – continued by inheritance to be steeped in both the Old Testament tradition of the Jews and in Roman mythology and its practices and rituals.[ii] Christians of the third and fourth centuries were exploring ways to express the mystery and significance of their religious faith, searching for ways to convey the redemption of mankind brought about by the birth of the Saviour.

The ox – often in the form of a bull – is an ancient symbol of sacrifice, a powerful beast, representing strength, held sacred in many traditions, myths and cultures (Egyptian, Assyrian, Sumerian, Greek, and others),[iii] and in all probability some of the rituals and practices continued to take place at the time of Christ's birth. The bull had played an important role in Mithraic cults, still widespread in the third and fourth centuries at the time when the Christian sarcophagi were made.

The text of the prophet Isaiah contains many references to the expected Messiah: 'The ox knows its owner, and the ass its master's crib', and continues 'but Israel has not known me, and my people have not understood' (Isaiah 1:3). Reading the Old and New Testaments in the light of one another, patristic commentators pinpointed references to the Messiah and to the ox and the ass, and reminded us that Mosaic law states: 'Thou shall not plough with an ox and an ass yoked together.' Exegesis explains the yoking of 'clean' and 'unclean'. Symbolically, the joining of extremes (represented by the Nativity animals), the union of the spiritual and corporal, the clean and unclean, the inside and outside, and ultimately the uncreated and the created, can only be accomplished by Christ, the Incarnation, and the Logos in the person of Jesus Christ.[iv] The ox and ass were associated with the words of the prophet Habakkuk in the Septuagint:[v] 'In the midst of two living creatures you will be recognised.'[vi]

The homily on Luke's Gospel preached in third-century Egypt by Origen (c. 185– c. 254) commented that the manger 'was that very one which the prophet [Isaiah] foretold, saying "The ox knoweth his owner, and the ass his master's manger."' Later, Ambrose (c. 340–97) and Augustine (354–430) both expand and interpret the prophet Isaiah's words, and characterise the symbol of the ox (bull) as the symbol of the chosen (Jewish) people, and the ass as the symbol of the heathen people.[vii] Gregory of Nazianzus (329–90) explained the presence of the ox and ass at the Nativity: 'Between the ox, yoked to the law, and the ass, loaded with the sins of idolatry, lies the Son of God who brings freedom from both burdens.' The contrast of the beasts was often stressed: the ass also symbolised ungodliness, especially lust, celebrated in fertility ceremonies in Mediterranian areas. A fearful insult to early Christians was depicted in a crude caricature that has survived in a Roman barracks: they are worshipping a crucified ass.[viii]

On a more prosaic and distinctly down-to-earth level, a more literal interpretation would suggest that the Christ Child was placed in the manger normally used by the ox. Was the ox the original occupant of the cave or stable? Might the logical explanation for the presence of the ass be accounted for by a longstanding popular tradition that the ass carried the heavily pregnant Mary on the

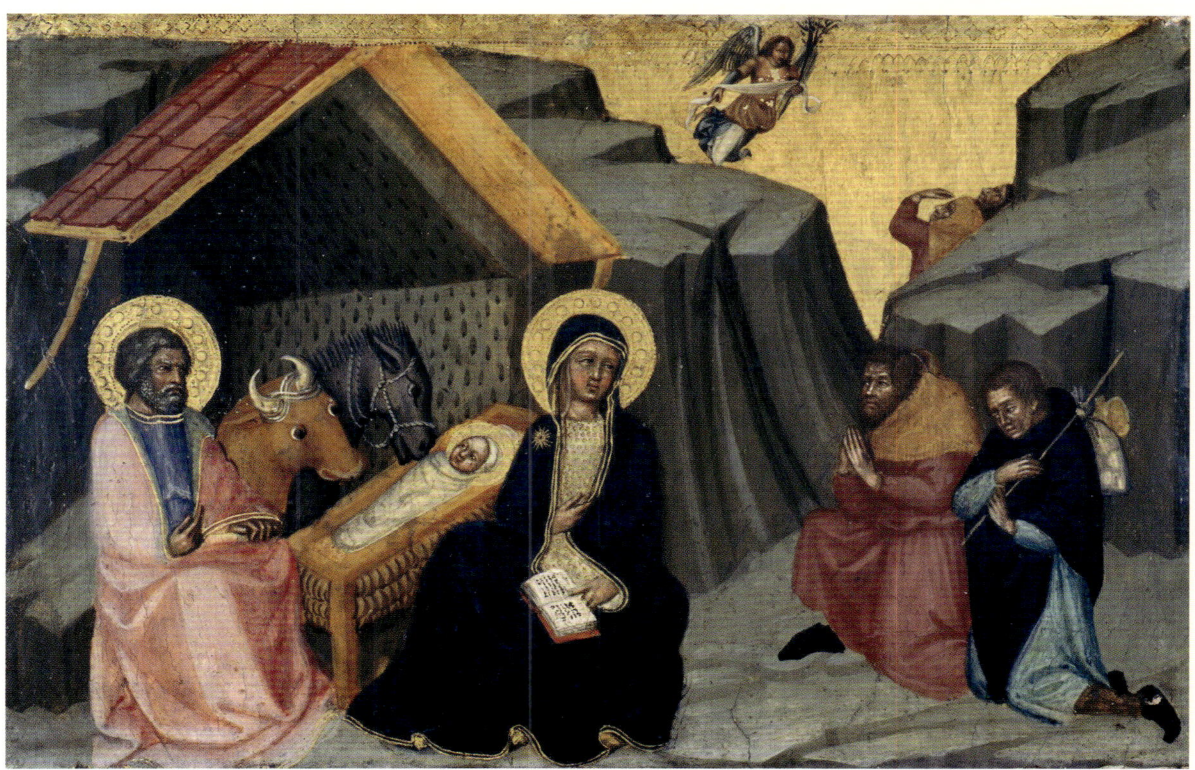

journey to Bethlehem?

The apocryphal gospels are rich in details: the mid-second-century *Protoevangelium Jacobi* tells us that when setting off to Bethlehem for the census Joseph had saddled his ass (she-ass, in some manuscripts) 'and sat Mary on it'.[ix] However, there is no mention of the ox. Later, the eighth-century Gospel of Pseudo-Matthew, describing the Nativity in detail in Chapters XIII and XIV, tells us how, on the third day, Mary and Joseph moved from the cave to the stable, where Mary 'placed the Child in the stall … Then was fulfilled that which was said by the prophet Isaiah saying: The ox knoweth his master, and the ass his master's crib.' The manuscript continues a little later, 'The very animals, therefore, the ox and the ass, having Him in their midst, incessantly adored Him. Then was fulfilled that which was foretold by Habbakkuk, the prophet, saying: "Between two animals thou art made manifest."' We are often shown the ox and ass adoring Christ on their knees.

FIG. 5. *Paolo di Giovanni Fei, The Nativity, c. 1400, tempera on panel, 22.2 x 23.5 cm, Lindenau Museum, Altenburg. The large-eyed ox and ass watch vigilantly, while the shepherds kneel in adoration. In an unusual detail, Mary holds a book.*

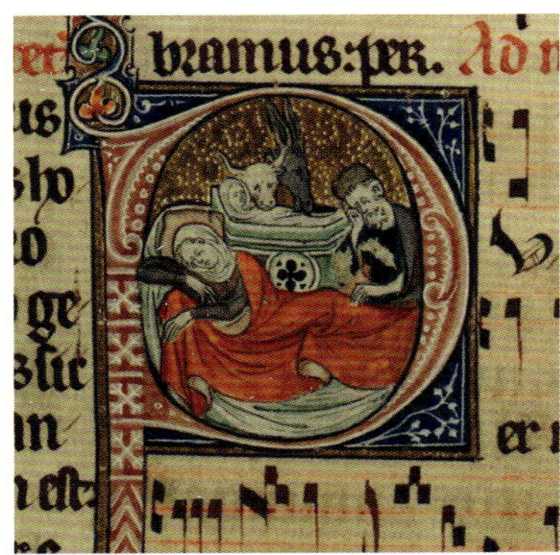

FIG. 6. *In this scene in the Sherbrooke Missal, c. 1310, National Library of Wales, MS 15536E, Mary reclines, resting after giving birth, Joseph sits, perhaps sleeping, or, as indicated by his hand held to his head, in thought, while the Holy Child lies peacefully in the manger, lovingly guarded by the ox and the ass.*

The mid-fourteenth-century *Meditationes Vitae Christi* embroider the Nativity legend like this: 'The ox and the ass knelt with their mouths above the manger and breathed on the Infant as though they possessed reason and knew that the Child was so poorly wrapped that He needed to be warmed, in that cold season' [FIGS 5–7]. It goes on to say that 'Joseph took the pack-saddle of the ass and pulled out the stuffing of straw or hair, placing it beside the manger that the Lady might rest on it'. These kindly acts soon found their way into depictions of the Nativity. The mid-thirteenth-century *Legenda aurea* tells us, on a practical note, that the hay, 'which the ox and the ass abstained from eating', was later brought to Rome by St Helena – as we learn from the *Historia scholastica* (compiled by Petrus Comestor *c.* 1173). Look closely, and you occasionally find examples where the beasts have eaten the straw or hay in the manger [FIG. 8].

In 1223 Francis of Assisi (1181/82–1226) obtained papal permission to erect a *praesepe* (a crib) on the altar at Greccio.[x] Inspired by his own pilgrimage to Bethlehem and his ardent wish to inspire prayerful attention to and interest in the birth of Christ, on Christmas Eve the holy friar set an ox and an ass on either side of the *praesepe* and in this manger he placed provender for the animals. The occasion was described in detail by St Bonaventure in his life of Francis (written in 1263), emphasising that Francis's intention was to stir the people to a more devout observance of the Nativity. Crowds gathered at Greccio, and in the words of Bonaventure, the night was 'made festal with clustered lights and glad sounds'. The manger served as altar, and Francis's eyes were suffused with tears of joy at the Christmas Mass, which he celebrated at night, singing the Gospel and preaching a sermon on the Nativity. Some witnesses even reported (fancifully?) to have seen a beautiful child sleeping in the manger. The hay preserved from the event later acted as a miraculous panacea for diseases of animals.

The fame of Francis's Christmas Mass celebrated over a manger attended by an ox and an ass spread fast, and instantly inspired a vogue throughout Christendom. Cribs were set up outside churches or inside them, in public squares, in places for private and public devotion. Occasionally real animals were used for a *tableau vivant* during the Christmas season.[xi] It is tempting to wonder whether Francis was aware of the use of *praesepe* in Christmas plays which took place during the liturgy. There is evidence that from the twelfth century structural cribs were familiar in dramatic performances,

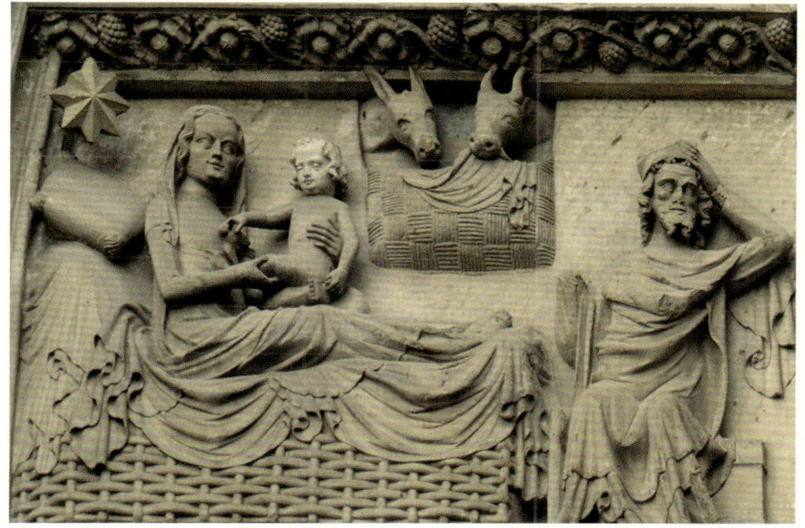

FIG. 7. *On the lintel just above the portal of the Frauenkirche, Esslingen, c. 1350, Mary sits up in her basketwork bed holding the naked Christ Child, awaiting the arrival of the Magi (in the right half of the lintel). The ass and the ox appear to prepare the covering for the Infant.*

sometimes provided with figures.[xii] So the Christmas crib was born, and from this time onwards prolific numbers of Nativity scenes were made for altarpieces [FIG. 9], devotional panels, illuminated manuscripts, sculpture, ivories, and stained-glass windows.

An image can be perceived and understood at different levels, and according to an ancient tradition, like scripture, an image describes the inner world of man rather than external life. It can act as a reminder of the sacred: we know that the deepest meaning of the Nativity lies in a spiritual interpretation, and the mystery is encountered in the present moment. The ox and the ass, silent witnesses, the beasts of burden accompanying the Divine Infant,

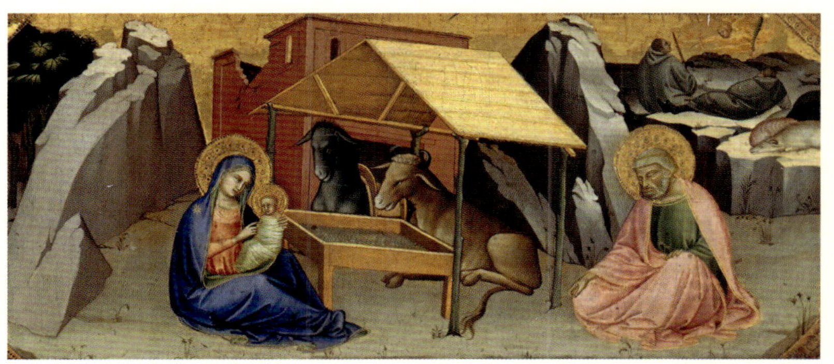

FIG. 8. *Lorenzo Monaco,* The Nativity, *in an altarpiece made for the Ardinghelli Chapel in Santa Maria del Carmine, Florence, c. 1398, tempera on poplar, 26.3 x 60.7 cm, Gemäldegalerie, Staatliche Museen, Berlin. The large seated ox and ass are shown looking across the manger towards the Virgin and Child, while Joseph ponders, in the setting of a rocky landscape.*

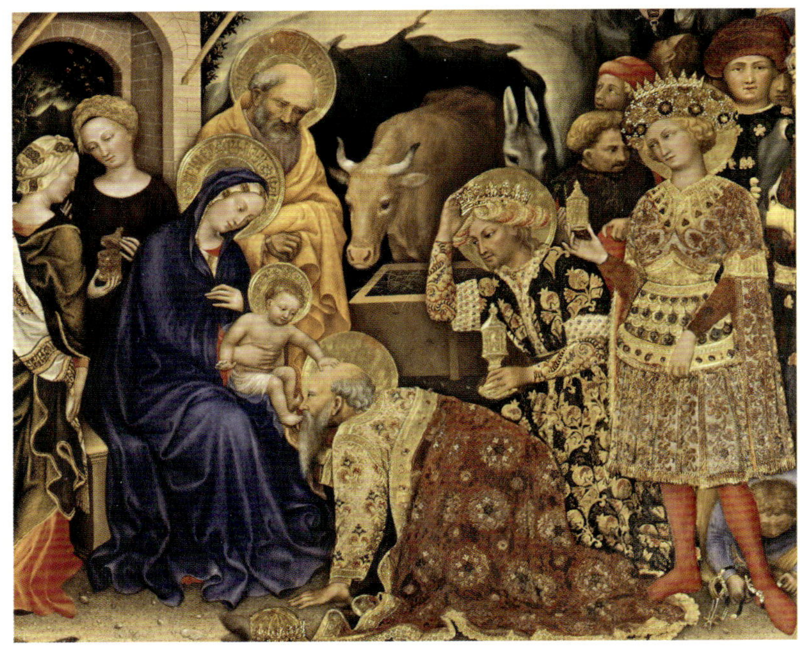

FIG. 9. *Gentile da Fabriano, detail from the Nativity scene in the great* Adoration of the Magi Altarpiece, *1423, originally in the Strozzi family chapel in Santa Trinità, Florence, tempera on panel, 283 x 300 cm, Uffizi, Florence. The animals act as foster parents, guarding the Christ Child amid the crowds coming to worship Him.*

offer the faithful homely, down-to-earth comfort, a grounding, a reminder of our own animal instincts – and they also evoke sacrificial archetypes that lie deeply buried in the subconscious. Consider the ox – steady, sturdy, strong – able to plough, entrusted to turn the earth so that seeds may be sown and later harvested, transformed into food; and consider the ass – gentle, patient, meek, sure-footed and stubbornly persevering – it is the ass who carries the Christ Child in His mother with Joseph to Egypt away from murderous Herod; it is the ass who is chosen to carry Christ in triumph into Jerusalem. The figurative foster parents who attentively watch over the Child enable us to recall our own role in the cosmos. The Christ Child they guard, human and Divine, alludes to the inner birth of the spirit. The ox and the ass have the power to evoke in man the need to work and to watch, the need to obey the Higher in order to allow this birth to take place in us.

II THE OX AND THE ASS: FOOTNOTES

i Pope Benedict XVI, writing as Joseph Ratzinger (2012), stated in his three volumes on the life of Jesus, 'No representation of the crib is complete without the ox and the ass.'

ii See Peter Brown, *The Rise of Western Christendom* (2nd edn, Oxford: Blackwell, 2003); also Robin Lane Fox, *Pagans and Christians* (London: Penguin, 1986).

iii See Jaś Elsner and Stefanie Lenk, *Imagining the Divine* (Oxford: Ashmolean Museum, exhibition catalogue, 2017).

iv ibid.

v The Greek version/translation of the Old Testament used before the time of Christ by the Jews in the diaspora.

vi It has also been suggested that Habakkuk was referring to the two cherubim on the mercy-seat of the Ark of the Covenant (Exodus 25:18), who both reveal and conceal the mysterious presence of God. See Christopher Howse, 'What the Ox and the Ass saw' (*Daily Telegraph*, 30 November 2012). Stories such as the talking ass of Balaam are seen as prefigurations of the Incarnation according to early sources, e.g. Irenaeus.

vii The ox is 'clean', the ass is 'unclean', according to dietary proscriptions in the Old Testament. Mixing the clean and the unclean related to mixing Jews and Gentiles. St Paul firmly warned Christians not to be 'yoked' to unbelievers.

viii See Gertrud Schiller, *Iconography of Christian Art* (London: Lund Humphries, 1971), vol. I, p. 61, n. 67.

ix '… his son led it, and Joseph followed. And they drew near to the third milestone. And Joseph turned round and saw her sad, and said within himself: "Perhaps that which is within her is paining her." And again Joseph turned round and saw her laughing. And he said to her: "Mary, why is it that I see your face at one time laughing and at another sad?" And she said to him: "Joseph, I see with my eyes two peoples, one weeping and lamenting and one rejoicing and exulting."' This is interpreted to mean that she saw the Jews weeping because they have departed from their God; and the people of the Gentiles rejoice because they have been made near to the Lord.

x Greccio is about 70 km from Assisi. St Francis founded the Friars Minor (and sought approval from Pope Innocent III for the Regula primitiva), the Poor Clares and the Third Lay Order.

xi Occasionally even now live animals are used in cribs, for instance in Brussels.

xii See Karl Young, *The Drama of the Medieval Church* (Oxford: Clarendon Press, 1933), vol. 2, p. 27.

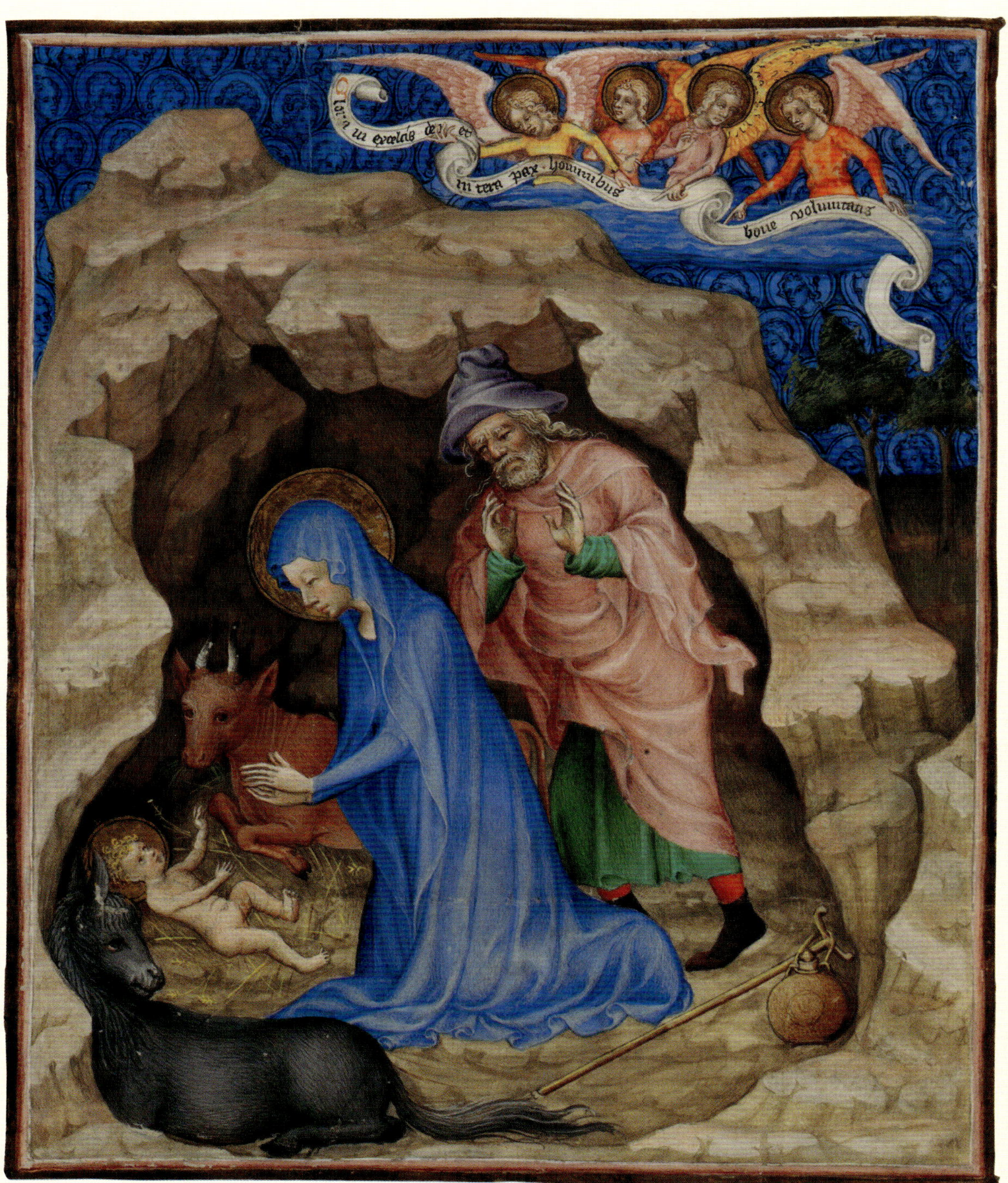
Gloria in excelsis deo et in tera pax homunibus bone voluntatis

III   THE CAVE

A CAVE IS OFTEN SHOWN AS THE SETTING for the Nativity [FIG. 1]. Both Luke and Matthew record that the Virgin 'brought forth her firstborn son' in Bethlehem, but we are not told where, though Luke (2:7) tells us 'she wrapped him up in swaddling clothes and laid him in a manger because there was no room for them in the inn'. According to the mid-second-century *Protoevangelium Jacobi*, Joseph 'found a cave and brought her into it'. Local legends concerning the birth of Christ are supported by the topography. To this day the area around Bethlehem is pitted with grottoes and caves in dry scrubby land. Cellars and stables are still hewn out of rock under houses; caves and grottoes provide shelter.[i]

Ancient commentaries support the story that Christ was born in a cave. Justin Martyr (*c.* 100–165) says, in *Dialogue with Trypho*, that the family found refuge in a cave outside the town: 'since Joseph could not find a lodging in that village, he took up his quarters in a certain cave near the village, and while they were there Mary brought forth the Christ and placed Him in a manger and here the Magi who came from Arabia found Him.'[ii]

Around the year 248 Origen wrote: 'In Bethlehem the cave is pointed out where He was born and the manger in the cave where he was wrapped in swaddling clothes. And the rumour is in those places and among foreigners of the Faith, that indeed Jesus was born in this cave, Who is worshipped and reverenced by the Christians.'[iii] At least as early as the fourth century a church was built over this grotto, now called the Basilica or Church of the Nativity.

The mystic light that appeared in this cave at Christ's birth is described in the *Protoevangelium* and also by the eighth-century Pseudo-Matthew, who tells us: 'When Mary entered the cave it began to shine as if the sun were there … thus the divine light illuminated the cave.'[iv] This passage resonates with the opening of John's Gospel (1:4–5): 'and the life was the light of men; And the light shineth in the darkness, and yet the darkness was not able to comprehend it.' Christ's own words are evoked: 'I am the light of the world' (John 8:12).

FIG. 3. *Adoration of the Christ Child in the* Turin-Milan Hours, *c. 1420, Museo Civico d'Arte Antica, Turin, inv. no. 47. Craggy rocks surround the cave, where the Christ Child, lying on the straw-strewn ground, reaches out towards the kneeling Mary. Joseph stands in a gesture of prayer, the ox and ass kneel, and the angels above sing in joy.*

In images in the Orthodox tradition the cave is an essential element of the Nativity scene [FIG. 2]. Light is shown pouring from on high down to the newborn Christ, and it is this light that illuminates the world. The great cosmic hierarchical order is shown, represented by different levels (more apparent in later icons): the heavens beyond the sky, the mountain, the cave, the earth, one set above the other, an ascending ladder linking man to God.[v] The shepherds, the angels, the Magi, the midwives and Joseph are all included in the icon. Essentially unchanged over the centuries, the Nativity icon could act as an *aide mémoire* to hold in the mind's eye – an image on which monks and the faithful could meditate, focusing on the various elements in prayer, as a means of preparation and purification necessary for Divine Birth to nourish the soul. We observe that the Christ Child, born in the cave, is often at the very centre of the image, at the midway point between heaven and earth.

Widely disseminated and much-loved legends and texts concerning the Nativity story were well known all over Christendom, familiar from early oral descriptions of the birth of the Saviour. For example, the Pseudo-Matthew, a source to which craftsmen and artists of the West were heavily indebted, narrates as follows: 'On the third day after the birth of our Lord Jesus Christ the most blessed Mary went forth out of the cave, and entering a stable, placed the Child in the stall, and the ox and the ass adored him.' With the intention of encouraging the reader and the listener to be witnesses to the events, the hugely popular mid-fourteenth-century *Meditationes Vitae Christi* embellish the cave setting of the Nativity like this: 'Looking for a place to rest, but not being able to find it because of the crowds ... when they saw an empty cave that men used when it rained, they entered to lodge themselves.' The account continues: 'And Joseph, who was a master carpenter, possibly closed it in some way.' The mid-thirteenth-century *Legenda aurea* tells us that 'they had to take shelter in a public passage'. This passage, according to the late twelfth-century *Historia scholastica*, was located between two houses; 'It provided some overhead covering and served as a meeting place for townspeople who came there to talk or eat together in their free time, or when the weather was bad.' The mysticism of the Cistercian Bernard of Clairvaux (1090–1153), with his intense love of the Christ Child and focus on the suffering of the Lord, was another powerful influence.

An illumination from an early fifteenth-century Burgundian

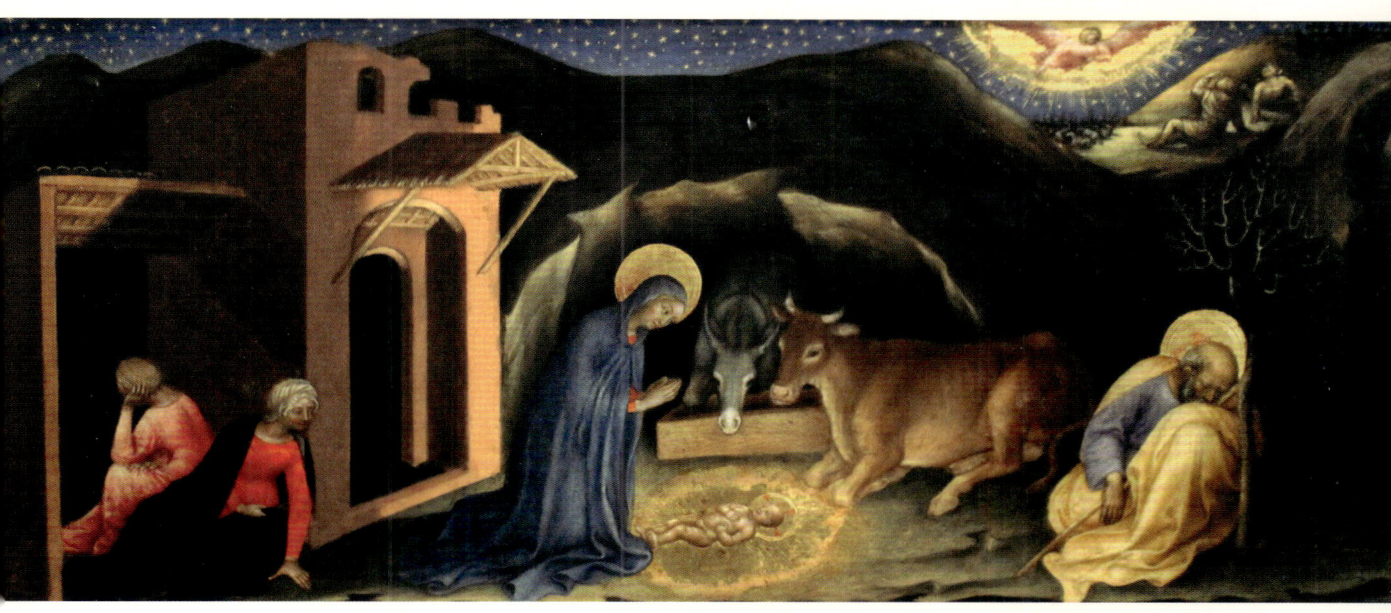

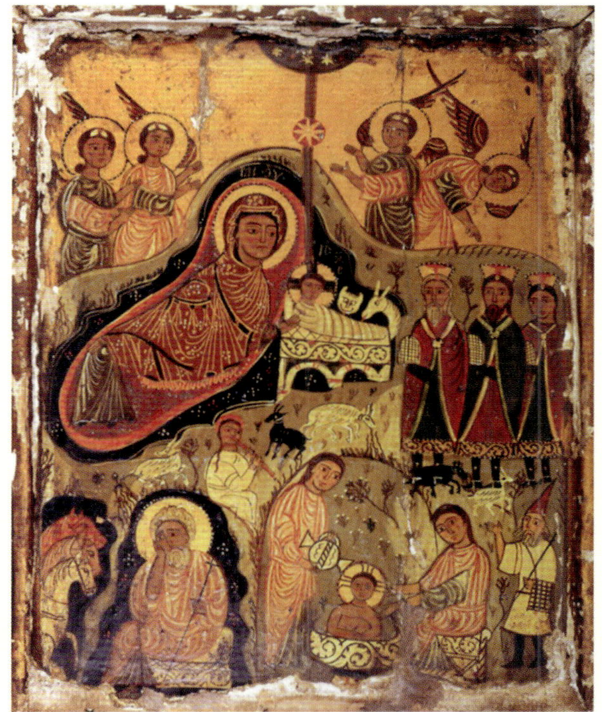

FIG. 1. *(above) Gentile da Fabriano, Nativity scene in the predella of* The Adoration of the Magi Altarpiece, *1423, originally in the Strozzi family chapel in Santa Trinità, Florence, tempera on panel, 25 x 62 cm, Uffizi, Florence. The Christ Child lies on the ground surrounded by mysterious light, in front of a cave where the ox and ass are shown gazing protectively at the Divine Child. Mary kneels beside the newborn, midwives sit to the side, Joseph sleeps in the foreground, and in the background shepherds see the angel.*

FIG. 2. *(left) Icon of the Nativity, in Coptic style, seventh century, in St Catherine's Monastery, Sinai, Egypt. The Virgin, almost cocooned, lies in front of the cave and attends to the Christ Child. The setting – which includes the Hand of God at the highest point, the angelic world, the light pouring down from above to the earth below – has remained traditional for Nativity icons over the centuries. The Christ Child is shown both in the manger and, in the foreground, at the bath with the midwives.*

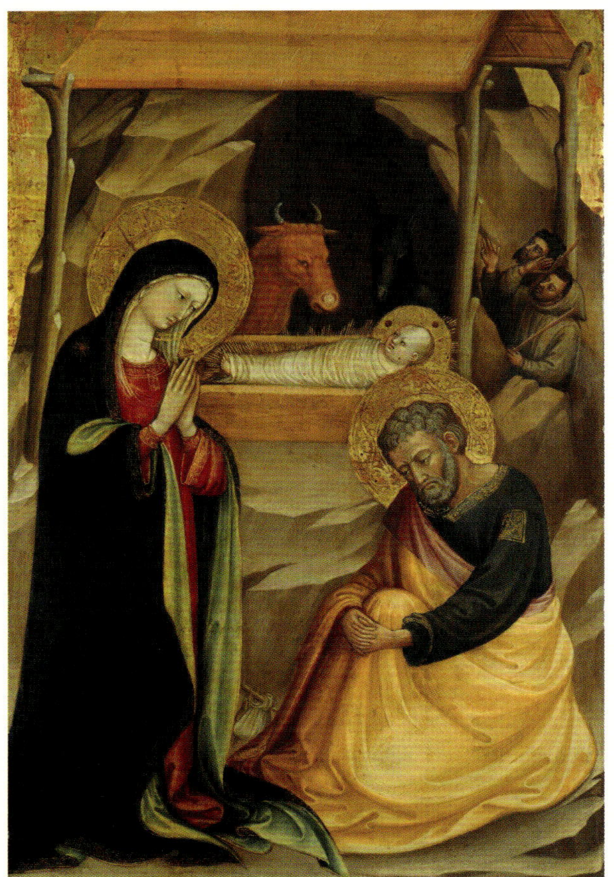

FIG. 4. *Bicci di Lorenzo,* The Nativity, *c. 1440, tempera on poplar, 88 x 58 cm, Private Collection. Here the cave is neatly cut into the rocks and the Christ Child lies tightly swaddled. Joseph, in yellow (the colour symbolising royalty, thus Joseph's descent from the royal house of David), is seen pondering.*

manuscript, the *Turin-Milan Hours*, depicts the event within the cave [FIG. 3]. It shows the Christ Child lying naked on the ground; Joseph stands protectively behind the Virgin, and angels in the sky sing in exultation.

What is the significance of the cave? The function of narrative events, written or depicted, is to draw attention to the threshold of another level of understanding. In ancient myth and mystical tradition the cave acts as the birthplace of gods, the focus of initiation, the dwelling place of unseen oracles. Traditionally the innermost cave was inaccessible to the profane, its access guarded. A metaphysical synonym for darkness and ignorance, as well as the unknown, a cave is essentially a secret place, a hiding place as well as a place of shelter, a place where treasure may be hidden.

The cave is also an allegory for the psychological prison into which mankind falls when expelled from Paradise. And a cave is the dark place within man, where one may be lost, where God has not yet entered. Man is born on the level of darkness and must ascend to the level where he can begin his ideal work.

Images in Western Christendom gradually replaced the cave of the Nativity with a stable, or a hut, a barn, a shed. The setting gradually evolved from one of infinite timelessness to a Europeanised context with emphasis on narrative details and down-to-earth familiarity, attempting perhaps to encourage the faithful to identify with the human aspects of the Divine birth in a more 'literal' interpretation, to bring the sacred events home. Poverty and humility are paramount. Yet the image of the cave persisted, notably in areas such as northern Italy, which had strong links with Byzantium, but now the cave was the darkened background set within a structure resembling a primitive stable [FIG. 4]. Look for instance, at Duccio's *Nativity* made for the *Maestà* altarpiece in Siena Cathedral [see Chapter V, FIG. 4], with its hierarchical Byzantine setting, the Virgin reclining, the Christ Child laid at her side on an altar-like manger, overlooked by the

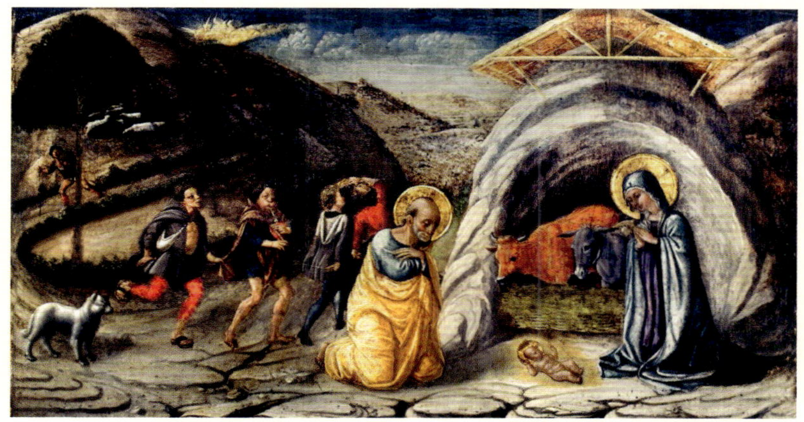

FIG. 5. *Niccolò da Foligno,* The Nativity, *c. 1480, fragment from a polyptych, oil on poplar, 48 x 76 cm, Musée du Petit Palais, Avignon. We see the ox and the ass sheltering in the cave, beneath a wooden roof structure, and the naked Christ Child on the ground. The shepherds are running – 'and they came with haste' – towards the cave, one still gazing up at the light, one playing pipes, accompanied by their dog.*

ox and the ass – and here the pedimented wooden structure has a dark cavernous backdrop, and, like an icon, is set into a steep rocky mountain, against a timeless gold background. Much later, *c.* 1480, another Sienese painter, Niccolò da Foligno, chose a cave for the Nativity, and set it below a wooden roof, all this in an Italianate landscape [FIG. 5]. Bartolo di Fredi's late fourteenth-century painting of the Adoration of the Shepherds, with a host of angels in the pinnacle of an altarpiece, depicts a tightly swaddled Christ Child with Joseph and Mary both kneeling beside the manger just outside the cave [FIG. 6].

Botticelli set his famous *Mystic Nativity* (*c.* 1500) in a blackened cave, surrounded by craggy rocks [FIG. 7] Here the cave is protected by a thatched overhanging stable roof, on which kneeling angels sing, holding their choir books, and the setting is transposed to a green meadow and a dark grove of trees behind. In the foreground men and angels embrace while demons scuttle away to hide, referring to Chapter 12 of the Apocalypse (Revelation) an interpretation based on Origen, known at this time as the 'Theologian of the Platonists'. He aimed to reconcile Platonism with

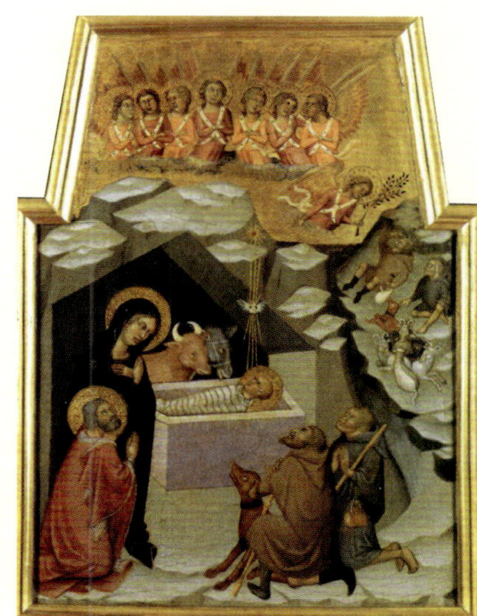

FIG. 6. *Bartolo di Fredi,* The Adoration of the Shepherds, *c. 1383, part of a polyptych made for the Chapel of the Annunciation in the church of San Francesco in Montalcino, tempera and gold on wood, 50 x 35 cm, Pinacoteca Vaticana. Outside the carefully cut-out cave the tightly swaddled Christ Child lies below the Holy Spirit, in the form of the Dove and the Light, descending from the invisible God the Father. The shepherds kneel at the crib, having received the tidings from the angel, shown in the background.*

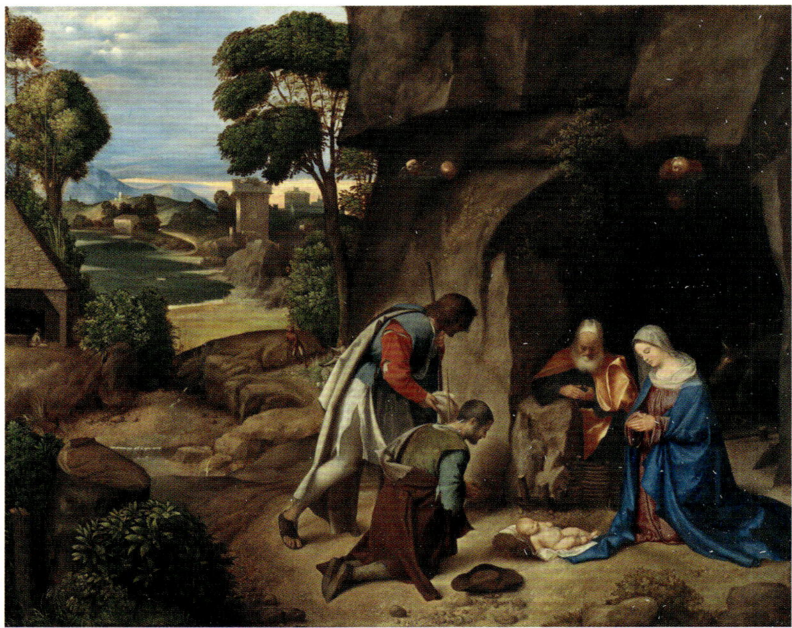

FIG. 8 . *Giorgione (Zorzo da Castelfranco),* The Adoration of the Shepherds, *1505–10, oil on panel, 90.8 x 110.5 cm, National Gallery of Art, Washington, D.C. Here the grotto is hollowed out of the rocks and beyond lies an Italianate landscape. The shepherds, modestly dressed, submit in humility beside the newborn Saviour. The picture was probably painted for a patron's private devotions.*

Christianity, and considered that man was an undecided angel. At the very top of the the painting, the Greek inscription mentions the 'troubles of Italy', a reference to the French invasions and civil strife in Florence, events that Botticelli associated with the Apocalypse.

In a completely different mode, Giorgione painted the *Adoration of the Shepherds* in a gloriously mellow landscape [FIG. 8], a setting often favoured by Renaissance artists of the time: the shepherds, simple, solid folk, kneel and bow before the Christ Child who lies on Mary's mantle outside the cave with rugged rocks around it, topped by the steep roof of a stable shed.

In Nativity images the cave of Christ's birth is intrinsically linked to the cave of His burial – a connection emphasised by the swaddling for the newborn that recalls the shroud wound about the dead Christ at His burial, a potent reminder that Christ was born to die for our sins and so to redeem mankind. Irenaeus, Bishop of Lyon (*c.* 120– *c.* 200), connected the cave of the Nativity to the cave of Hades, linking Christ's Incarnation with the Descent into Limbo.[vi] *Anastasis* – Resurrection – has long been a subject for icon and fresco painters in the Eastern Church, as we see for example in the magnificent fresco in the Chora Church [FIG. 9].

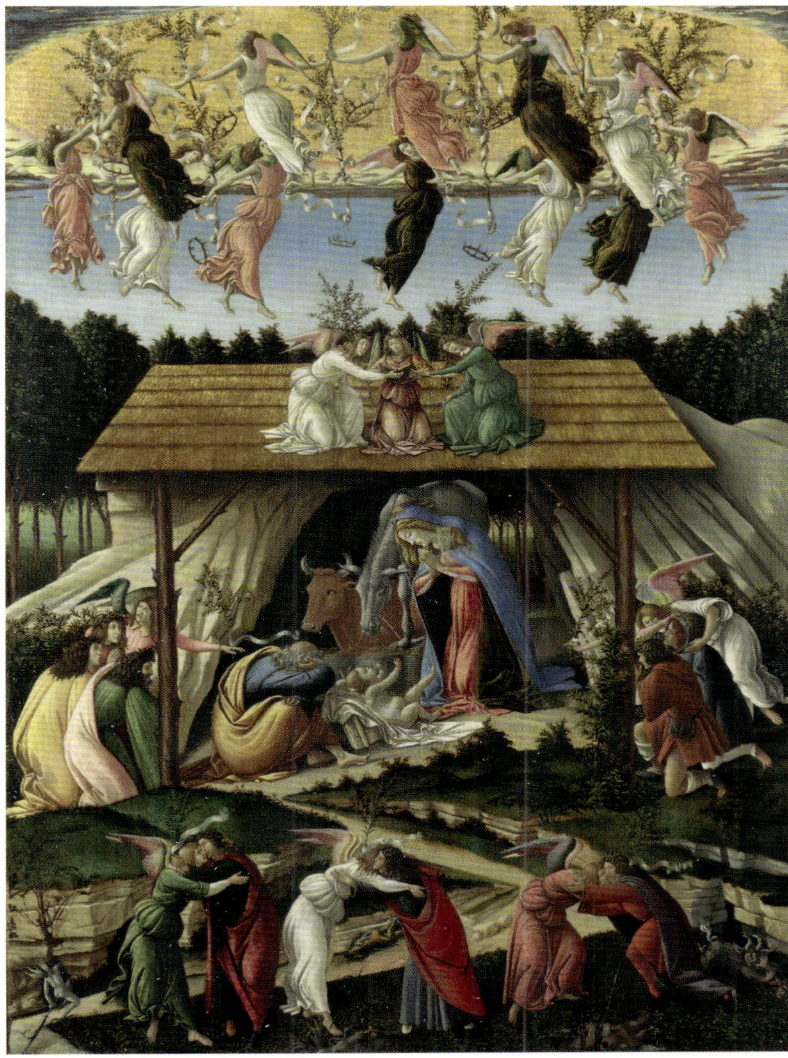

FIG. 7 . *Sandro Botticelli*, Mystic Nativity, *c. 1500, oil on canvas, 108.6 x 74.9 cm, National Gallery, London. In the glade of a forest, a thatched roof shelters the cave. The Christ Child reaches towards Mary, Joseph sleeps, shepherds and Magi are all present. Angels celebrate the glorious event.*

The 'cave of the heart' is a well known traditional expression: the word *guhā* in Sanskrit generally denotes a cave, and is also applied to the cavity of the heart, and so to the heart itself.[vii] Like the axis of the wheel, this dark, mysterious interior symbolised by the cave in the image of the Nativity represents the heart, our own centre. It is this that connects us with the periphery. The heart is the dwelling place of the Divine.[viii]

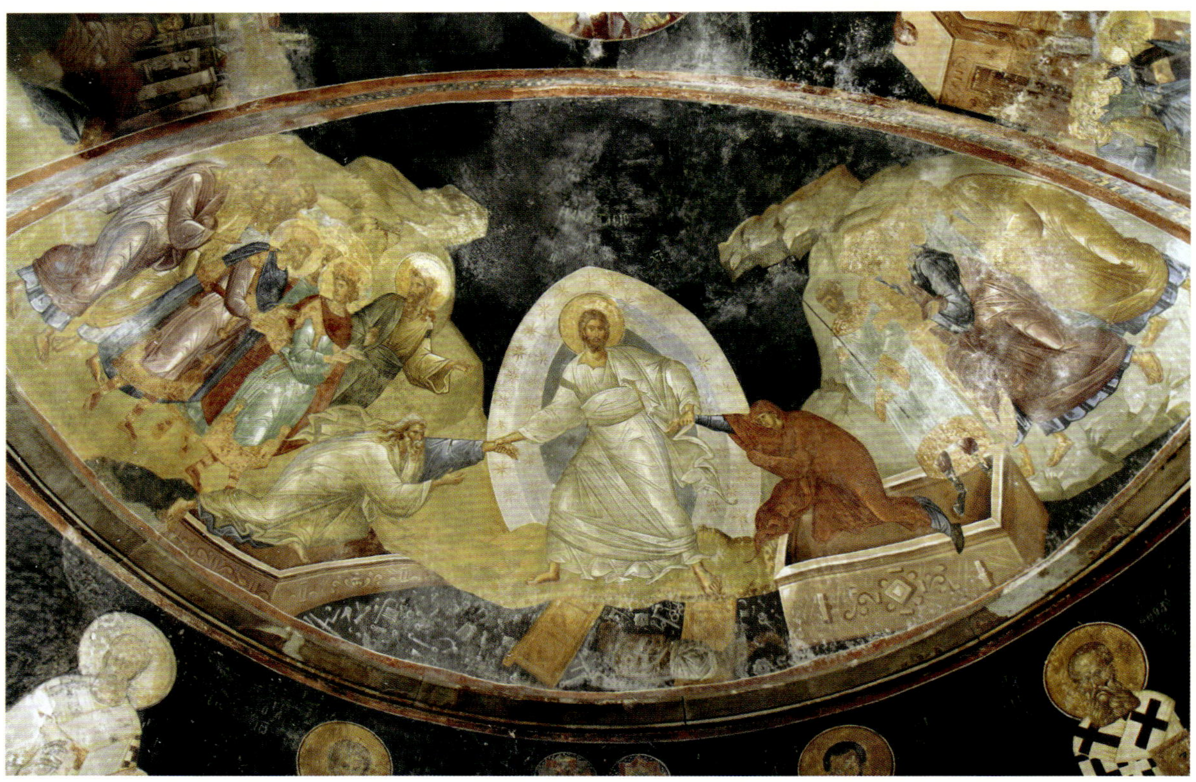

FIG. 9. The Anastasis *(the Resurrection), c. 1315–20, a famous Byzantine fresco in the apse of the Church of the Holy Saviour in Chora, Istanbul. Enclosed in a luminous oval mandorla, decorated with stars, the glorious figure of the risen Christ, clad in glowing* white robes, descends into hell and vanquishes Satan. *Emblems of hell – chains, keys, nails, shackles – are depicted in the circular cave of darkness. Christ pulls Adam and Eve out of their tombs upwards, an allegory of the spiritual journey from darkness to light.*

III THE CAVE: FOOTNOTES

i According to the Ethiopian *Book of Adam and Eve* (*c.* sixth century) Eve gave birth to her firstborn, Cain, in a cave in the Mountain of Paradise. Eve, the first mother, is taken as prototype for Mary. Adam, in his grief at Eve's travail during labour, is associated with Joseph, often depicted expressing a gesture of sorrow.

ii Justin Martyr, *Dialogue with Trypho*, ch. LXXVIII.

iii Origen, *Contra Celsum*, bk 1, ch. 1.

iv See David R. Cartlidge and J. Keith Elliot, *Art and the Christian Apocrypha* (London and New York: Routledge, 2001).

v See Richard Temple, *Icons and the Mystical Origins of Christianity* (Shaftesbury: Element, 1990). See also Christian Heck, *L'Échelle céleste dans l'art du Moyen Age* (Paris: Flammarion, 1997).

vi Theologically termed the 'harrowing of hell'.

vii This word comes from *guh*, which means 'covering' or 'hiding', as does *gup*, whence *gupta*, which is applied to everything secret, not outwardly manifested. It is equivalent to the Greek *kruptos*, from which comes the word 'crypt', a synonym of 'cave'. See www.studiesincomparativereligion.com. René Guénon, 'The Mountain and the Cave', in *Studies in Comparative Religion*, vol. 5, no. 2 (Spring 1971), and 'The Heart and the Cave', ibid., no. 1 (Winter 1971).

viii See Jonathan Pageau, www.orthodoxartsjournal.org/the-recovery-of-the-arts-pt-3-memory-of-the-heart

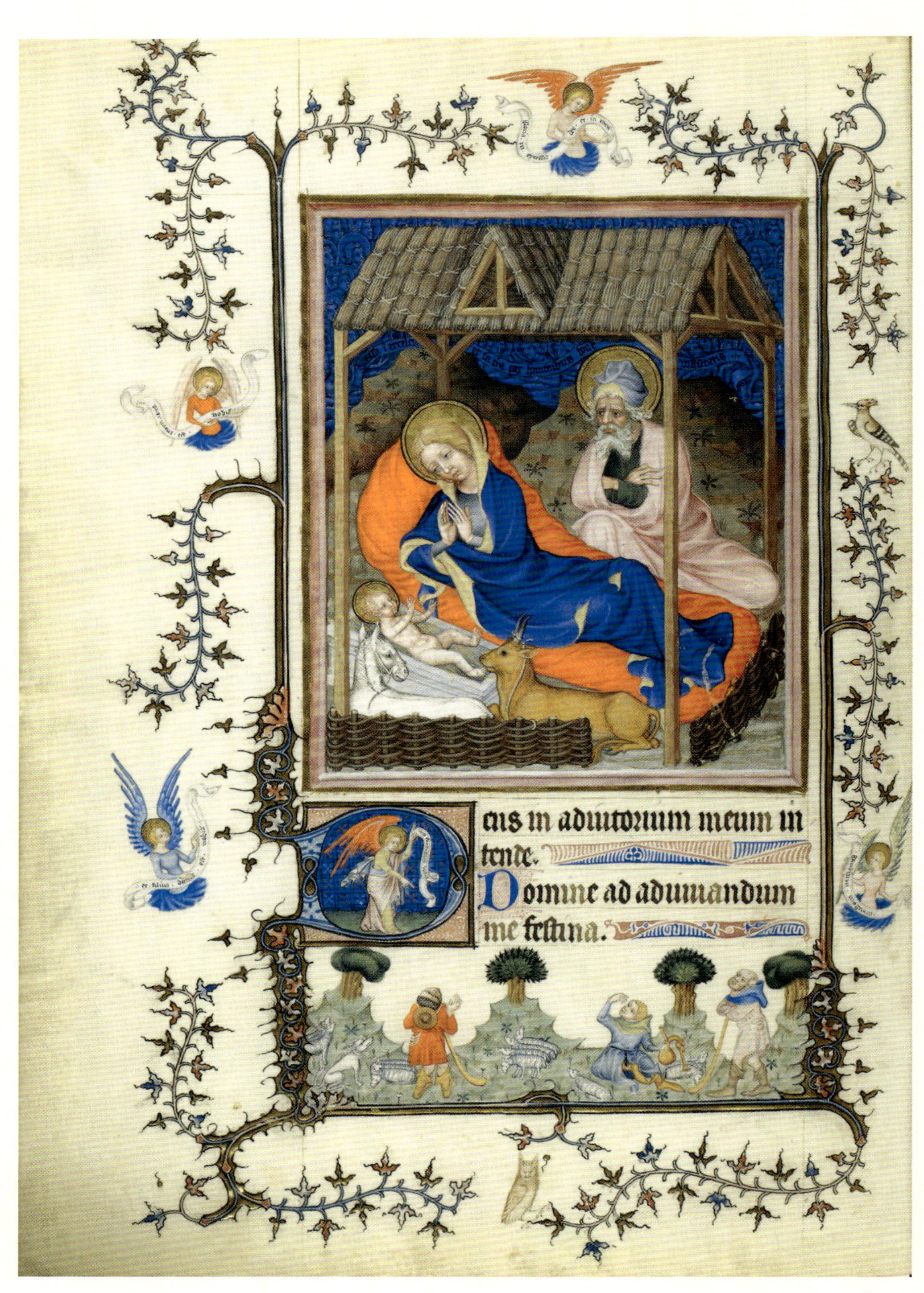

eus in adiutorium meum in
tende.
Domine ad adiuuandum
me festina.

IV   THE MANGER

'AND SHE BROUGHT FORTH HER FIRSTBORN SON, and wrapped him up in swaddling clothes, and laid him in a manger; because there was no room for them in the inn' (Luke 2:7) [FIG. 1].

The history of the manger begins in the grotto in Bethlehem, traditionally venerated as the birthplace of Christ. According to Origen in the third century, this veneration was well established in his own day, and a specific manger in a specific cave was the centre of pious devotion, as we saw in the previous chapter.

Over this sacred spot the Empress Helena (who visited Bethlehem in 325–26), mother of Constantine the Great, erected a basilica, probably begun in the year 330, and dedicated in 339.[i] The site was visited during the fourth century by numerous pilgrims, among them Jerome (*c.* 347–420), who spent the last years of his life living in a nearby cave, and wrote of the 'spiritual edification' of seeing holy places. Other literary evidence informs us that the grotto was richly decorated, the manger adorned with gold and silver, and some unproven reports assert that figures of the Holy Family were placed here as early as the year 400.[ii] Early visitors included the anonymous Pilgrim of Bordeaux, author of *Itinerarium Burdigalense*, an account of the journey from Bordeaux to the Holy Land in 333/34; also Eusebius of Caesarea (*c.* 260–340), Church historian and geographer, and Egeria (possibly from Roman Galicia), who wrote a detailed account of her pilgrimage to the Holy Land in the 380s.[iii]

According to legend, relics of the manger, consisting of boards of sycamore wood, were brought from Bethlehem to Rome by pilgrims as early as the fourth century, and soon attracted large numbers of the faithful. The *praesepe* relics were enshrined and venerated in the church then called Sancta Maria ad Praesepe, now known as Santa Maria Maggiore.[iv] It was here, in the year 432, that Pope Sixtus III commissioned magnificent mosaics in honour of the Virgin *theotokos* – bearer of God (for Mary *theotokos* see Chapter VIII). While celebrating Mass on the eve of the Nativity, the Pope laid the consecrated Host directly on the enshrined crib relics which

FIG. 1. *Nativity scene in the* Très Belles Heures de Notre-Dame, *c. 1380, Bibliothèque nationale de France, Paris, MS nouv. acq. lat. 3093. Against a blue background made up of choirs of angels, Mary, with Joseph beyond, gazes in awe at the Christ Child. He lies in a simple manger, watched by the ox and ass, enclosed by a low wattle fence. Below is the Annunciation to the Shepherds.*

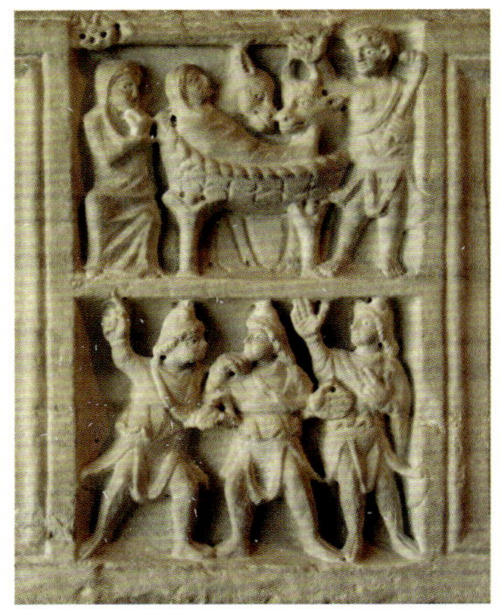

FIG. 2. *Basketwork manger guarded by the ox and the ass, carved on the lid of a sarcophagus, first half of the fourth century, Musée de l'Arles et de la Provence antiques, Arles. Mary sits at one end, a young shepherd stands at the other. Below, the Magi are shown searching.*

had been placed on the altar. The story of the celebration of this Christmas Mass rapidly spread throughout Christian Europe, and we can presume that 'manger altars' were set up in imitation in other churches to celebrate Christ's Nativity on the feast day.

In the middle of the seventh century another sycamore board from the manger of Christ's birth was brought from Jerusalem through the diplomatic negotiations of the Pope, Theodore I (born in Jerusalem, of Greek descent).[v] Together these precious relics were enshrined in the 'Cave of the Nativity' – an area that had been carved out of rock under the high altar of the basilica, in imitation of the cave in Bethlehem. Much later, in the sixteenth century, the relics were encased in a crystal urn (the reliquary was trimmed with silver and gold in the early nineteenth century), and the 'cave' was moved – lock, stock and barrel – to the crypt below a huge newly built side chapel in the church, the Sistine Chapel, named in honour of Pope Sixtus V.[vi] At its entrance are placed the remains of Arnolfo di Cambio's remarkable freestanding crib figures, sculpted in stone in 1291. Now the relics of the sacred manger, in their ornate urn, are in a crypt directly beneath the high altar – the Crypt of the Nativity, or Bethlehem Crypt.

The form of the manger in images of the Nativity varies considerably, as does the design of the altar that alludes to the manger.[vii] It may be a plain solid feeding-trough or an osier basket [FIG. 2] or made of brick [FIG. 3]; it may be a large chest-like object [FIG. 4], or resemble a wooden box [FIG. 5]. It may be depicted as a tall structure resembling an altar [FIG. 6], and so replace the small crib. Sometimes

FIG. 3. *Panel from Gaul or northern Italy depicting a brick manger on which the tightly swaddled Christ Child lies, first quarter of the fifth century, ivory, 7.2 x 12.8 cm, Musée de la Faïence et des Beaux-arts, Nevers. The ox and the ass stand in arched niches. The adjoining scene shows the Adoration of the Magi.*

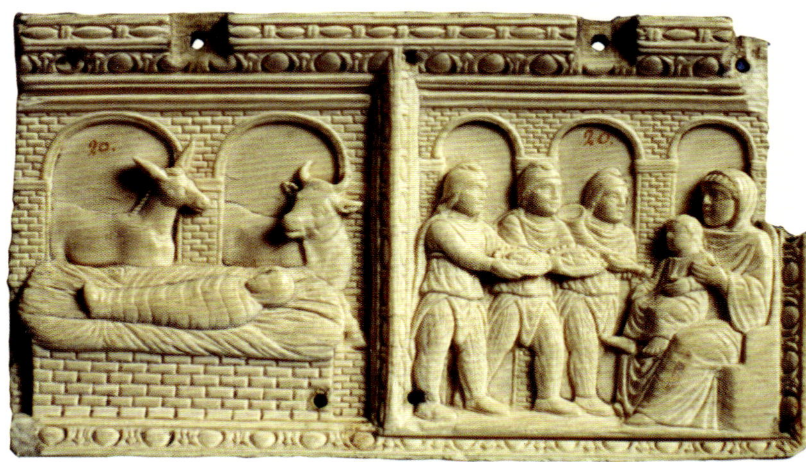

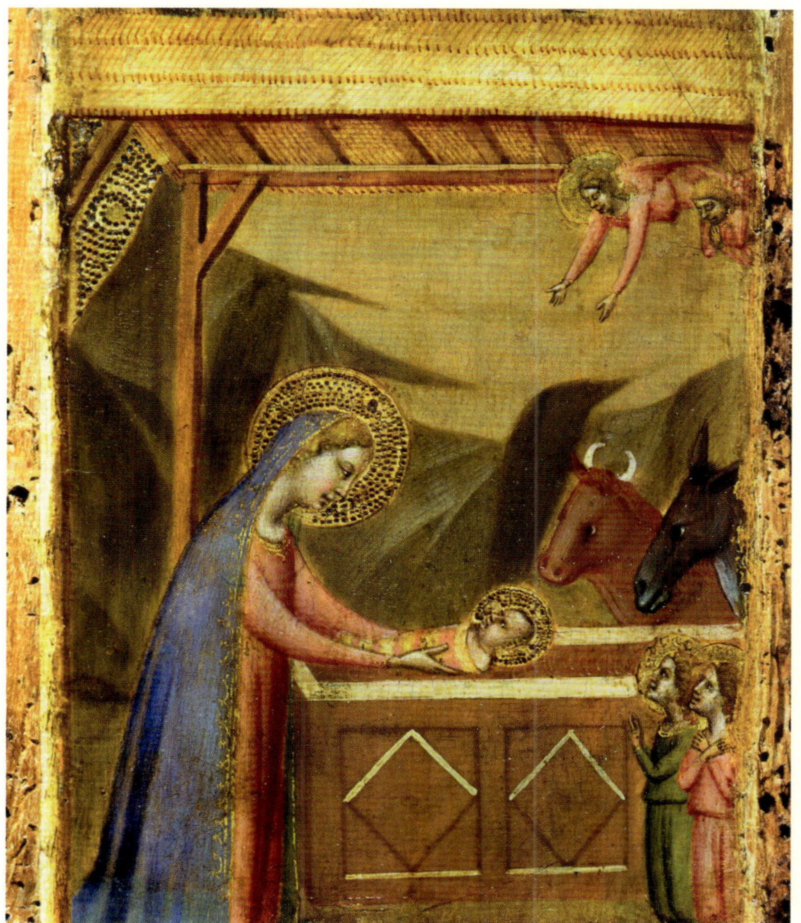

FIG. 4. The Nativity, *fragment of a triptych from the studio of Bernardo Daddi, tempera on poplar, 14.1 x 12.1 cm, Wallace Collection, London. The Virgin is placing the Child – in red swaddling clothes patterned like a liturgical vestment – in a deep box manger. Rejoicing angels and benevolent beasts participate in this tender rendering of the event.*

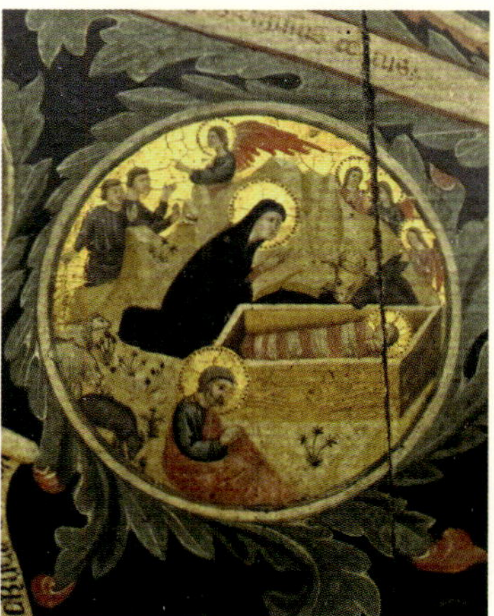

FIG. 5. *Pacino di Bonaguida, Nativity scene in a circular panel of the* Arbor Vitae *from the convent at Monticelli, c. 1310–15, tempera and gold leaf on poplar, Galleria dell'Accademia, Florence. The Christ Child, whose swaddling is reminiscent of burial bindings, lies in a simple wooden box manger. The overall effect is tomb-like: birth and death, sacrament and sacrifice are evoked.*

we are shown one, two or three little rounded openings below the flat top [FIG. 7] – a reference to pilgrims' accounts of their experience of looking through an opening, like a *confessio*, built over the grotto, and gazing down into the specific site of the Nativity in the church at Bethlehem. There this sacred spot is now marked by a fourteen-pointed silver star (inserted in 1717) with a Latin inscription that reads: *HIC DE VIRGINE JESUS CHRISTUS NATUS EST* (Here Jesus Christ was born of the Virgin Mary).

Traditionally a manger provides fodder for beasts (as the French verb *manger*, to eat, reminds us). So by analogy the image of the newborn Christ Child placed in a manger is linked to nourishment. On the manger-altar during the sacrifice of the Mass, at the

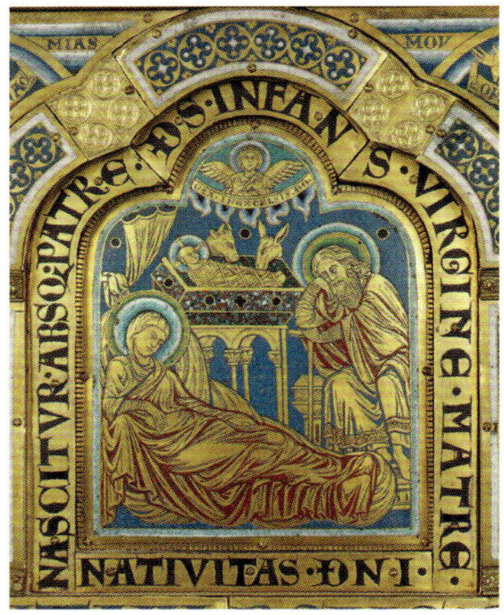

FIG. 6. *An elegant manger-altar on spindly legs, on a plaque from an ensemble completed in 1181 by the renowned goldsmith Nicholas of Verdun, champlevé enamel on copper with gilding, 20.5 x 16.5 cm. One of forty-five plaques for the pulpit of the Abbey of Klosterneuburg near Vienna, reassembled to become a triptych altarpiece after a fire in 1320. Christ's halo contains a cross.*

FIG. 7. *Relief showing a confessio below the manger where the Christ Child lies, 1140–60, walrus ivory, 21 x 19 cm, Victoria and Albert Museum, London. There are arched openings, as described by pilgrims to the birthplace in the cave at Bethlehem. This panel may have formed part of the facing of an altar.*

Consecration, the bread is changed into the Body of Christ and the wine into the Blood of Christ, in commemoration of the Last Supper.[viii] Jerome says that when his disciple Paula first saw the cave of the Nativity she cried out, 'I salute thee Bethlehem, House of bread, where the bread was born that came down from heaven.' In the Eastern Orthodox tradition, the space behind the iconostasis (the screen) used for the preparation and storage of the Holy Bread is named Bethlehem.

On our earthly level, bread is a universally fundamental food, offering sustenance to both body and spirit. In many traditions and cultures, the breaking of bread together, the sharing of a meal, is a sacred act. The word 'companion' – 'with bread' – bears testament to this, as do wall paintings in the catacombs. In the Lord's Prayer Jesus taught His disciples to pray to the Father 'to give us this day our daily bread' – this nourishment coming from another level, a

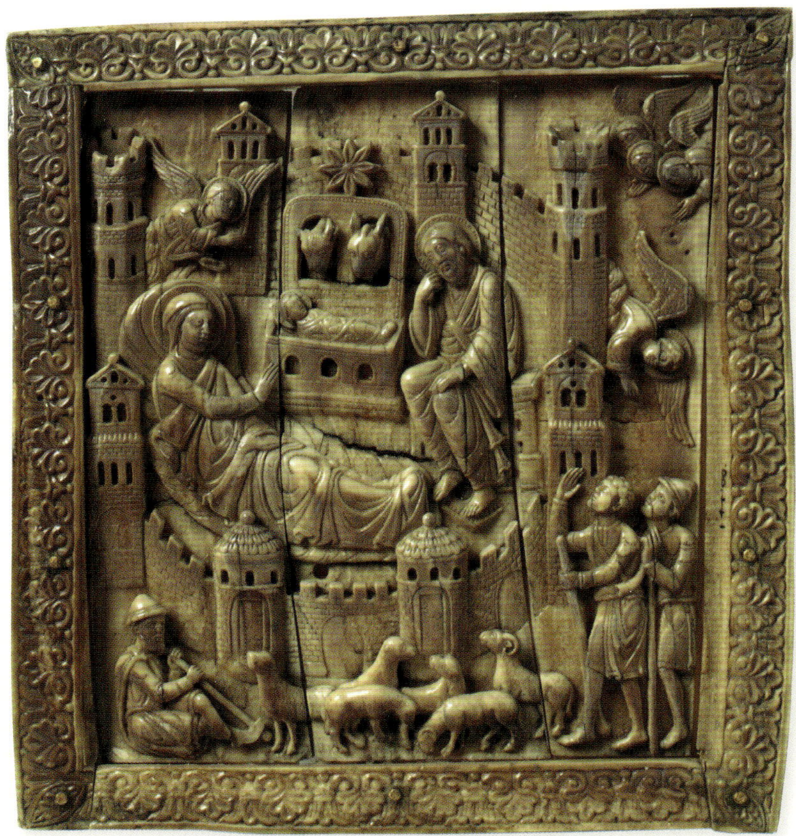

higher truth that imparts new vitality to mind and body.[ix] The word 'Eucharist' comes from the Greek *eucharistia*, meaning thanksgiving, and derives from the Hebrew *berekah* – praise and thanks.

From a very early date the Incarnation of Christ was given a Eucharistic interpretation in Greek and Latin theology and homilies. Athanasius (*c.* 296–373) connects the birth of Christ with the Eucharist; the Christological controversies of the fourth century led to an intensive analysis of the mystery of the Incarnation. Ambrose, John Chrysostom and Gregory the Great all expanded and developed the Eucharistic theme in homilies and sermons, as did later mediaeval theologians, among them Aelred of Rievaulx (1110–67) and Meister Eckhart.[x] Increasingly the Church Fathers considered that by accepting the word and the body of Christ, the individual believer could become the new Bethlehem, and the Church was characterised as the true *domus panis*.

An eleventh-century manuscript illumination in the Gospel Book of Bishop Bernward of Hildesheim depicts the Nativity scene, showing the Christ Child lying on a manger-altar [FIG. 8]. The three Magi, their backs to the viewer, dressed to resemble three priest-kings celebrating Mass, worship the Child. Elsewhere in paintings,

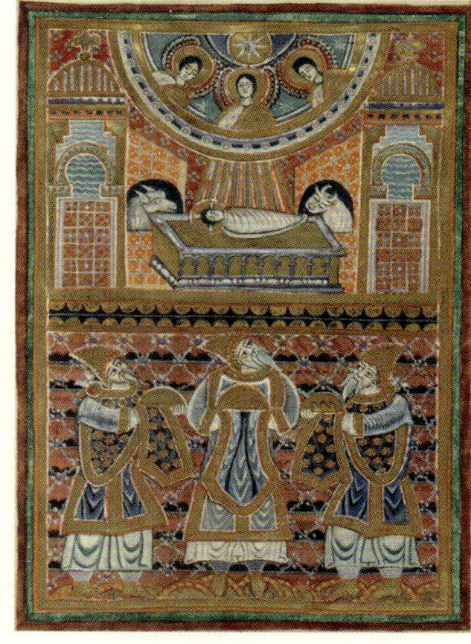

FIG. 8. *Two scenes in the Gospel Book of Bishop Bernward of Hildesheim, 1011–14, Hildesheim Cathedral Treasury, Cod. 18. Above is the Nativity with a manger-altar; below we see the Magi, the priest-kings, robed in liturgical vestments, worshipping the Child.*

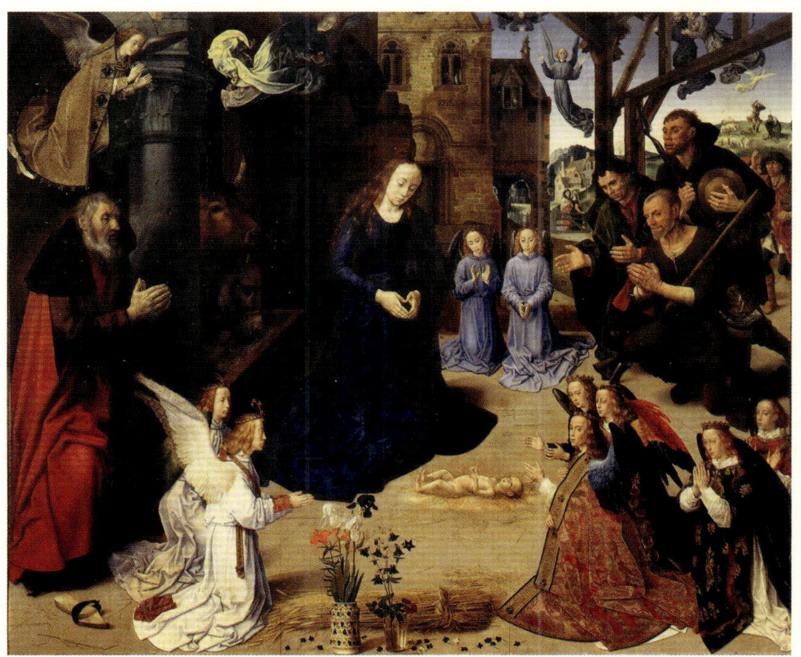

FIG. 9. *Hugo van der Goes, Nativity scene, c. 1475, in the altarpiece commissioned by Tommaso Portinari, representative of the Medici bankers in Bruges, for the hospital of Santa Maria Nuova in Florence, oil on wood, 240 x 340 cm, Uffizi, Florence. The Adoration of the Shepherds contains several Eucharistic evocations – the sheaf of corn in the foreground, ready to become the Eucharistic bread, and the angels in liturgical vestments worn by priests during the celebration of High Mass.*

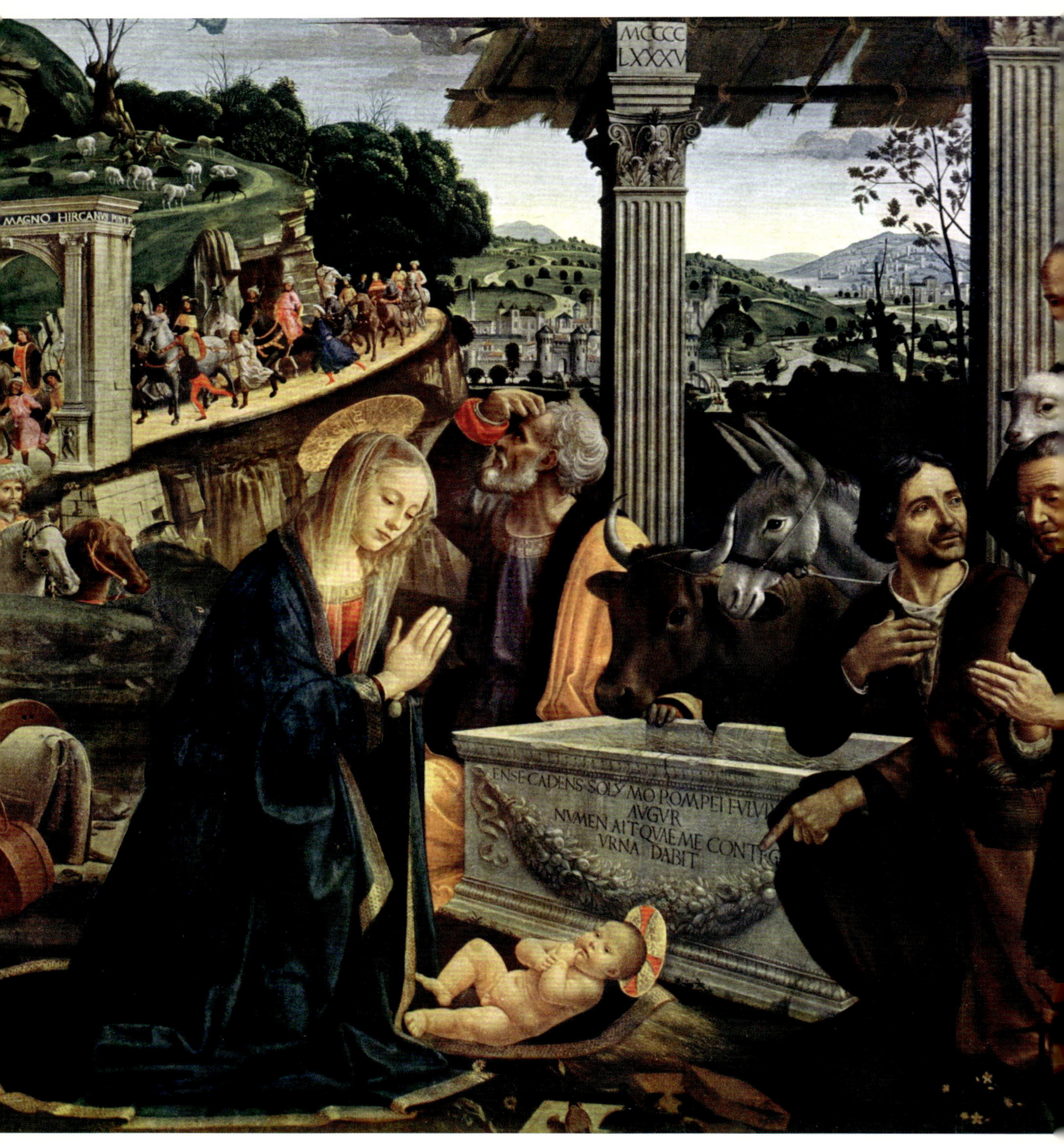

the sacramental significance of the Incarnation is evoked by the motif of the angels censing the Child or by the lamp above the manger-altar, recognisable as the sacristy lamp found in churches to this day, and popular in medieval French illuminated manuscripts. In later paintings of the Middle Ages we find sheaves of corn or ears of corn, representing bread, depicted near the newborn Christ Child. Look, for instance, at the *Portinari Altarpiece* [FIG. 9].

However, images of Christ's birth, His Incarnation, also recall Christ's death. With shock we perceive that the carefully swaddled bands protecting the Christ Child lying in the manger resemble the winding sheet of a shroud. Swaddling clothes that envelope the newborn Christ Child are a symbol of His birth, His humanity, His frailty, and equally of His death, the Saviour born to die for mankind, to redeem humanity. In a scene from the studio of Bernardo Daddi, the Infant's swaddling is coloured blood-red, as we have seen [FIG. 4]. Some Nativity scenes intentionally depict the manger to look like a sarcophagus [FIG. 10, and Chapter V, FIG. 6] and the swaddling at Christ's birth [FIG. 11] echoes the linen cloths wrapped around His body at His entombment. Occasionally the swaddling bands are shown to be embroidered with little crosses, resembling a corporal, the small cloth laid on the altar on which elements of the Eucharist are placed.

Birth and Death are evoked, the Sacrament of the Eucharist, and the Sacrifice of Christ's Death. Inside Chartres Cathedral, the thirteenth-century rood screen, now in fragments, shows the manger's dual role – both altar and tomb – in a sculpture which remains remarkably tender and moving despite the damage of time and the headless figure offering the Virgin covering [FIG. 12].

The sculpture at the entrance to Chartres Cathedral clearly expresses the sacramental nature of the Nativity. Christ is revealed as both human and Divine. On the west front, the right door of the Portail Royal (1145–55) shows us the following [FIG. 13]: in the lowest register, Mary lying on her bed, and directly above her the Christ Child (this figure now destroyed) lying between the ox and the ass, and flanked by figures on a flat surface akin to an altar top – an evocation both of the Child in the manger and the Bread on the altar. Above this register, we see the Presentation in the Temple, where the Christ Child stands on the altar. At the summit, in the tympanum, the Christ Child sits enthroned in His mother's lap. Thus on this axis we see Christ born to man, ascending to Divine Wisdom, Kingship and Divinity.

FIG. 10. (opposite) Domenico Ghirlandaio, The Adoration of the Shepherds, fresco in the Sassetti Chapel in Santa Trinita, Florence, 1482–85. The marble manger is more like a sarcophagus, resonating with the Classical architecture in the painting. The artist has included his self portrait as the shepherd at the front of the group, pointing to the Christ Child.

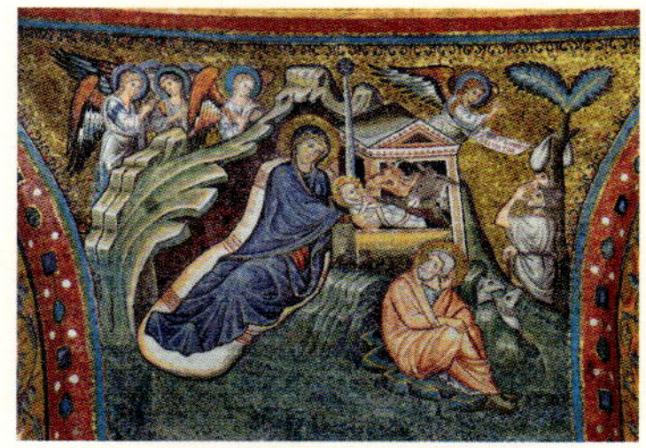

FIG. 11. Jacopo Torriti, mosaic of the Nativity in the apse of Santa Maria Maggiore, Rome, 1296. The manger is reminiscent of a Classical tomb, and the Christ Child's swaddling evokes burial bindings as well as swaddling bands.

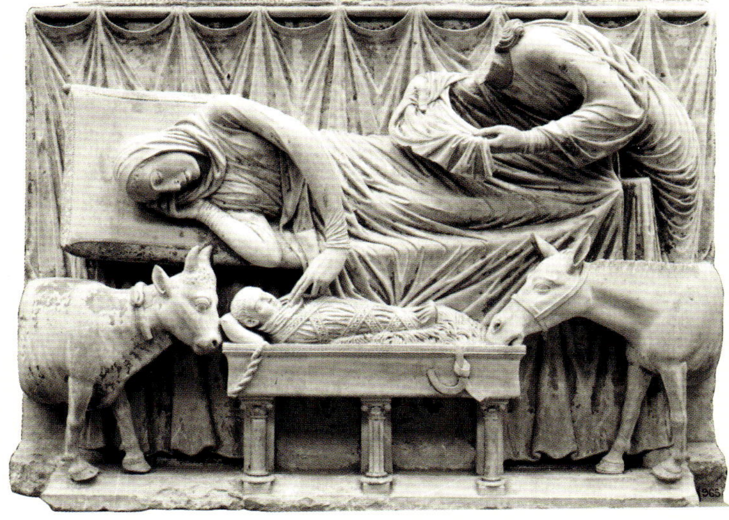

FIG. 12. *Nativity scene on a fragment of the rood screen of 1240–50 in Chartres Cathedral, 93 x 133 cm. Tender motherly love for the Divine Child is powerfully expressed. The manger evokes both a Classical tomb and an altar.*

Origen's homily on Luke's Nativity Gospel (preached in Egypt around the year 240) ends with this: 'Having understood this manger, let us strive to know the Lord and become worthy of the knowledge of Him, and to receive His birth, the resurrection of His flesh and also His glorious return to majesty; to Him be glory and dominion unto all ages. Amen.'

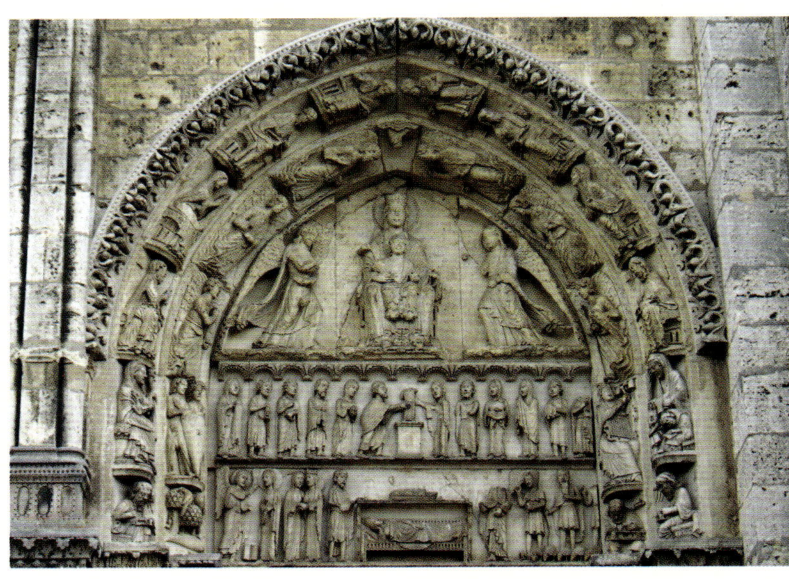

FIG. 13. *Birth, sacrifice and kingship, sculpted in the tympanum of the right door of the Portail Royal on the west front of Chartres Cathedral, 1145–55. In the centre of the lowest register is the Nativity: directly above the Virgin Mary, who lies on the bed, was the figure of the Christ Child (destroyed) lying on a flat surface, suggesting an altar top, between the ox and the ass. At the centre of the next register is the Presentation in the Temple; at the top, the Child enthroned on His mother's lap.*

IV THE MANGER: FOOTNOTES

i The basilica has endured many changes: it was destroyed by fire during the Samaritan uprising in the sixth century and subsequently rebuilt under Justinian; during the Crusades there were numerous repairs, changes and additions. The Church of the Nativity (as it is generally known nowadays) was made a UNESCO World Heritage Site in 2012.

ii See Karl Young, *The Drama of the Medieval Church* (Oxford: Clarendon Press, 1933), vol. 2, p. 24.

iii The author of the *Itinerarium Burdigalense* journeyed from modern-day Bordeaux through northern Italy, the Danube valley, Constantinople, into Syria, and on to Jerusalem. Egeria wrote a detailed account of her pilgrimage: see *Egeria's Travels* transl. and ed. by John Wilkinson (3rd edn, Warminster: Aris and Phillips, 2006). See also E.D. Hunt, *Holy Land Pilgrimage in the Later Roman Empire AD 312–460* (Oxford: Clarendon Press, 1982).

iv One of the first churches built in honour of the Virgin Mary, and one four major basilicas in Rome, the church changed names many times – Sancta Maria ad Praesepe, the Liberiana (under Pope Liberius), Our Lady of the Snows. Constantly enlarged and embellished, despite its Baroque exterior it retains the basilica interior with its famous fifth-century mosaics.

v Theodore's pontificate (640–49) was dominated by the struggle against monotheism.

vi Designed by Domenico Fontana.

vii See M. Hassett, 'History of the Christian Altar', in *The New Catholic Encyclopaedia* (New York: Robert Appleton & Co., 1967).

viii It was at the Fourth Lateran Council in 1215 (sometimes called the Great Council), convoked by Pope Innocent III, that the teaching on transubstantiation was defined, by which the bread and wine offered in the sacrament of the Eucharist become the actual blood and body and Christ. See 'Fourth Lateran Council' in *The New Catholic Encyclopaedia*, op. cit. in the preceding note.

ix See Maurice Nicoll, *The New Man* (London: Vincent Stuart and Richards, 1950), and *The Mark* (London: Vincent Stuart, 1952).

x For example, Gregory the Great in Homily 8, and Aelredus, Sermo 2. See Ursula Nilgen, 'The Epiphany and the Eucharist in the Interpretation of Eucharistic Motifs in Medieval Epiphany Scenes', in *Art Bulletin*, vol. 49, no. 4 (1967), pp. 311–20.

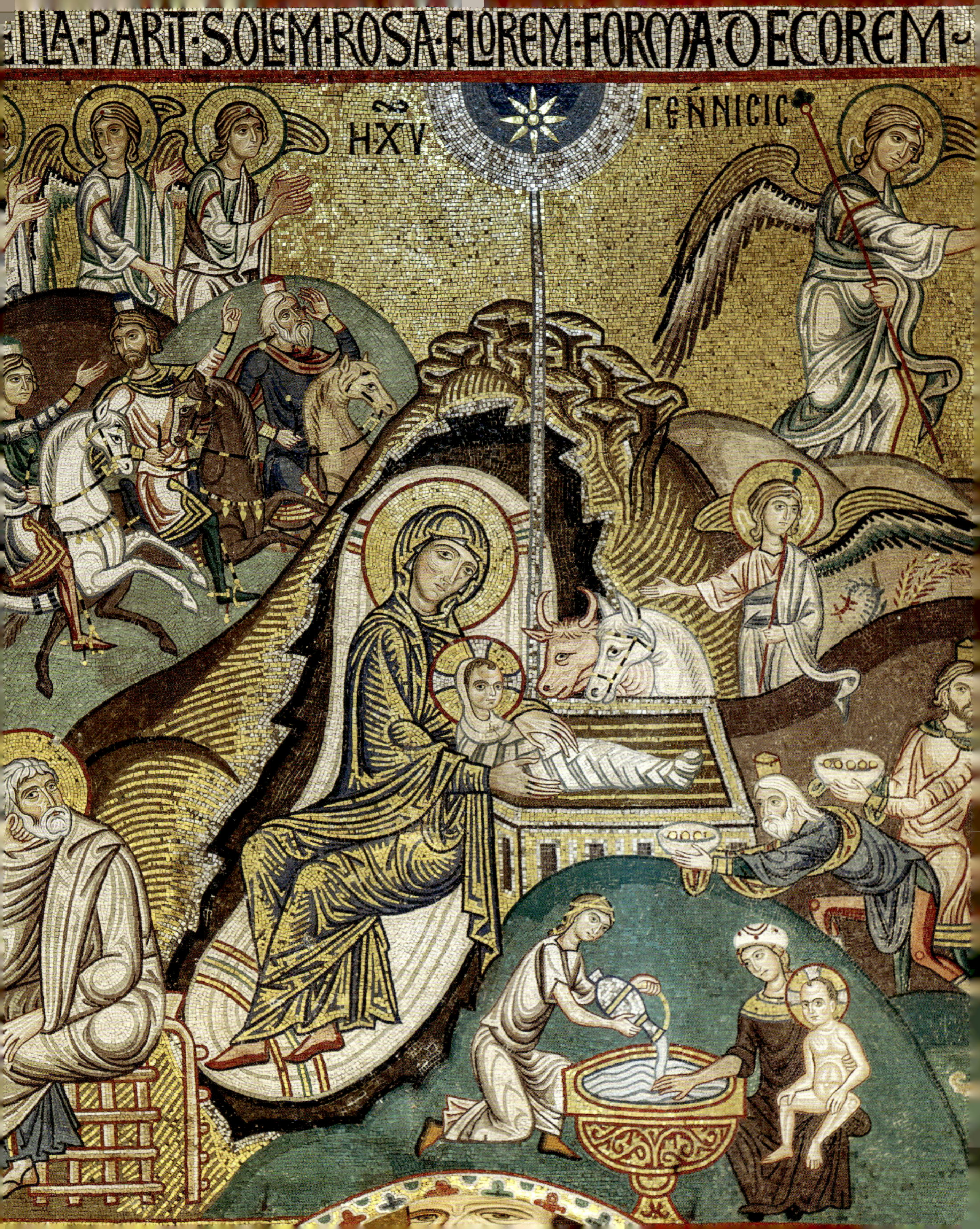
LLA·PART·SOLEM·ROSA·FLOREM·FORMA·DECOREM
HXV
ΓΕΝΝΙCΙC

V THE MIDWIVES

TWO MIDWIVES ARE OFTEN SHOWN present at the Nativity – and in the Orthodox tradition no icon of the scene is complete without them. They are usually seen bathing the newborn Christ Child [FIG. 1]. In later depictions of the Nativity in the Latin West the midwives might be taken simply as the Virgin's attendants or maidservants (whether one or two), as we observe in works by Giotto and Melchior Broederlam.

The story of the midwives attending the birth of Christ is nowhere to be found in the Gospels of Matthew, Mark, Luke or John, but is told in detail in the account of the Nativity in the *Protoevangelium Jacobi* (*c.* 150). We read that when Joseph and Mary arrived in Bethlehem

> He [Joseph] found a cave there and brought her into it and left her in the care of his sons and went out to seek for a Hebrew midwife in the region of Bethlehem … And he found one who was just coming down from the hill-country, and he took her with him, and said to the midwife: 'Mary is betrothed to me, but she conceived of the Holy Spirit after she had been brought up in the Temple of the Lord.' And the midwife went with him. And they went to the place of the cave, and behold, a dark cloud overshadowed the cave. And the midwife said: 'My soul is magnified today, for my eyes have seen wonderful things; for salvation is born to Israel.' And immediately the cloud disappeared from the cave, and a great light appeared in the cave, so that our eyes could not bear it. A short time afterwards that light withdrew until the child appeared, and it went and took the breast of its mother Mary. And the midwife cried: 'How great is this day for me, that I have seen this new sight.' And the midwife came out of the cave, and Salome met her. And she said to her, 'Salome, Salome, I have a new sight to tell you: a virgin has brought forth, a thing which nature does not allow.' And Salome said: 'As the Lord my God lives, unless I put my finger and test her

FIG. 1. *Nativity in mosaic in the central dome of the Palatine Chapel, Palermo, c. 1143. The scene is in the Byzantine tradition, with the cave and the journey of the Magi on the left, and also on the right, offering their gifts. The angel (top right) appears to the shepherds (not shown here). Joseph sits (bottom left), and in the foreground the midwives prepare to bathe the Christ Child, one pouring the water, the other testing the temperature of the water in a bath that resembles a baptismal font.*

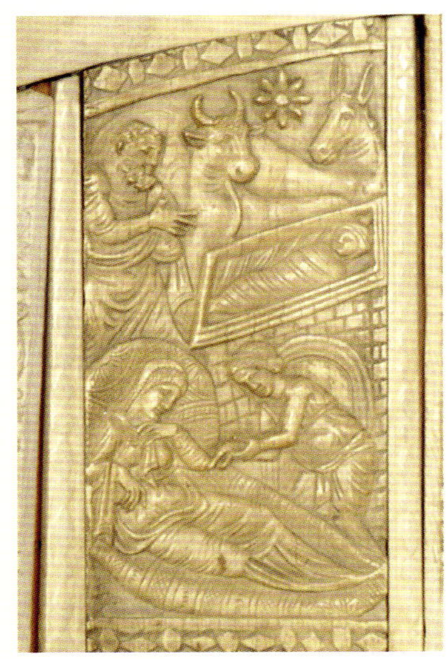

FIG. 2. *Panel of Archbishop Maximian's Throne, made in Ravenna or Constantinople, c. 545–53, ivory, 21 x 11.3 cm, Archiepiscopal Museum, Ravenna. Above, the Christ Child lies in the manger, watched over by the ox and the ass beneath a star, and Joseph stands to the side. Below, Mary reclines, and the midwife Salome extends her hand, now apparently miraculously cured.*

condition, I will not believe that a virgin has brought forth.' And Salome went in and made her ready to test her condition. And she cried out, saying: 'Woe for my wickedness and my unbelief; for I have tempted the living God; and behold, my hand falls away from me, consumed by fire.' In response to her prayer, an angel stood before Salome and said to her: 'Salome, the Lord God has heard your prayer … Stretch out your hand to the Child and touch Him … so will healing and joy be yours.' And full of joy Salome came to the child, touched Him … And Salome was healed at once.

Salome's doubting statement instantly reminds us of Thomas's expression of disbelief when told by the other apostles that the risen Christ had appeared to them (John 20:24–29): 'Except that I see in His hands the print of the nails and put my finger into the print of the nails and thrust my hand into His side, I will not believe.' The event concerning Salome's burnt hand and the miraculous healing is very rarely depicted. Was the subject too intimate, even too offensive, to be illustrated? But we witness the incident in a few intriguing images. In a panel of Maximian's Throne in Ravenna, probably made by Byzantine craftsmen, Salome is extending her hand to the Virgin [FIG. 2]. In another sixth-century ivory relief Salome is shown in the act of reaching out to touch the Christ Child. On the famous bronze doors at Hildesheim,[i] the Virgin lies on her pallet; above her, the swaddled Christ Child sleeps in the manger – and standing between the recumbent forms we observe a figure extending one arm, hiding her face with her other hand, generally considered to be the doubting midwife. The subject also appears in later paintings [FIGS 7, 8].

The narrative of the midwives was adopted and adapted, at times simplified, at times embroidered, both in the mid-thirteenth-century *Legenda aurea*, which simply tells us 'when Zebel, probing and realising that Mary was virgin, cried that a virgin had given birth, Salome did not believe it', and in the *Meditationes vitae Christi* a century later. Among the apocryphal Infancy Gospels, only the sixth-century Arabic gospel (variously dated between the seventh and the ninth century) mentions Salome, while the author of the Gospel of Pseudo-Matthew (eighth century) names the first midwife Zelami.[ii]

Centuries after the canon of the New Testament Gospels (Matthew, Mark, Luke and John) was established at the end of the fourth century,[iii] the popularity of the midwives' story recounted in

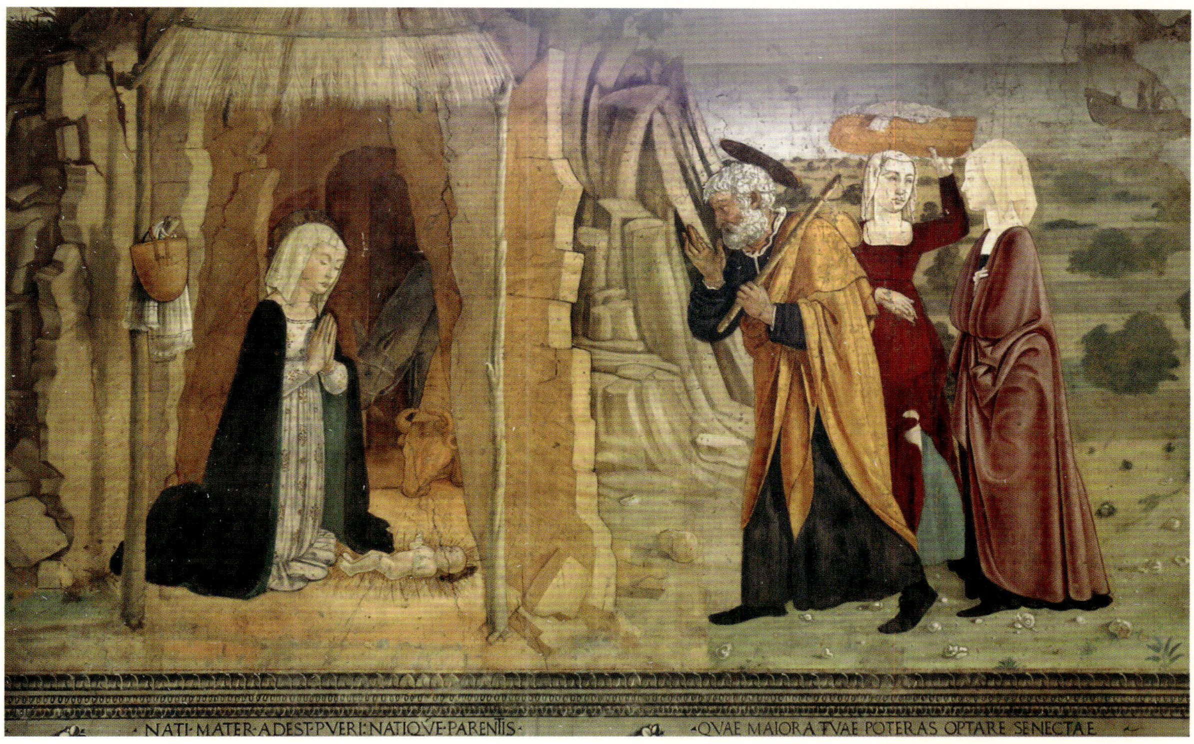

startling detail refused to be uprooted in the Latin West. Though the influential Jerome (who died at Bethlehem in 420) fiercely denied the reliability of the tales,[iv] and subsequent theologians and Church Fathers firmly dismissed the legends (the sixteenth-century Council of Trent even outlawed the midwives and the bathing of Christ as 'ignoble, apocryphal and unsound'[v]), that did not deter such a cherished and familiar event from being included in representations of Nativity scenes. There have been claims that the origin of the bathing of Christ can be traced to Egypt or that it derives from Classical scenes showing the bathing of the god Dionysus.[vi]

A very unusual example illustrating the tenacity in Western Christendom of the *Protoevangelium* story of the midwives is seen in a fresco of 1469 in the church of Santa Maria della Verità at Viterbo [FIG. 3]. On the left, the Christ Child lies on the ground, and Mary kneels over him in prayer. On the right we see Joseph arriving with two midwives (note the hill country in the background), one carrying

FIG. 3. *Lorenzo da Viterbo, fresco of the Nativity in the Mazzatosta Chapel in the church of Santa Maria della Verità, Viterbo, 1469. The depiction is unusual, showing on the left Mary kneeling by the newborn Christ Child, with the ox and ass perhaps warming His naked body, and on the right Joseph returning with two midwives. The figure carrying a basket of linens required for midwifery on her head, seems to be in the act of explaining to her sceptical companion, Salome, the wonders 'which nature does not allow'.*

a basket on her head containing linens essential to a midwife in the course of her work.

In the sacred dramas that took place during the festive Mass at Christmas, the roles of the midwives, *obstetrices*, were taken by the deacons. The altar now represented the manger (in the Easter plays it symbolised the tomb), and the 'dialogue' was sung across it. At Rouen in the fourteenth century (and soon elsewhere) a manger was set behind the main altar with a curtain in front of it, and at the appropriate moment the *obstetrices* pulled the curtain open to reveal Mother and Child.[vii]

Although Nativity icons of the Orthodox tradition always show the midwives bathing the Christ Child, the incident is never described in the *Protoevangelium Jacobi* (or any other apocryphal gospel). Bathing and cleansing of a newborn infant is, of course, as every mother knows, an essential episode in the miraculous event of giving birth. In Nativity scenes the bathing of the newborn Christ intentionally brings to mind baptism, and the ritual cleansing of sin, the entry to a new spiritual life. Significantly we observe that in icons the ritual bath administered by the midwives takes place in the lower part of the image, that is, on the ground, on the level of the earth.

The bathing of the Christ Child appears in Western art too, initially under Byzantine influence during the reigns of Greek and Syrian popes in the eighth and ninth centuries, and gradually the ritual event entered the artists' repertoire, a subject proffering its deepest meanings for the faithful to ponder. We are reminded that birth scenes of great heroes and divinities in the Greco-Roman world (such as Alexander the Great) sometimes showed the bathing of a child, and the bathing of a newborn infant was an important social event.[viii] Symbolically, water represents clarity and truth, purity and transparency.[ix] We recall the 'living water' that Christ spoke of to the Samaritan woman at the well (John 4:13–14). We are also reminded of Christ's words to Nicodemus, 'Except a man be born of water and the spirit, he cannot enter into the Kingdom of God' (John 3:5). It is significant that in the earliest days of Christianity the celebrations of the Birth of Christ, the Adoration of the Magi, the Baptism of Christ and His first miracle – the changing of the water into wine – were all celebrated on the same feast day, on 6 January.

We see the bath itself resembling a baptismal font in Duccio's *Nativity* scene [FIG. 4], one of the three predella panels for his great *Maestà* made for Siena Cathedral. Giotto also includes the

FIG. 4. *(opposite) Duccio,* The Nativity, *in a predella panel from the* Maestà, *1308–11, tempera on poplar, 43 x 43.9 cm, National Gallery of Art, Washington, D.C. The midwives are busy with bathing the Christ Child in what resembles a font.*

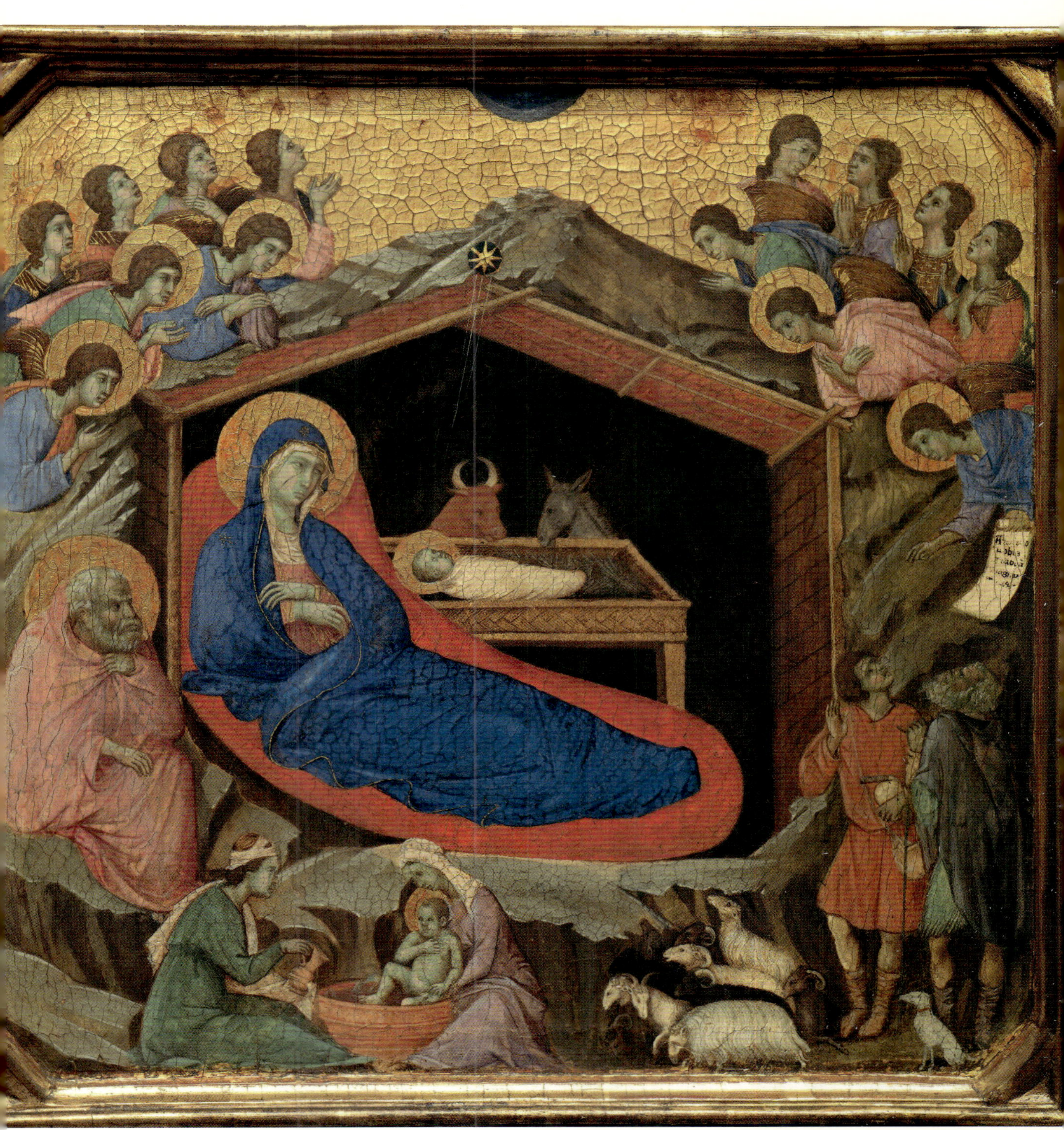

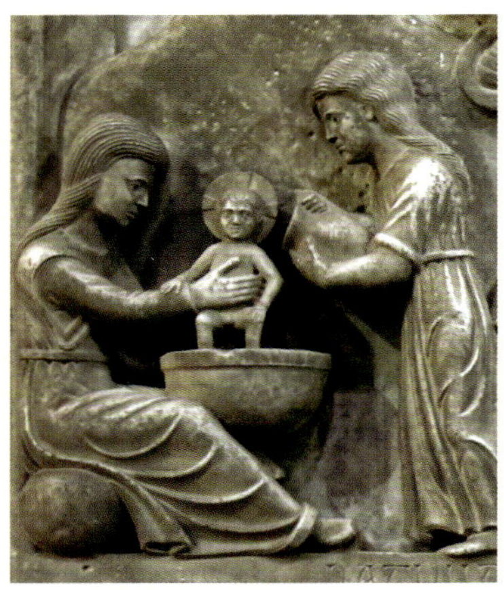

FIG. 5. *Guido da Como (also known as Guido Bigarelli), Nativity scene on the pulpit of San Bartolomeo in Pantano, Pistoia, 1250. The midwives bathe the Child, who is seen swaddled and sleeping in another section on the pulpit.*

FIG. 6. *Sculpture on the west front of Orvieto Cathedral, c. 1310–30, showing the midwives preparing the Christ Child's bath. (The crib, with its striated patterns, is notably similar to a sarcophagus.)*

FIG. 7. *(opposite) Jacques Daret, The Nativity, c. 1434–35, in an altarpiece dedicated to the Virgin in the funerary chapel of Abbot Jean du Clercq in the Abbey of St Vaast in Arras, oil on panel, 59.5 x 53 cm, Museo Nacional Thyssen-Bornemisza, Madrid. Both midwives are shown in contemporary dress; Salome extends her hand close to the Infant, while an angel hovers above.*

two midwives giving the Christ Child a bath in a fresco in the Lower Church at Assisi. We witness the popularity of the subject in sculpture, particularly on pulpits in Tuscany – at San Bartolomeo in Pantano in Pistoia [FIG. 5], at Siena, and – in a relief – at Orvieto [FIG. 6], both reminiscent of baptism. The motif has inspired some charmingly human details – the Infant's clothes held in preparation, the water being tested for its heat, Joseph helping to fill the bath, the drying, and so on, and sometimes we are shown the midwives in contemporary dress [FIGS 7, 8].

Images depicting sacred events offer the possibility to act as a doorway, a threshold that may lead to another vista, even another level. Witnessing the midwives ritually bathing the Christ Child at the Nativity we receive the impression of Christ's dual nature – His humanity and His Divinity, the Incarnation, the Word made flesh. The bathing of the Christ Child in Nativity scenes offers us an allegory of spiritual birth, a rebirth. The role of the midwives is essentially to assist and to serve this birth, to prepare, to nurture, to cleanse.

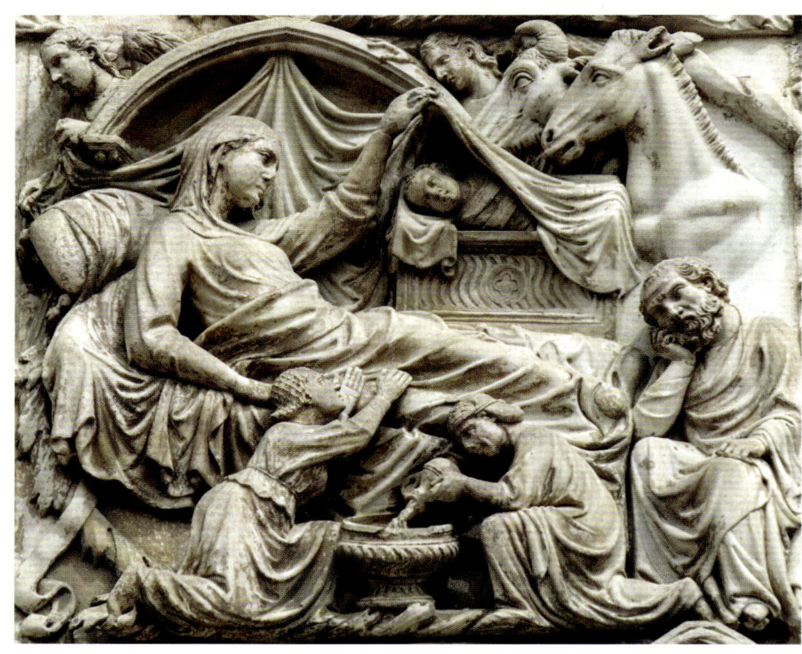

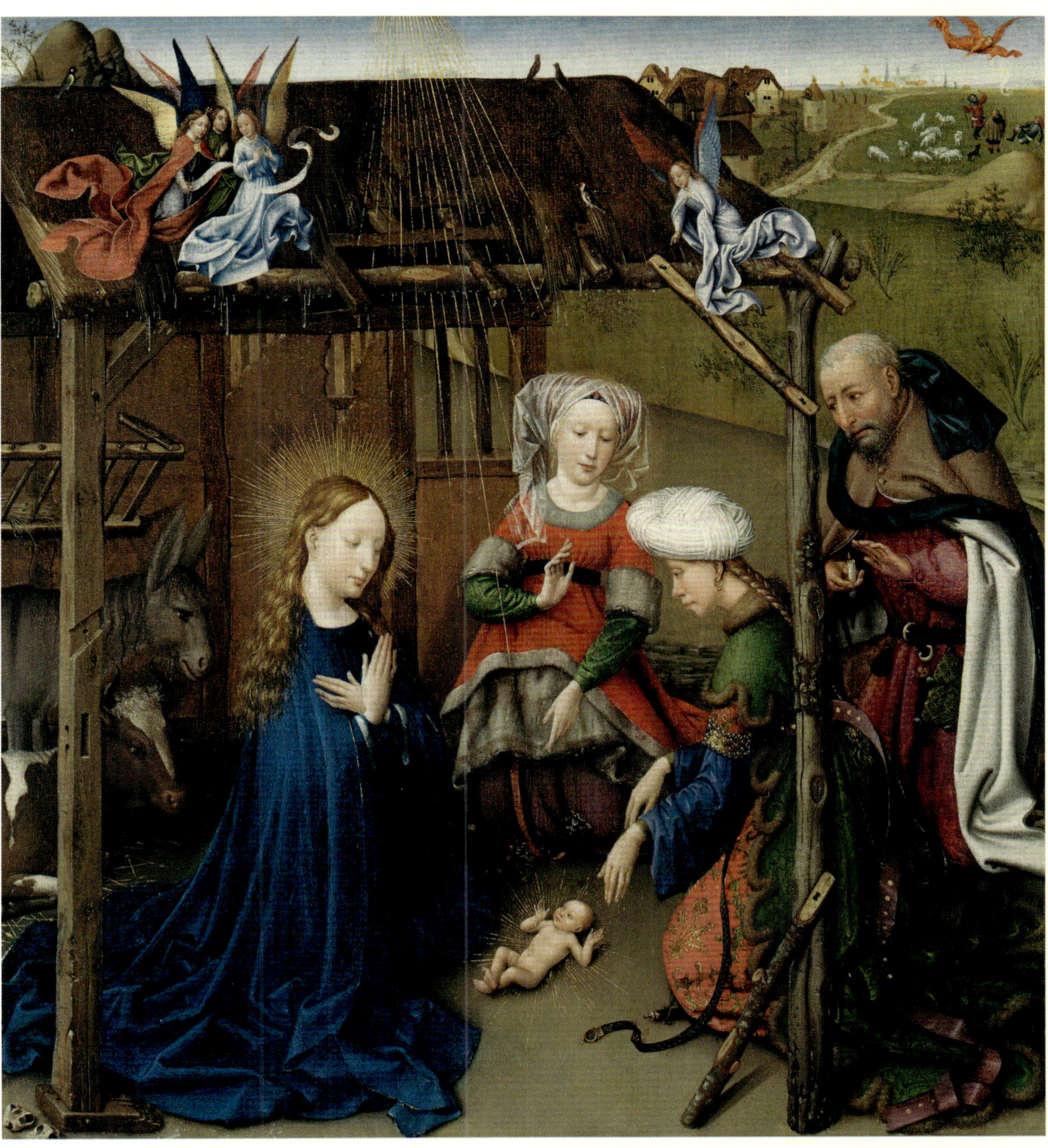

FIG. 8. *Robert Campin*, The Nativity, *c. 1420, oil on wood, 87 x 70 cm, Musée des Beaux-Arts, Dijon. The midwives are clad in chic contemporary dress, in stark contrast to the poverty of the setting. Salome extends her arm, and above her an angel hovers holding a banner that reads 'Tangue puerum et sanabaris' (Touch the Child and you will be healed).*

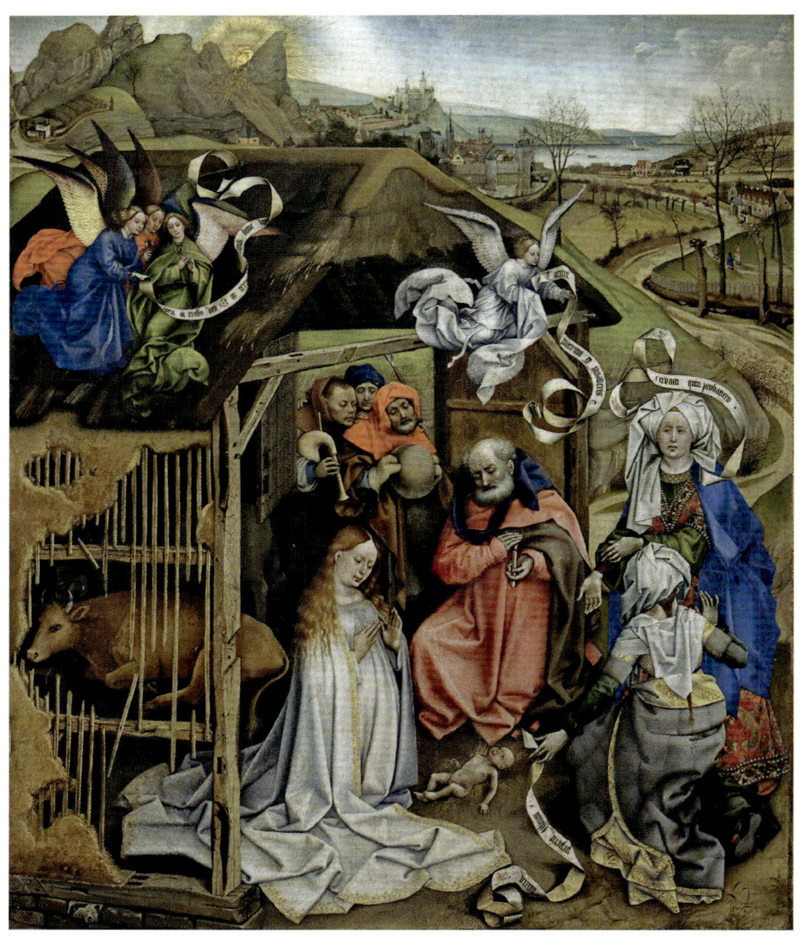

V THE MIDWIVES: FOOTNOTES

i Archbishop Bernward of Hildesheim drew up the programme for the double doors of the Cathedral, the Mariandom, pairing events in the Old Testament (on the left door) with events from the Life of Christ (on the right door). The sacrifice of Cain and Abel is paired with the Nativity scene.

ii Perhaps a corruption of the name Salome?

iii By Damasus I, Pope 366–84.

iv Jerome was fiercely against the midwives, as we read in *Against Helvidius*.

v The ox and the ass were also banned by the Council of Trent.

vi *Encyclopaedia Britannica*.

vii See Karl Young, *The Drama of the Medieval Church* (Oxford: Clarendon Press, 1933).

viii See David R. Cartlidge and J. Keith Elliott in *Art and the Christian Apocrypha* (London and New York: Routledge, 2001).

ix See Maurice Nicoll, *The New Man* (London: Stuart and Richards, 1950).

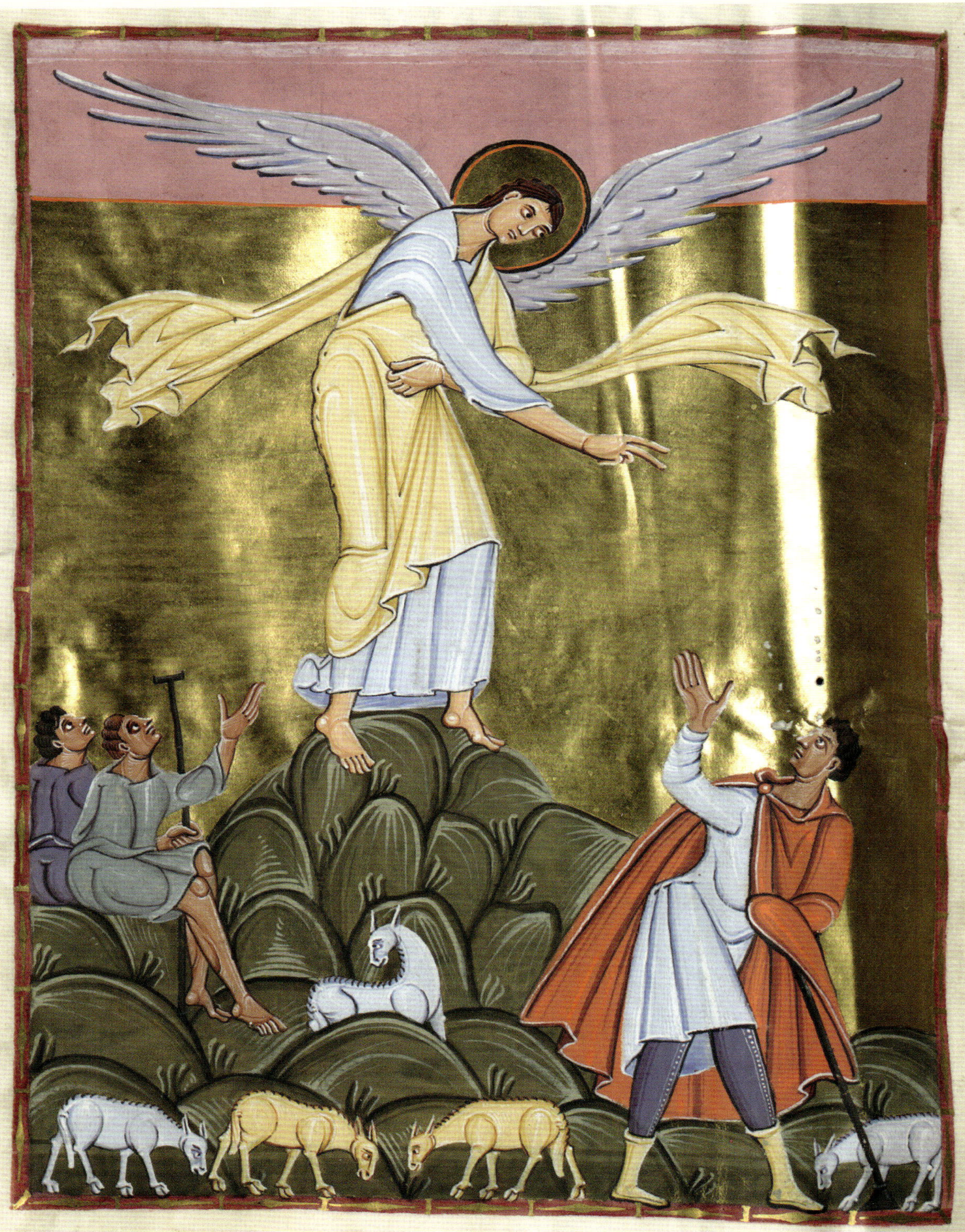

VI   THE SHEPHERDS

A shepherd is the first human figure to be shown accompanying the Christ Child in Nativity images [FIG. 1]. He holds his crook, and lifts his hand in a gesture of awe, gazing down at the Divine Child lying in the manger, guarded by the ox and the ass. He wears the *exomis*, the short girdled tunic worn by Roman shepherds. This somewhat crude representation is one of the earliest surviving images of the Nativity scene that we know, and was carved on a sarcophagus; another is on a contemporary sarcophagus [see Chapter II, FIG. 2]. Only two centuries later do we find the mother of Christ, the Virgin Mary, depicted at the manger – although she is shown on very early sarcophagus carvings depicting the Adoration of the Magi (as we shall see in Chapter VII).

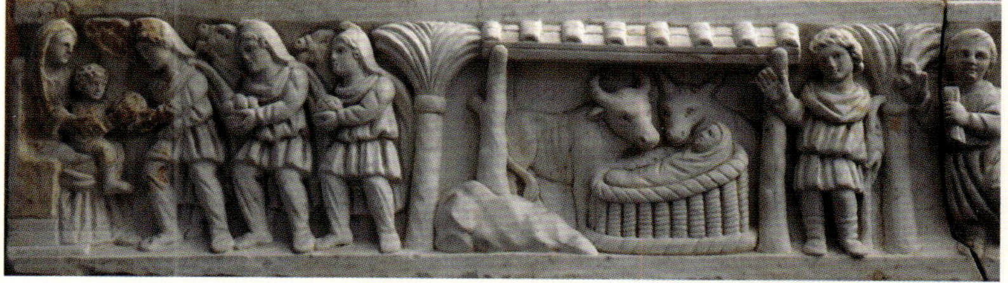

FIG. 1. *(right) Detail of the cover of a sarcophagus, first third of the fourth century, Lateran Museum, Rome. The shepherd, his hand raised, stands at the head of the manger beside the Christ Child.*

FIG. 6. *(left) The Annunciation to the Shepherds on a hillside, in the* Pericopes of Henry II, *Reichenau School, 1007–12, 27.2 x 19.6 cm, Bayerische Staatsbibliothek, Munich, Cod. lat. 4452. The monumental angel appearing to the shepherds is shown against a timeless background indicating higher worlds.*

Immediately following the story of the birth of Christ, Luke's Gospel continues (2:8): 'And there were in the same country shepherds abiding in the field, keeping watch over their flock by night.' We can wonder why the presence of a shepherd was considered to be essential at the Christ Child's manger? Why did Christians of the fourth century (and perhaps earlier) choose to include a shepherd in their search for imagery to evoke the mystery of the Nativity?

The figure of the shepherd is deeply embedded in the human psyche and crops up in images and legends since time immemorial in widely different cultures and traditions. Yet the shepherd archetype remains essentially the same, representing watchfulness and care. His role is to 'keep watch', to round up and take care of the 'sheep' that stray and are endangered – a powerful allegory of our own

FIG. 2. *The Sacrifice of Noah, mosaic in the Cathedral of Monreale, Sicily, 1167–69. The lamb is shown as the sacrificial victim. The rainbow is a sign of God's covenant, linking Noah, the sacrificial lamb, and God: 'I set my bow in the clouds and it shall be a sign of the Covenant between me and the earth.' (Genesis 9:13).*

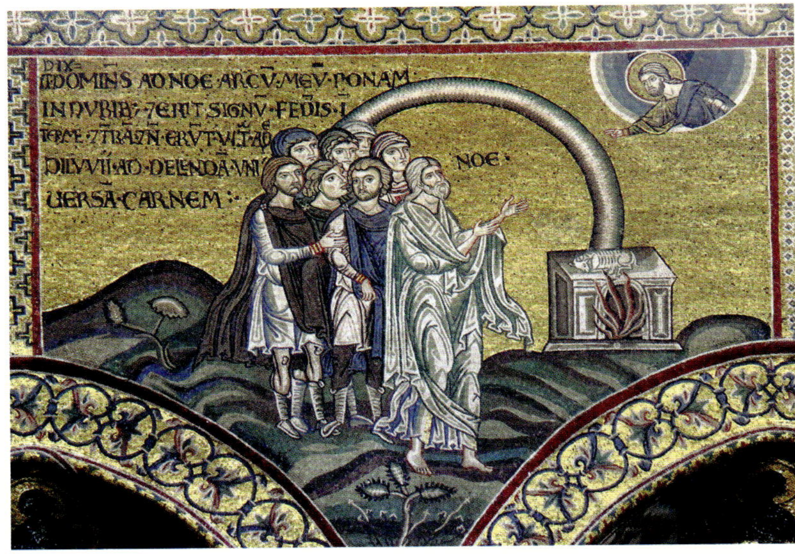

disordered, sometimes chaotic, inner lives, invaded by thoughts that wander. The quietening of the mind is seen as an essential primary step in all traditions towards finding and maintaining a state of inner harmony. Luke continues with the revelation to the shepherds (2:9–14):

> And lo, the angel of the Lord came upon them, and the glory of the Lord shone round about them: and they were sore afraid. And the angel said unto them, Fear not, for behold, I bring you good tidings of great joy, which shall be to all people. For unto you is born this day in the city of David a Saviour, which is Christ the Lord. And this shall be a sign unto you: Ye shall find the babe wrapped in swaddling clothes, lying in a manger. And suddenly there was with the angel a multitude of heavenly host praising God, and saying, Glory to God in the highest, and on earth peace, to men of good will.

To Christians the image of the shepherd inevitably connects us with Christ's words 'I am the good shepherd' (John 10:11), and with it the parable of the Lost Sheep.[i] The Gospels, like the Old Testament, are littered with references to shepherds and sheep.[ii] The good shepherd lays down his life for his sheep (John 10:11) and

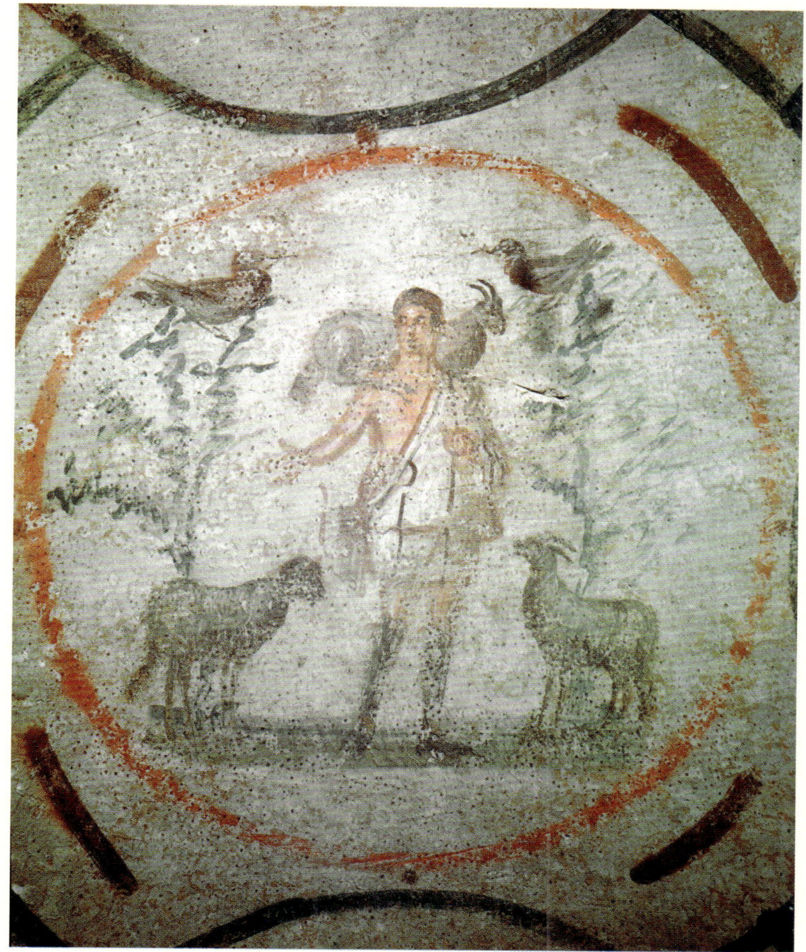

FIG. 3. The Good Shepherd, *c. 250, painted on the ceiling of the Cubiculum of the Veiled Woman in the Catacomb of Priscilla outside Rome. A young beardless figure, presumed to be Christ, bears a ram on his shoulders; doves in the trees.*

Psalm 23 famously claims 'the Lord is my shepherd/I shall not want'. The lamb is an ancient symbol of sacrifice, as we are reminded in the twelfth-century mosaics in Monreale Cathedral depicting Noah and his family offering the sacrificial victim over the fire below the altar [FIG. 2]. David, Moses, Abraham, Jacob and others were all described as shepherds. However, the Gospels also warn us against false shepherds (John 10:1–5) who are but thieves and robbers, and to 'beware of false prophets who come to you in sheep's clothing but inwardly are ravening wolves'.

Writing at the end of the second century or possibly very early

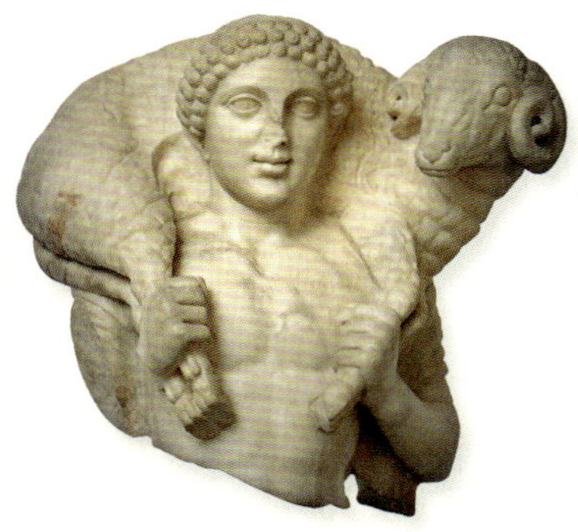

FIG. 4. Hermes-Kriophoros, *late Roman copy of the Kriophoros – ram-bearer – by Kalamis, marble, Museo Barracco, Rome.*

in the third century, Tertullian reported (in *De Prudentia*) that the image of the shepherd was used on Communion vessels to demonstrate that 'the flock is the people of the Church, the Good Shepherd is Christ'. In the Catacomb of Priscilla (*c.* 250) we see the figure of a youth holding a ram around his neck, a personification of Christ the Good Shepherd [FIG. 3].[iii] This familiar image was frequently used in antiquity, borrowed and adapted from the pagan *Kriophoros*, ram-bearer [FIG. 4].

While in icons the shepherds are depicted on a mountainside, in Western images they are often shown on a rock-strewn hillside [FIGS 5, 6]. Both representations can be interpreted in the ancient language of allegory as on a higher level. In images of Western Christendom the Annunciation to the Shepherds is repeatedly taken as a subject on its own [FIGS 6, 7], a trope especially popular in illuminated manuscripts. Memling in an unusual combination juxtaposes the Annunciation to Mary and the Annunciation to the Shepherds [FIG. 8].

In the darkness of the winter solstice the Light appears, and with

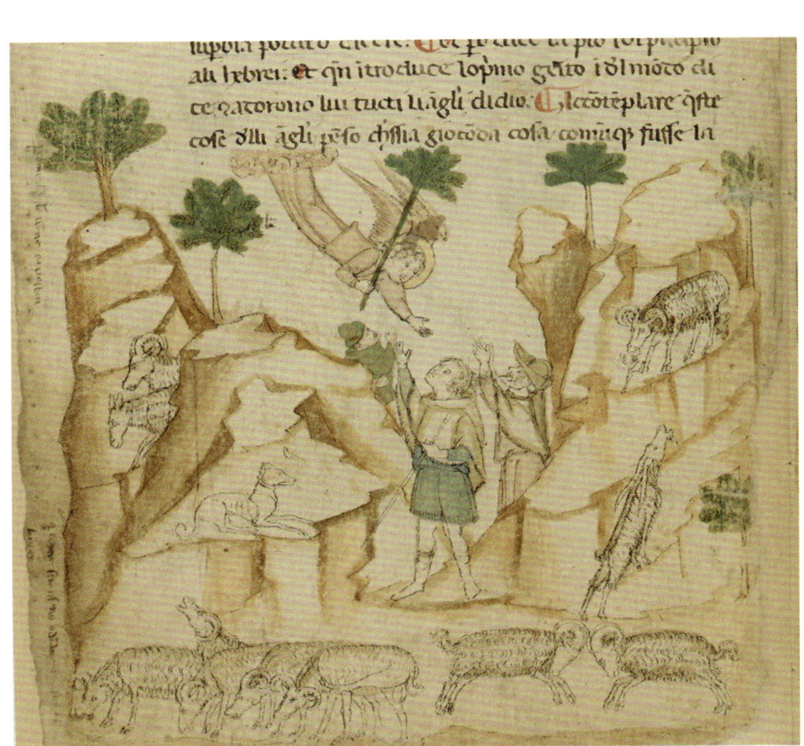

FIG. 5. *The shepherds on a spectacularly rocky hillside, in a fourteenth-century illustrated copy of the* Meditationes Vitae Christi, *drawing with colour wash, Bibliothèque nationale de France, Paris, MS ital. 115. Undoubtedly the most influential devotional text of the time, hugely popular and widely disseminated.*

it there is a welcome sense of hope, of redemption. Sometimes we see the shepherd with his hand raised – a gesture that may be expressing joy, awe, or salutation. We observe that the shepherd is astonished: what is witnessed is beyond his understanding, and yet he is irresistibly attracted by the Light [FIG. 9], pointing unwaveringly up to the heavens as he listens to the angel's message and the 'heavenly host praising God' [FIG. 10]. The shepherds respond instantly to this revelation and together the companions follow the summons, guided by the Light to the place of the Nativity. 'And it came to pass, as the angels were gone away from them into heaven, the shepherds said one to another, Let us now go even unto Bethlehem, and see this thing which is come to pass, which the Lord has made known unto us. And they came with haste, and found Mary and Joseph and the babe lying in a manger' (Luke 2:16).

This annunciation event is also very often included in Nativity scenes, though sometimes scarcely visible, taking place in the background or at the side of the image [FIG. 11]. We are shown the

FIG. 7. The Annunciation to the Shepherds, *painted on the vault of the funerary chapel of the kings of Leon in San Isidoro, Leon, c. 1100. The shepherds are scarcely distracted by the appearance of the angel in this almost pagan bucolic scene, where the animals include goats, pigs, deer and cattle; one shepherd feeds a dog, another has his pipes.*

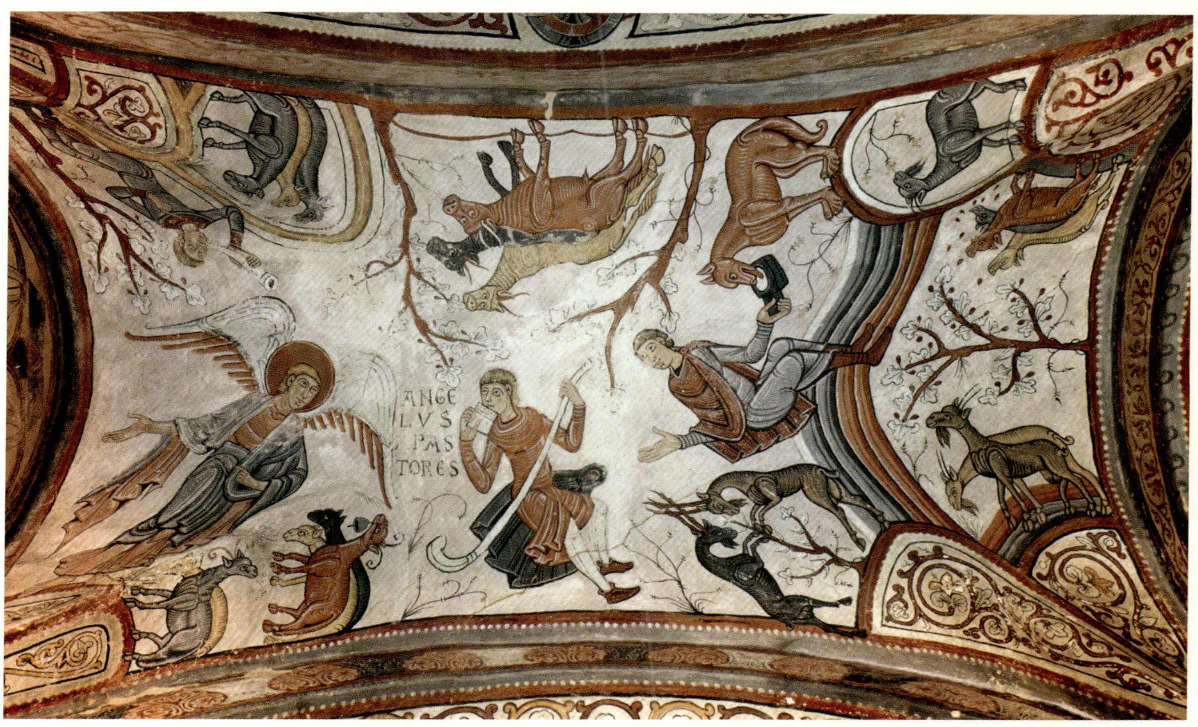

FIG. 8. Hans Memling, the Annunciation to the Shepherds, detail from The Seven Joys of Mary *(also known as* The Advent and Triumph of Christ*), 1480, commissioned for the Chapel of the Tanners in the Frauenkirche, Bruges, oil on wood, 189 x 81 cm, Alte Pinakothek, Munich. A peaceful down-to-earth depiction of the event, with dogs and sheep, directly below the Annunciation to Mary.*

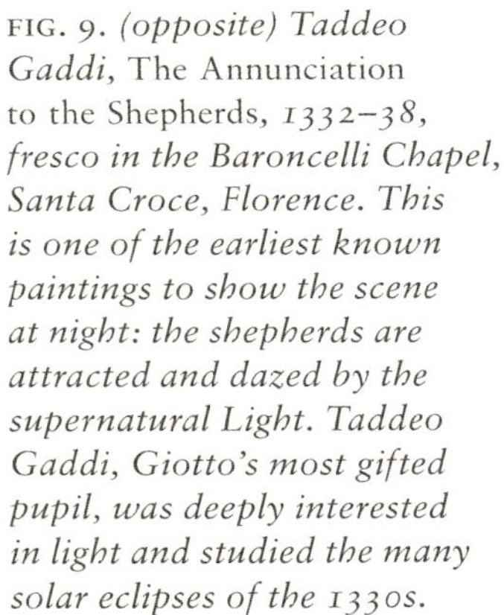

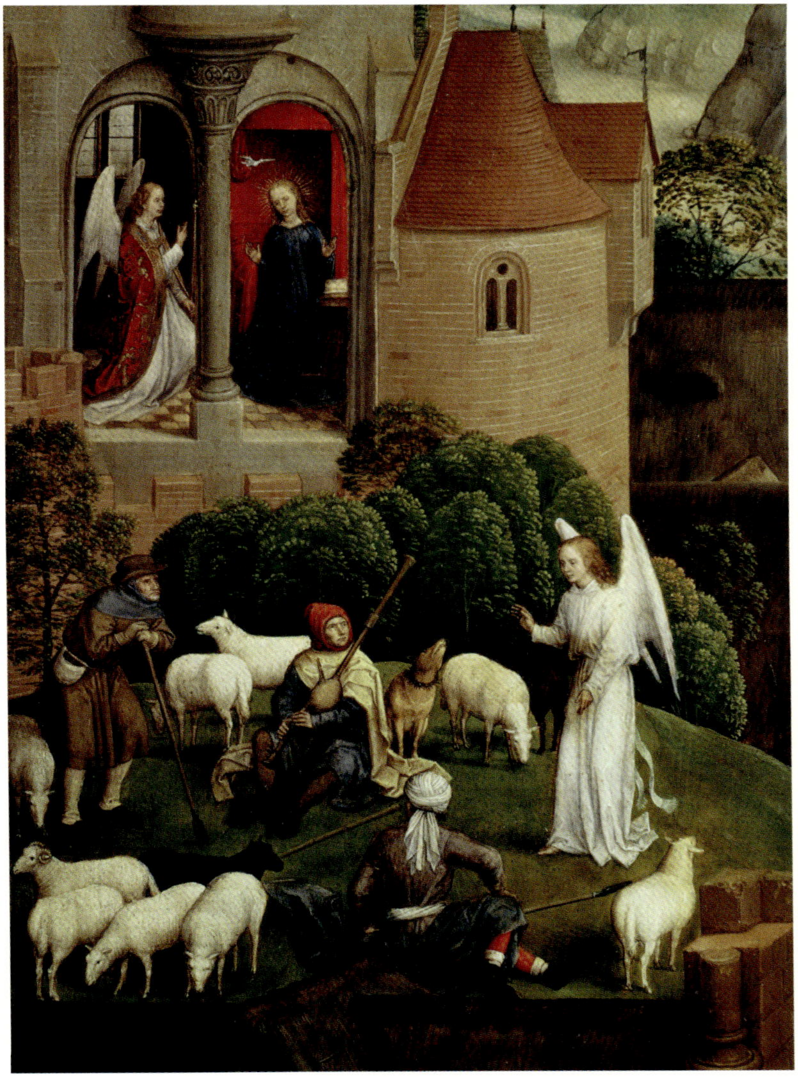

FIG. 9. (opposite) Taddeo Gaddi, The Annunciation to the Shepherds, *1332–38, fresco in the Baroncelli Chapel, Santa Croce, Florence. This is one of the earliest known paintings to show the scene at night: the shepherds are attracted and dazed by the supernatural Light. Taddeo Gaddi, Giotto's most gifted pupil, was deeply interested in light and studied the many solar eclipses of the 1330s.*

shepherds' arrival at the manger accompanied by sheep, possibly a dog, presenting gifts (a lamb, flowers). We witness their rural simplicity and poverty in impoverished, well-worn clothing [FIG. 12]. Humble, close to Nature, close to the earth, close to instinct and animal life – all this acts as a reminder that folklore and ancient wisdom go hand-in-hand.

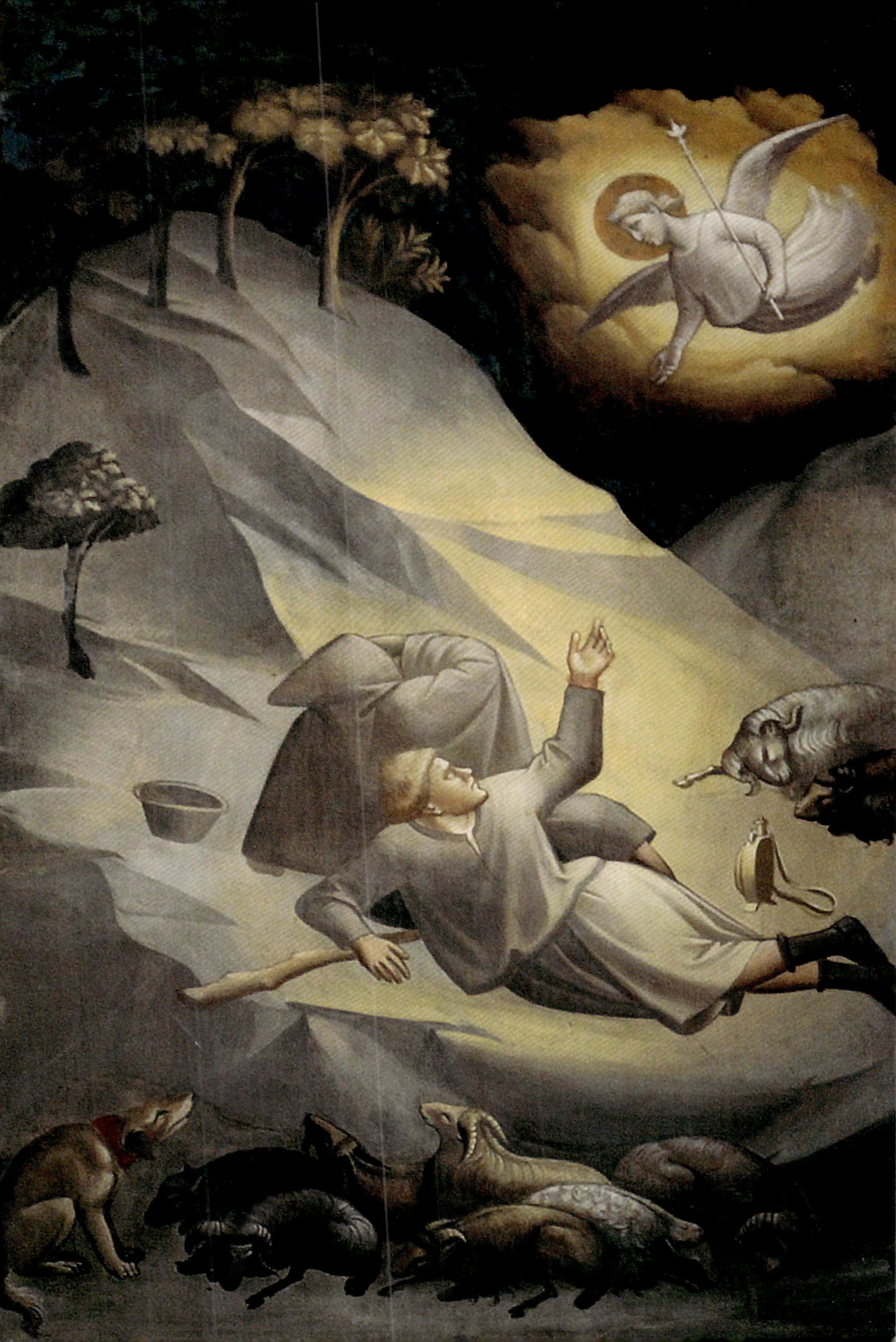

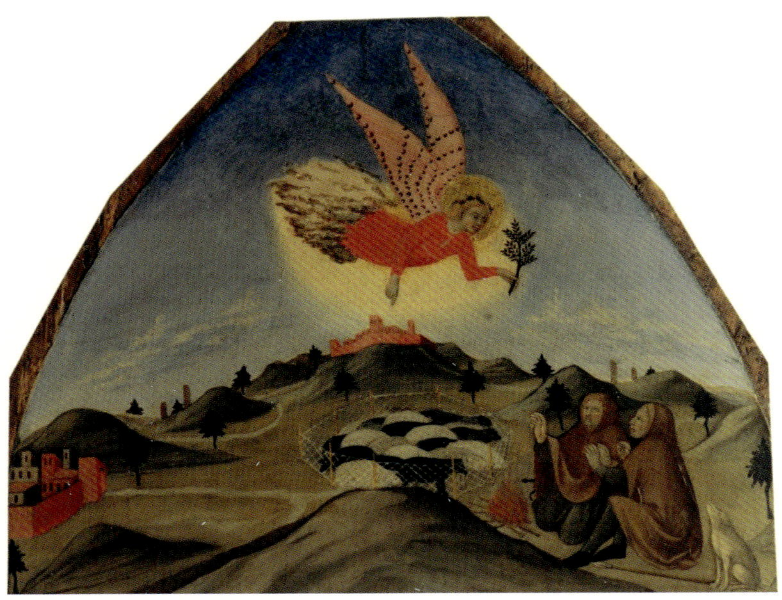

FIG. 10. *Sano di Pietro*, The Annunciation to the Shepherds, *pinnacle of a polyptych, 1450, tempera on board, Pinacoteca Nazionale, Siena. The sheep are all penned in for the night; the shepherds, accompanied by their dog, huddle by the fire and listen to the angel, who points downward to the Nativity scene below.*

During the liturgy of the Mass on the feast day of Christmas, the natural centre of a dramatic performance was, of course, the *praesepe* at Bethlehem, and the action chosen was the visit of the shepherds. In the earliest extant texts dating from the eleventh century of Christmas plays performed in churches, the shepherds, *pastores* (roles played by cantors), are found conversing with the midwives, *obstetrices* (played by deacons).[iv] The altar took the place of the manger. Initially the trope was attached to the Introit of the Mass; later it was transported to the end of the office of Matins, usually performed at the end of the normal liturgical service on the feast of the Nativity at Christmas.[v] There are descriptions of five youths (dressed with amices, albs, tunics and staffs) representing the shepherds who take their place in the church, while one choir boy, high up in the vaults where he is accompanied by other 'angels', sings the announcement of the Nativity to the shepherds – *Nolite timere* (Do not be afraid) – followed by his companion choristers singing *Gloria in excelsis Deo* (Glory to God in the highest). The shepherds then proceed towards the manger singing a responsorial poem, *Pax in terra* (Peace on earth), as they traverse the choir, and as they round the altar, they sing the verse *Transeamus Bethlehem* (We travel on to Bethlehem). However, evidence of such liturgical Christmas plays is relatively meagre, overshadowed by the magnificence of opportunities offered by the Epiphany plays of the Magi.

The ancient language of the Gospels uses words and descriptions allegorically in order to explore truths beyond space and time. So, too, images seek ways to lead the viewer towards a higher level, approaching the mystery by symbolic and metaphorical means that offer a psychological language that conveys man's spiritual path and the difficulties he must overcome.

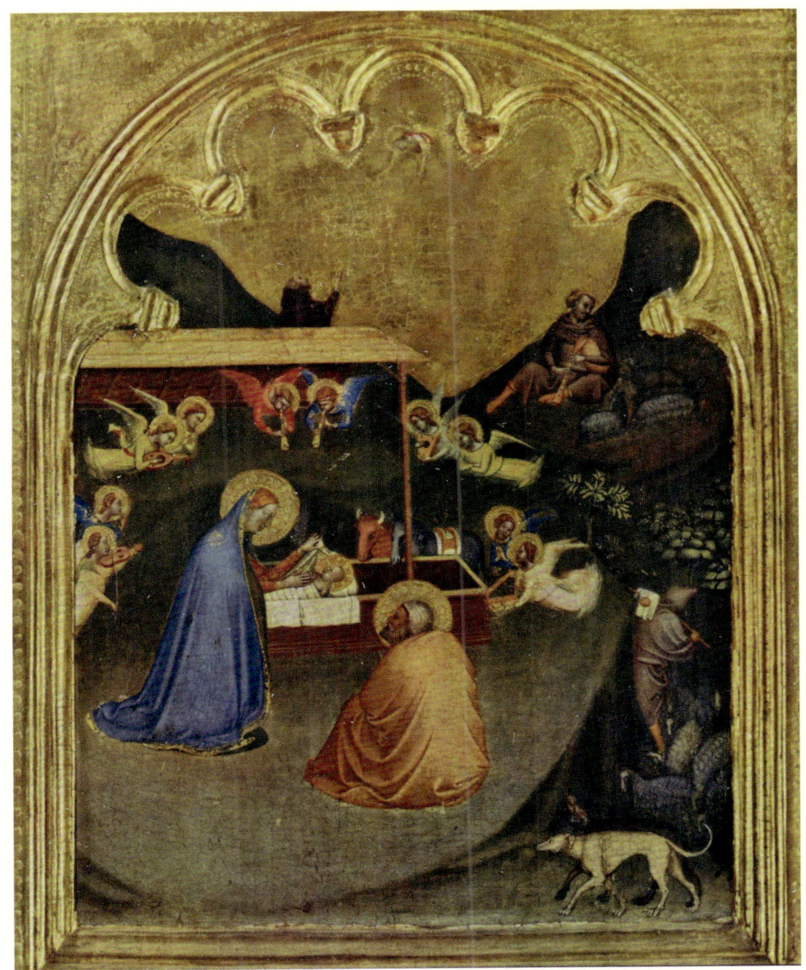

FIG. 11. *Bernardo Daddi,*
the Nativity, predella panel
of the San Pancrazio Polyptych,
1338, tempera on wood,
23.6 x 30.3 cm, Uffizi, Florence.
The Annunciation to the
Shepherds is shown taking
place up the hill, and then their
journey, preceded by dogs and
sheep, to the stable.

Perhaps we can identify the figure of the shepherd at the Nativity
as representing mankind, a metaphor for man's quest for deeper
meaning and more profound understanding in his search for his role
in the cosmos. The shepherds watch 'by night' – an ancient parallel
with darkness and ignorance. Watching entails being alert, aware,
awake. They listen – and they respond instantly: they affirm the call
from the Higher. 'And they came with haste, and found Mary and
Joseph and the babe lying in a manger.' How can we awaken to the
mystery of the Sacred? How to be vigilant?

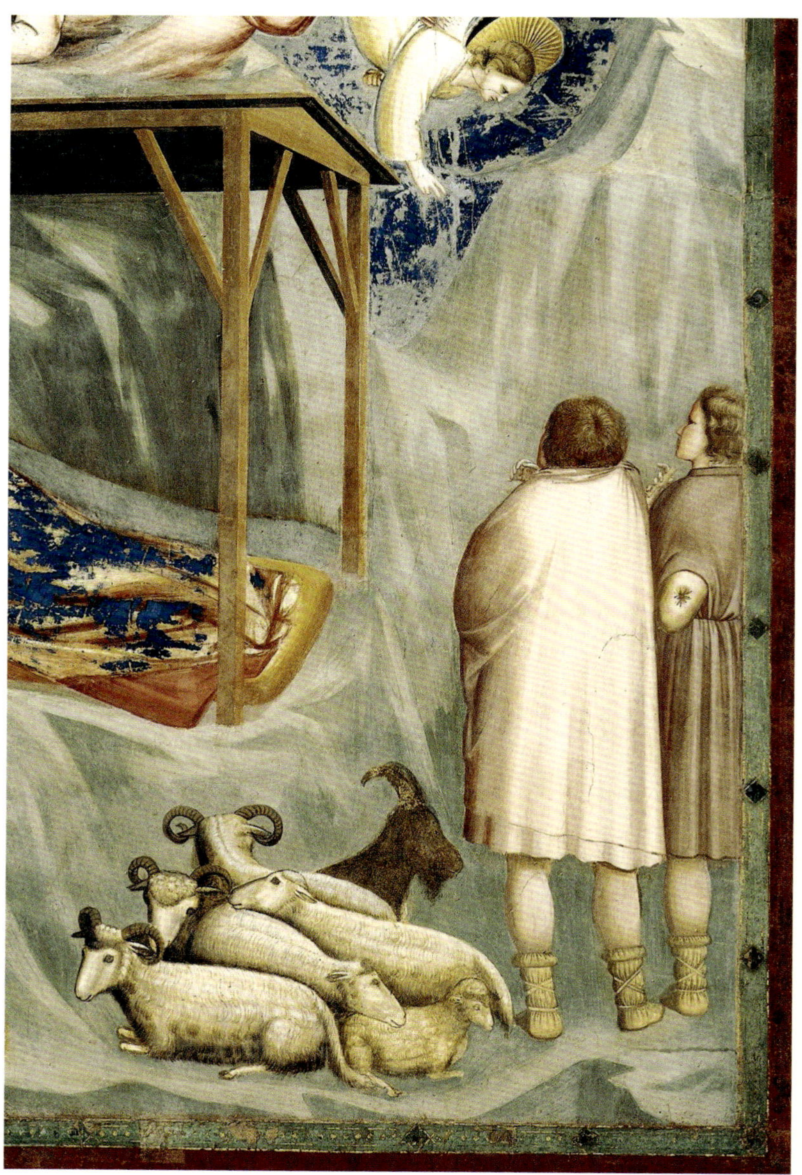

FIG. 12. *Giotto, detail from one of the Nativity frescoes in the Arena Chapel, Padua, c. 1305. The shepherds have arrived at the manger; with sheep and a goat at their feet, they gaze up at the angel. We notice a patched sleeve, warm rough clothes, and leather-thonged footwear.*

VI THE SHEPHERDS: FOOTNOTES

i Luke 15:3–7; Matthew 18:12–14.

ii See for instance Matthew 9:36, 25:32, 26:31; Mark 6:34, 14:27; Luke 15:3–7; John 10:11–18. Sheep are mentioned over five hundred times in the Bible.

iii Figures of Christ carrying a sheep around his neck are found in the Lateran Museum and in the Pio-Cristiano Museum, the Vatican.

iv See Karl Young, *The Drama of the Medieval Church* (Oxford, Clarendon Press, 1933). vol. 2, ch. xvii, 'Shepherds at the Holy Manger'. Texts for Easter plays pre-date texts for Christmas plays.

v Occasionally, for instance in the thirteenth century in the Cathedral at Padua, the play preceded Matins, immediately following the arrival of the Bishop. Young, op. cit. in the preceding note, pp. 3–28.

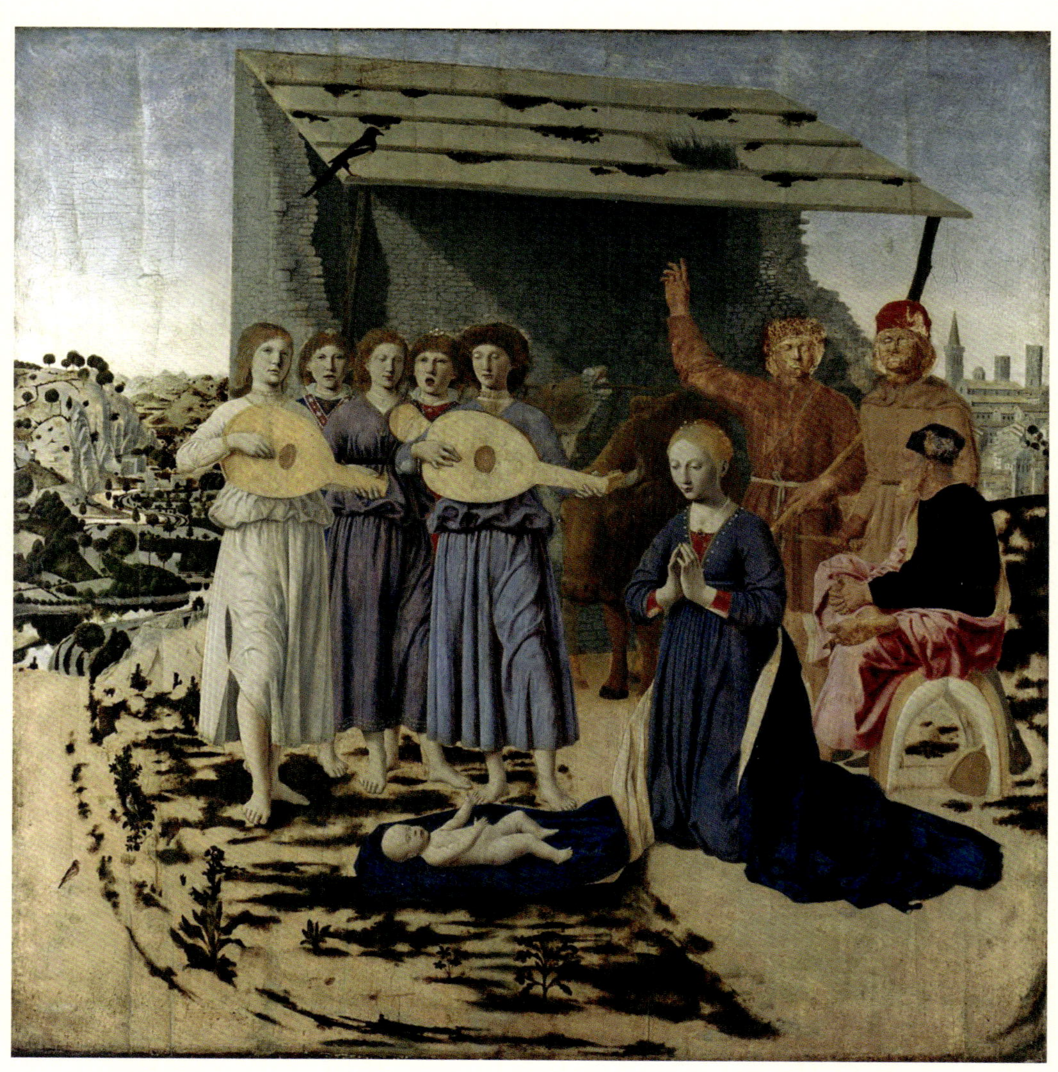

VII BIRGITTA'S VISION

IN 1373 IN THE CHURCH AT BETHLEHEM (now the Basilica or Church of the Nativity) Birgitta – known to us as St Bridget of Sweden – received a vision of the Nativity. She saw the Virgin, dressed in a white mantle and a finely woven tunic, through which her swollen belly was visible. Joseph prepared the cave and went outside; Mary removed her mantle and veil, and made ready the garments for the Baby. Birgitta's vision revolutionised the way artists depicted the scene [FIG. I]: the Saviour is shown lying on the earth. This is is Birgitta's description of her vision:[i]

FIG. I. *Piero della Francesca, The Nativity, 1470–75, oil on poplar, 124.4 x 122.6 cm, National Gallery, London. One of the artist's last works, probably made for his family's private chapel at Sansepolcro, the fortified city seen in the background. In a ramshackle lean-to the Virgin meditates with wondrous serenity on the birth of her divine Son, who, following the description in Birgitta's vision, lies on Mary's mantle, a layer of protection on this stony earth. Joseph sits on the donkey's saddle facing the two shepherds, while angels make music, but nothing disturbs the intense silence of the scene.*

And when all these things had been prepared, the Virgin knelt with great reverence, she began to pray; and she kept her back towards the manger and her face lifted to heaven towards the east. And so with raised hands and with her eyes intent on heaven she appeared to be suspended in ecstasy of contemplation, inebriated with divine sweetness. And while she was thus in prayer, I saw something lying in her womb move; and then, in a moment and the twinkling of an eye she gave birth to a son, from whom there went out such great and ineffable light and splendour that the sun could not be compared to it. Nor did the candle that the old man had put in place give light at all because that divine splendour totally annihilated the material splendour of the candle. And so sudden and momentary was that manner of giving birth that I was unable to notice or discern how or in what part of her body she was giving birth. But yet, at once, I saw that glorious Infant lying on the earth, naked and glowing in the greatest gracefulness. His flesh was most clean of all dirt and uncleanness. And the Virgin's womb, which before the birth, had been very swollen, at once retracted, and her body then looked wonderfully beautiful and delicate … Having bowed her head and joined her hands, with great dignity and reverence she adored the boy and said to Him: 'Welcome my God, my Lord, my Son!' … the old man entered; and prostrating himself on the ground, he adored Him on his knees and wept for joy. [For the Virgin there was] no infirmity as usually happens in other women giving birth ... Then she arose, holding the boy in her arms, and together both of them, namely, she and Joseph, put Him in the manger, and on their knees they continued to adore him with gladness and immense joy.

Birgitta's father, one of the richest Swedish landowners of his time, was Governor of Uppland, and her mother's family were related to the King.[ii] Birgitta was born in 1303, and had her first vision (of the crucified Christ) when she was ten years old. Many more visions followed, all meticulously recorded by Birgitta in her journals. Married at the age of fourteen or fifteen to Ulf Gudmarsson and mother of eight (two children died in infancy; her daughter Catherine became St Catherine of Sweden), in her early thirties Birgitta was summoned to act as lady-in-waiting to the new Queen of Sweden, Blanche of Namur. In 1341 Birgitta and Ulf made a pilgrimage to Santiago de Compostela, and not long afterwards Ulf died. Birgitta joined the Third Order of St Francis, and later she founded her own order, the Order of the Most Holy Saviour, also known as the Brigittine Order of Augustinian nuns.[iii] In due course Birgitta set up double monasteries – joint communities of men and women (with separate cloisters), where books were very firmly encouraged. Seeking approval of her Order, Birgitta made a pilgrimage to Rome, and while waiting for the Pope's return from Avignon she sent back instructions on the building of a new church and convent, Vadstena Abbey on Lake Vättern in southern Sweden.[iv] She lived in Rome until the end of her life, working for the poor (she was especially interested in single mothers),[v] agitating for Church reform, and renowned for her outspoken criticism of ambitions within the Church. She was constantly hounded by debts, largely caused by building works. In 1373 Birgitta made a pilgrimage to Jerusalem and to Bethlehem – where she received the vision of the birth of Christ. She died shortly afterwards, in the same year, in Rome.

The accounts of Birgitta's visions were translated from Swedish into Latin, with her permission, during her own lifetime, by her confessor, Peter Olafsson, prior of Alvastra, and Matthias, canon of Linköping. *Revelationes Coelestes – Celestial Revelations –* comprises four volumes, with eight books in all, and from its first appearance it

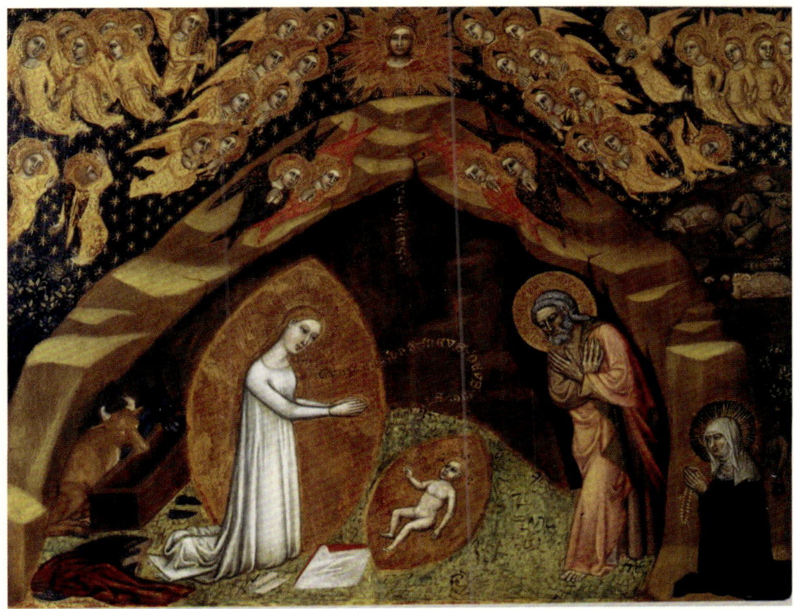

FIG. 2. *Niccolò di Tommaso,* The Nativity with St Birgitta, *c. 1380–1400, tempera on wood, 44 x 54 cm, Pinacoteca Vaticana. Birgitta is an onlooker, kneeling outside the cave of the Nativity. The Virgin's words of prayer are shown as a scroll, and angels surround the Creator.*

enjoyed a great vogue which persisted throughout the Middle Ages.[vi] It was first printed (in Lübeck) in 1492.

Birgitta saw herself as present at the Nativity. The late fourteenth-century Tuscan painter Niccolò di Tommaso was one of the first to make allusion to Birgitta, in a panel now in the Vatican, where the Virgin's words of welcome to the Child are painted as a scroll and we see Birgitta holding a rosary [FIG. 2]. A Pisan Master, *c.* 1400, shows the kneeling saint nimbed (she was canonised in 1391[vii]), flanking the cave, as is Joseph [FIG. 3]; we see the Virgin's blue mantle lying prominently heaped at the front of the image, and the shepherds (clad in garments closely resembling those of Franciscan friars) receiving the Annunciation in the background. Masolino included Birgitta in the foreground of a Nativity fresco in Castiglione d'Olona in Piedmont. The new iconography took root quickly, especially in areas of Birgitta's influence. Four churches in Naples claimed early paintings of Birgitta's Nativity vision.[viii] In the church of Santa Maria Novella in Florence one of the three predella scenes below the Annunciation, painted by Pietro de Miniato *c.* 1400, [FIG. 4] shows Birgitta present, a kneeling witness to the Nativity. The ox and the ass are also depicted on their knees.

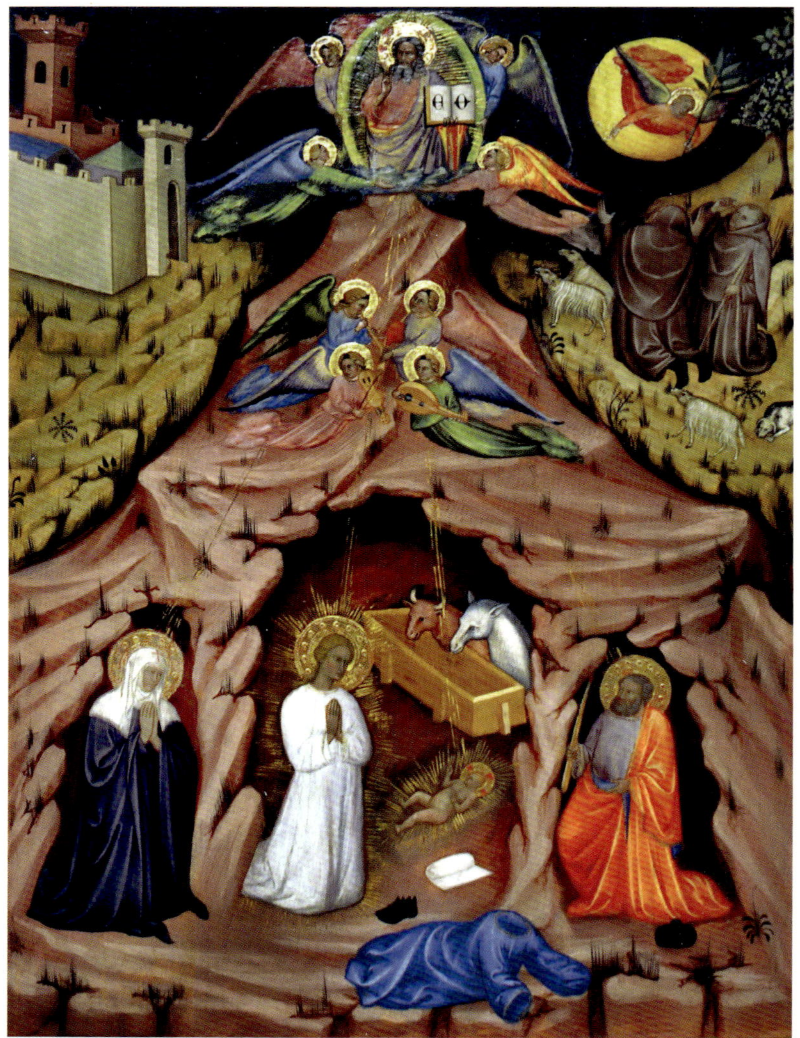

FIG. 3. *Pisan Master (possibly Turino Vanni),* The Nativity with St Birgitta, *c. 1400, tempera on wood, 30.6 x 41.5 cm, Museo San Matteo, Pisa. Birgitta, wearing the habit of the order of nuns that she founded, is shown present as a spectator, following her own description of her vision at Bethlehem. The ineffable light surrounds the naked Christ Child, and pours down from the heavens, where God the Father reigns.*

With astonishing speed artists in Western Christendom, initially in Italy, adopted Birgitta's visionary details of the Nativity. By the early fifteenth century the iconography had been established. Joseph is sometimes absent, or shown as the old man putting a candle in place (as described in Birgitta's vision). Painters rapidly adopted her revolutionary revelations, depicting the luminous naked Christ Child lying on the ground, on Mary's mantle – but sometimes just on the bare earth – before being placed in the manger. He is shown surrounded by a mystic brilliance evoking another dimension, timeless, invisible and all-pervading [FIGS 4–6]. Like the air we breathe, this light calls us (at least for the fraction of a moment) from the habitual darkness of ignorance and sleep. Artists now depict Mary, and sometimes Joseph, kneeling [FIG. 7] or standing in adoration and prayer. These are startlingly new departures from traditional iconography, where we see Mary lying back, resting after giving birth. Perhaps this is a reference to the effortless childbirth described by Birgitta, who comments that the Virgin suffered no infirmity as 'usually happens in other women giving birth'. All these innovations – the newborn Christ Child placed on the ground, the surrounding light, the adoring Virgin – quickly became firmly established in the repertoire of artists.

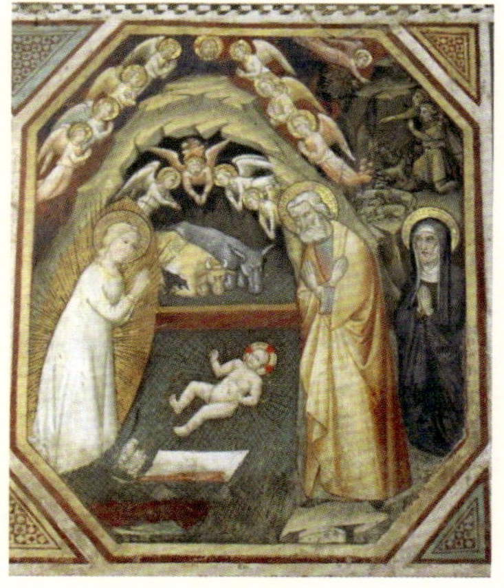

FIG. 4. *(above) Pietro di Miniato, predella scene in fresco (below the Annunciation), c. 1400, in Santa Maria Novella, Florence. Birgitta kneels behind Joseph, the ox and the ass are on their knees, the Christ Child lies on the ground.*

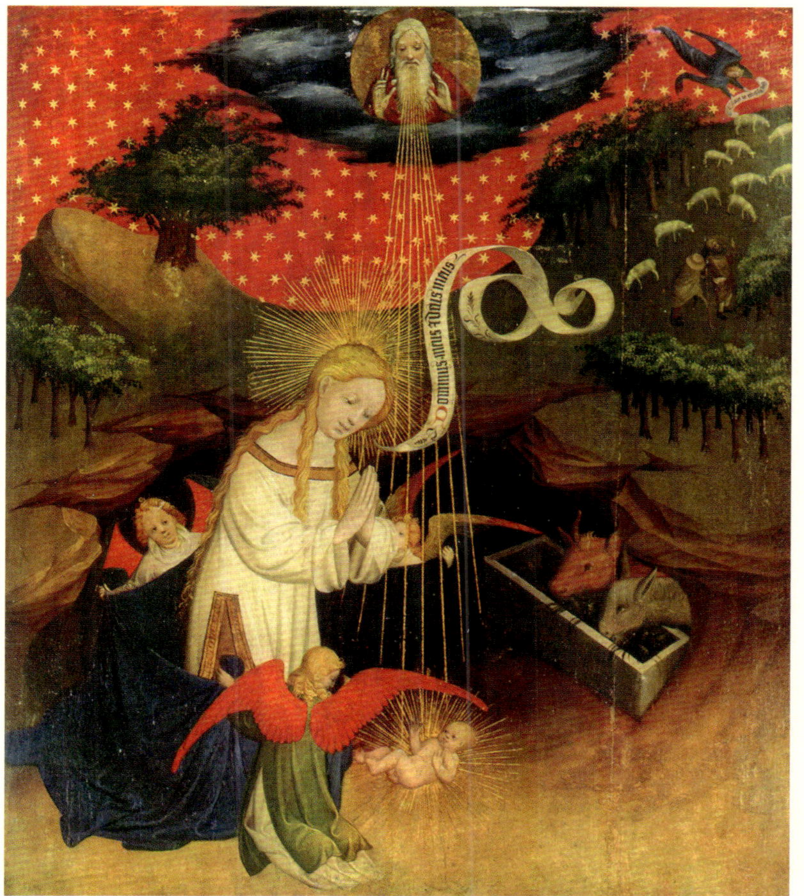

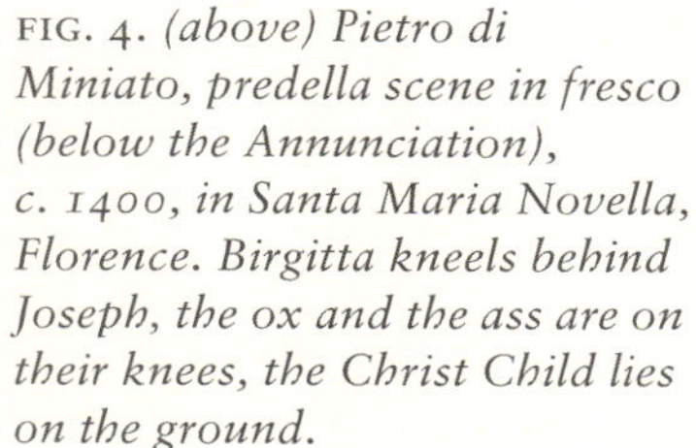

FIG. 5. *(left) Meister Francke, The Nativity, c. 1426, tempera and oil on oak, 91.8 x 81.5 cm, Kunsthalle, Hamburg. This is a panel of an altarpiece commissioned in Hamburg by the Society of Merchants trading with England, originally in the former Dominican church of St John in Hamburg, where Meister Francke was a friar. Joseph is absent; in the background up the hill we see the Annunciation to the Shepherds.*

FIG. 6. *(right) Giovanni di Paolo di Grazia, the Nativity, detail of the Monte dei Paschi Altarpiece, c. 1435, tempera and gold on wood, 38 x 43 cm, Pinacoteca Vaticana. The scene is set in an orchard, lit by Divine light from the heavens and by the radiant newborn. Mary adores the Christ Child while Joseph sleeps, and the midwives sit by the stable.*

FIG. 7. *(below) Detail. Sano di Pietro, The Nativity, c. 1445, tempera on wood, 31.5 x 45 cm, Pinacoteca Vaticana. The Virgin (dressed in white) and Joseph both kneel beside the Christ Child lying on the ground, the ox and ass breathing warmth on His fragile little body. Above Him the Holy Spirit hovers, and celestial light pours down from God the Father. The Annunciation to the Shepherds – wearing heavy cloaks, beside a fire – takes place on the hillside, a blaze of light in the night sky. Not shown here, the Annunciation to the Shepherds takes place in the distance.*

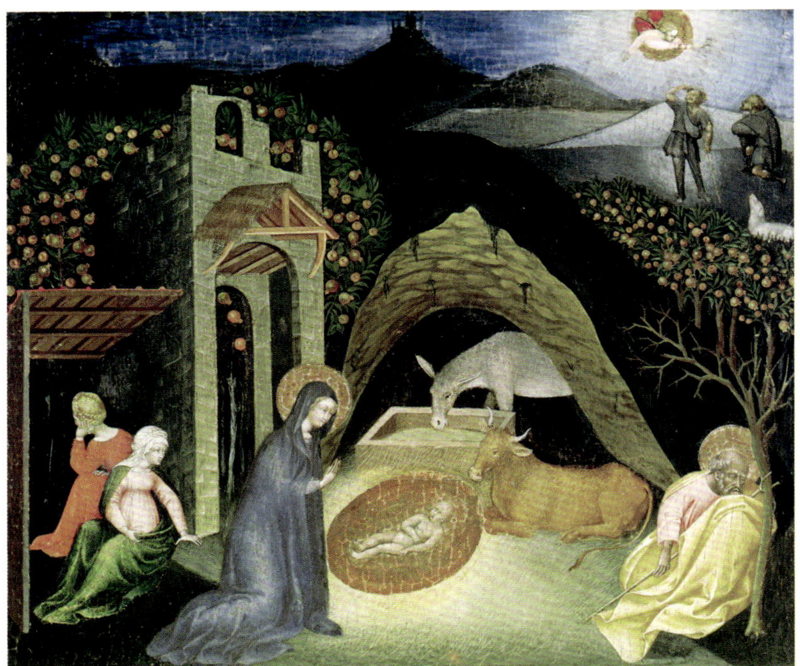

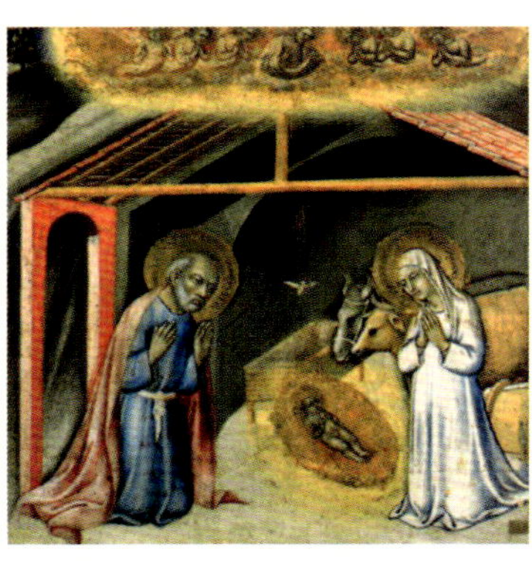

Birgitta noted the events she witnessed with precision, which no doubt captivated and seemed to add authenticity for her devoted followers. She was no prude, and not squeamish. She describes intimate details concerning the Nativity:

I saw also the afterbirth, lying wrapped very neatly beside Him. And then I heard the wonderfully sweet and most gentle songs of the angels … Then sitting on the ground, she put her Son in her lap and deftly caught His umbilical cord with her fingers. At once it was cut off without any flow of liquid or blood … And at once she began to wrap Him carefully, first in the linen cloths and then in the woollen ones, binding his little body, legs and arms, with a ribbon that had been sewn into four parts of the outer woollen cloth. And afterwards she wrapped and tied on the boy's head those two small linen cloths that she had prepared for this purpose.[ix]

Throughout the fourteenth century personal piety and devotion were encouraged and developed. Lay men and women, and groups of

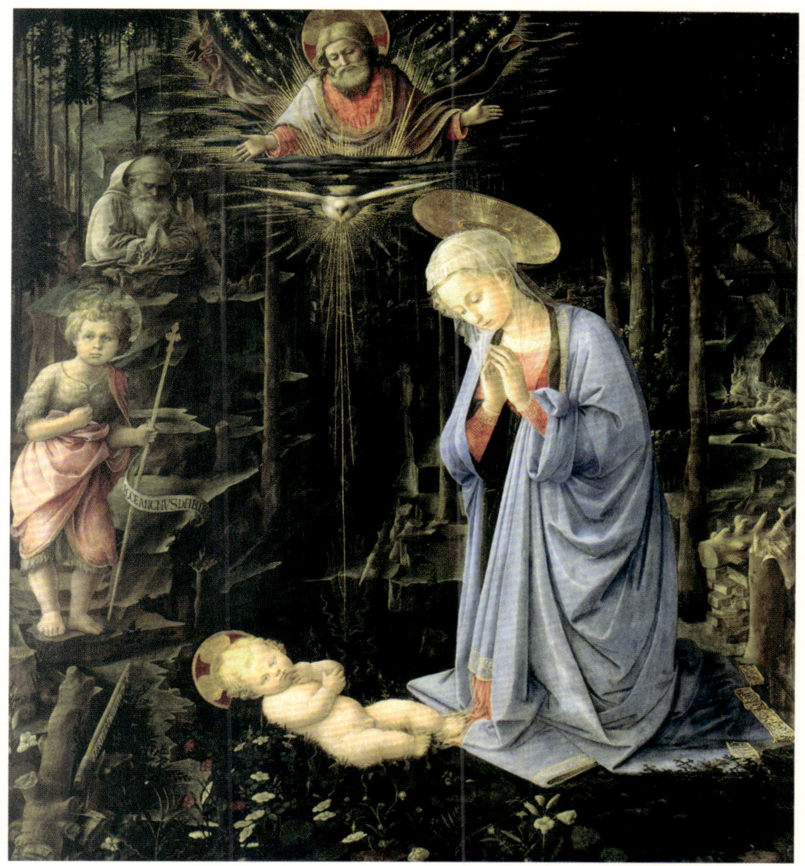

FIG. 8. *Filippo Lippi,* Mystical Nativity, *c. 1459, painted for the newly built chapel in the Medici Palace in Florence, oil on poplar, 127 x 116 cm, Gemäldegalerie, Staatliche Museen, Berlin. The Virgin kneels in adoration, and the Child (partly covered with a transparent gauze cloth) lies in a richly detailed flowering meadow in a dark forest. John the Baptist and Bernard of Clairvaux are seen in the background.*

companions such as the Beguines and the Brethren of the Common Man, like monks and nuns in monasteries and convents, were taught to practise spiritual exercises in their daily lives, and urged to pray, to study, to read.[x] Through hearing and reading treatises, listening to homilies and exhortations, the faithful were recommended and inspired to contemplate and to visualise sacred events, to be an eyewitness – 'as if you yourself were present', as Bernard of Clairvaux had advocated in the twelfth century. Among numerous mystics and visionaries of the fourteenth century we find Margery Kempe, Thomas à Kempis, Julian of Norwich, Richard Rolle and Catherine of Siena. Both *The Cloud of Unknowing* and *Piers Plowman* were written in the second half of the fourteenth century. The anonymous *Cloud* emphasises intense contemplation motivated by love, and

FIG. 9. *Rogier van der Weyden, the* Bladelin Nativity, *c. 1450, painted for the new church at Middleburg, oil on panel, 91 x 89 cm, Gemäldegalerie, Staatliche Museen, Berlin. This follows Birgitta's vision, showing the Virgin kneeling and Joseph holding a candle, and also includes some unusual features – the metal grating and cistern in the foreground, and the Romanesque window arches in the ruined stable. The patron's portrait is included – probably Pieter Bladelin, an influential and pious burgher, dressed in the fashion of those close to the Duke of Burgundy.*

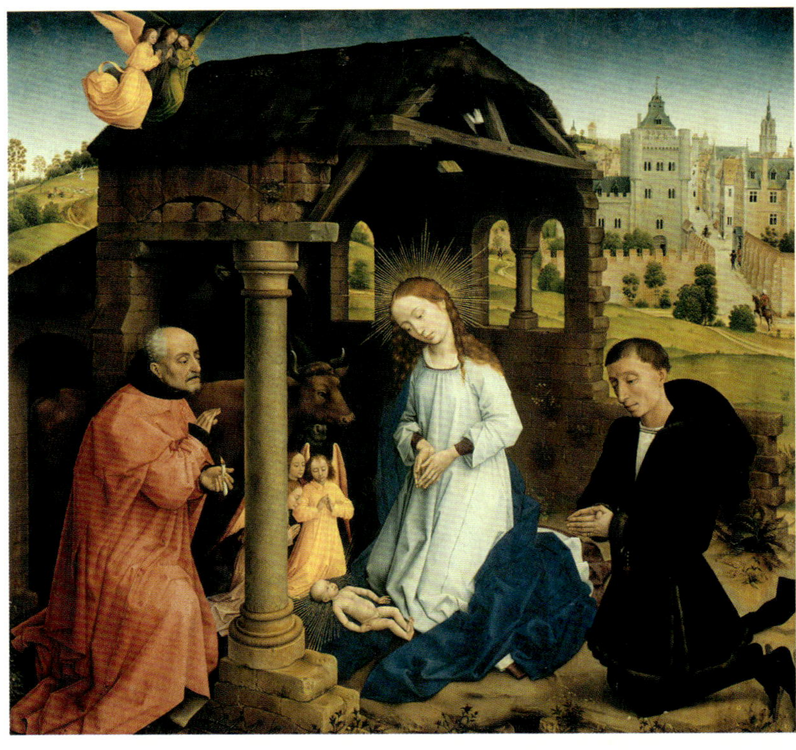

FIG. 10. *(opposite) Fra Angelico, Nativity scene with St Peter Martyr and St Catherine of Alexandria, c. 1445, fresco in cell 5 of the Dominican convent of San Marco, Florence. The cells in this corridor were used by friars training to become preachers; the image in each cell was a means of contemplation and of learning to embody the central values of the Order – Humility, Chastity and Obedience.*

urges the reader to worship God with one's 'substance', coming to rest in 'naked blind feeling of being'. In his Christmas Sermon 1, Meister Eckhart reminded the faithful that 'Here, in time, we are celebrating the eternal birth which God the Father bore and bears unceasingly in eternity.'

Why were Birgitta's visionary details of the Nativity so attractive to artists and to the faithful? Was this an innovative way of exploring and understand the meaning of the Nativity? In the *Mystical Nativity* Filippo Lippi (Cosimo de' Medici's favourite painter) depicts the Son lying among lushly growing plants [FIG. 8]. In his only definitively known Nativity scene Rogier van der Weyden places the newborn Saviour on the ground on the Virgin's mantle [FIG. 9]. Inspired and intensified through the influence of Franciscans and Dominicans with their insistence on simplicity [FIG. 10] and the frailty of human nature, Birgitta's down-to-earth organic, almost matter-of-fact description of the birth scene, the supernatural light, now struck a totally new chord with artists, and found an echo in the faithful. However, perhaps

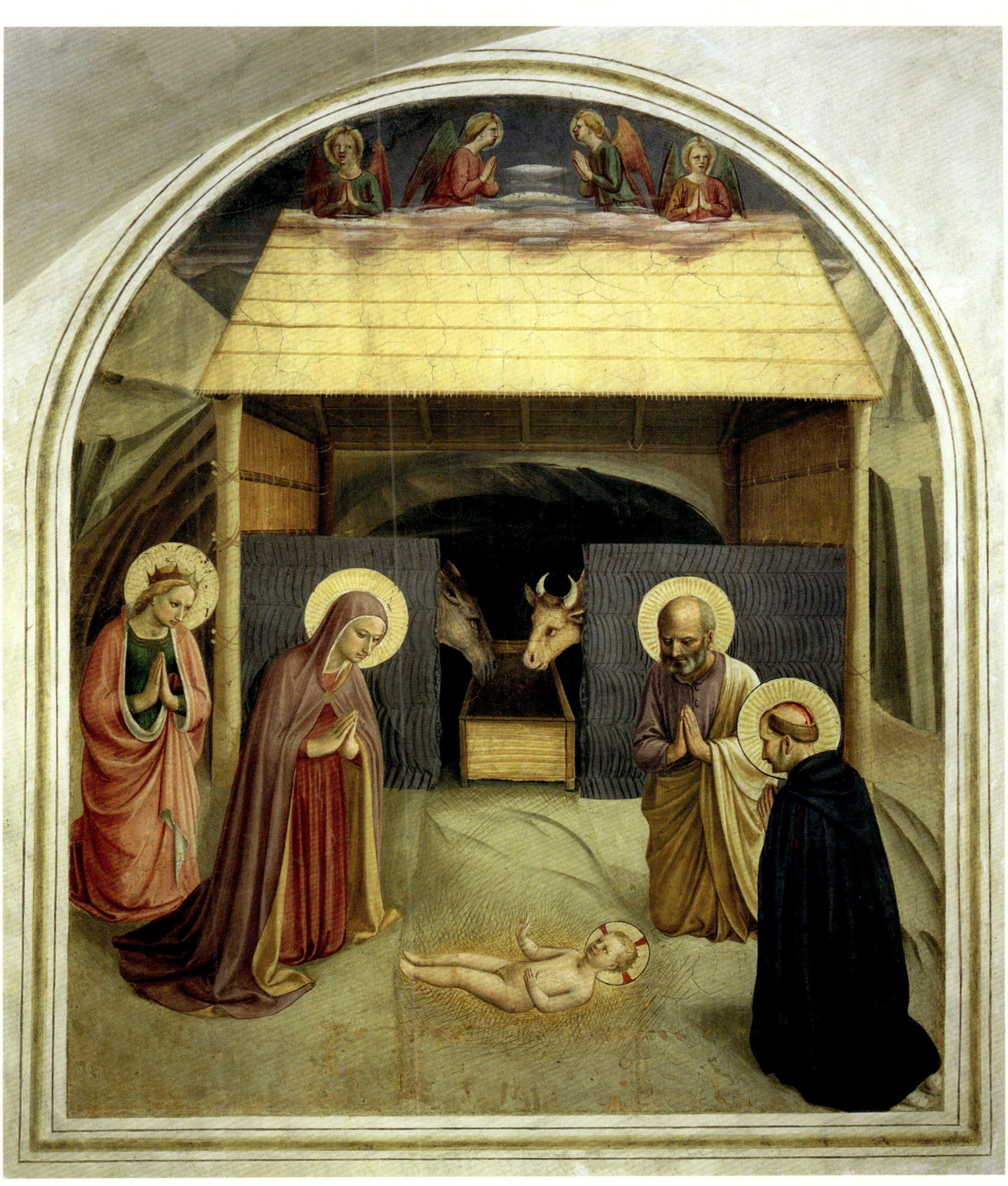

depictions of the Nativity were evolving in this direction: was this a natural evolution for craftsmen? Artists, like Birgitta herself, were surely familiar with the numerous details concerning the Nativity described in the apocryphal Infancy Gospels.[xi]

Birgitta's vision of the Nativity encompasses myriad aspects at every level – from mundane bodily functions to the ineffable Light, mysterious, pervasive, the life-giving Source. For artists and the faithful, Birgitta's vision revealing the Christ Child surrounded by Light, the unifying principle of relationship everywhere in the universe, offers profound means of meditation. The newborn Christ is now revealed as a human baby, naked, fragile, defenceless. The shock of this impression may evoke a wish to protect, to cherish, to nurture the secret Life in ourselves. And the tiny naked newborn is also a vivid reminder that at death the soul is traditionally represented in art as a naked infant being borne up to another level.

VII BIRGITTA'S VISION: FOOTNOTES

i *Revelationes Coelestes*, bk VII, ch. 21.

ii Her father was Birger Persson, knight, landowner and lawspeaker.

iii In England the Brigittine abbey was at Syon, its foundation stone laid by Henry V in 1415. It was one of the last religious communities to be dissolved at the Reformation, in 1539, when nuns and monks fled to Portugal and Holland.

iv Known as the Blue Church, from the colour of the granite. At its head was the abbess, in honour of the Blessed Virgin Mary. Vadstena, richly endowed by King Magnus IV, became the principal house of Birgitta's order in Sweden.

v Birgitta was known from her earliest years as constantly smiling, and for her charitable work with the sick and the poor.

vi See *The New Catholic Encyclopaedia*, vol. 2, St Bridget of Sweden.

vii The only woman to be canonised in the fourteenth century.

viii See Bridget Morris, 'St Birgitta of Sweden', in *Studies in Medieval Mysticism* (Woodbridge, Boydell Press, 1999), vol. I, pp. 135–39.

ix The vision itself is followed by three further revelations: one is a commentary on the vision, confirming the truth and novelty of the descriptions; the second describes the visit of the shepherds; the third tells of the Virgin's comment that what had been ordained and foreknown had now come to pass. See Bridget Morris, op. cit. in the preceding note.

x See Ross Fuller, *The Brotherhood of the Common Life* (New York: State University of New York Press, 1995).

xi The Pseudo-Matthew recounted that Mary was alone at the time of giving birth, because Joseph had set off in search of a midwife; the *Protoevangelium Jacobi* described the mystic Light.

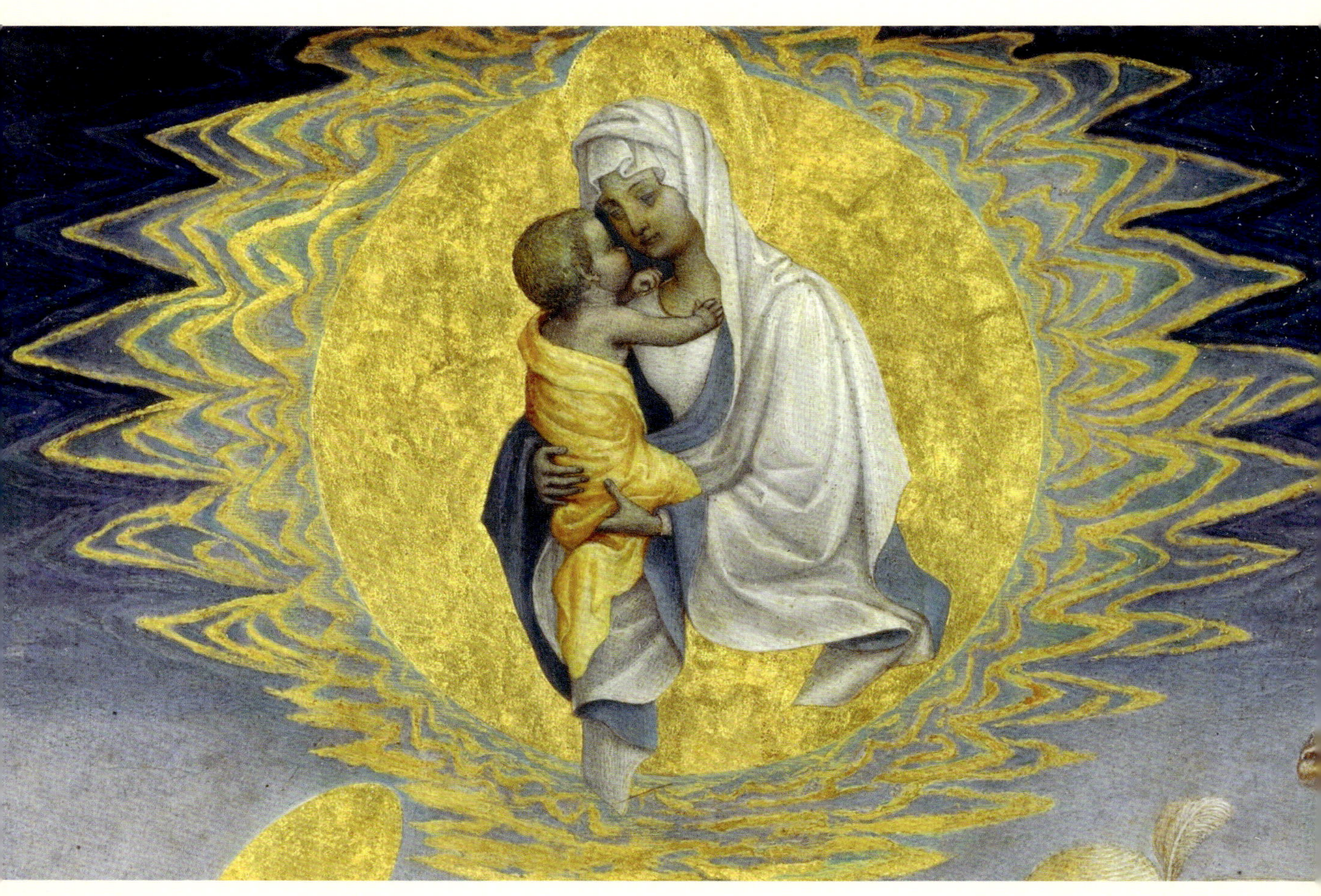

Detail from FIG. 7, *Pisanello,* The Virgin and Child with St Anthony Abbot and St George, *c. 1435–41, egg tempera on poplar, 46.5 x 29 cm, National Gallery, London*

VIII   THE VIRGIN MARY

THE CULT OF MARY as the Virgin Mother of God emanated from Egypt (Isis), Syria and Palestine. Yet in the very earliest days of Christian imagery the Mother of Christ only appears in Nativity scenes when a shepherd or the Magi are also depicted. Part of the carving on an early fourth-century sarcophagus shows the seated Virgin with the Child on her lap [FIG. 1]; the Magi, carrying their gifts and accompanied by their camels, process towards them to pay homage; the leading Magus points to the star. We see the Virgin Mother, a slight young girl, sitting regally, the Christ Child upright on her lap. Mary, symbol of the Church, is shown both as the Mother of the Saviour and as the Throne of Wisdom, *sedes sapientiae*.[i]

The traditional carvings on sarcophagi of the Adoration of the Magi are a reminder that in the years before the Feast of the Nativity was fixed to be celebrated on 25 December (the Roman feast of Saturnalia) around the year 350, it had been combined with the gloriously important Epiphany holy day celebrations on 6 January. This day commemorated the birth of the Saviour and His manifestation to the Gentiles, represented by the Magi, and His baptism. Though the figures on the sarcophagi, all carved in profile, are relatively small, the impression is monumental.

The Child shown on His mother's lap in these early carvings

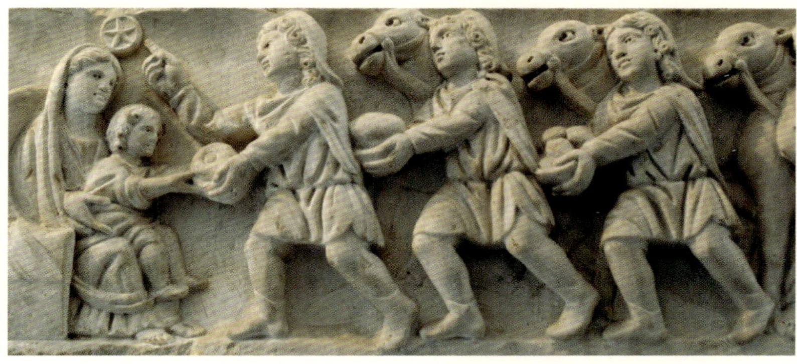

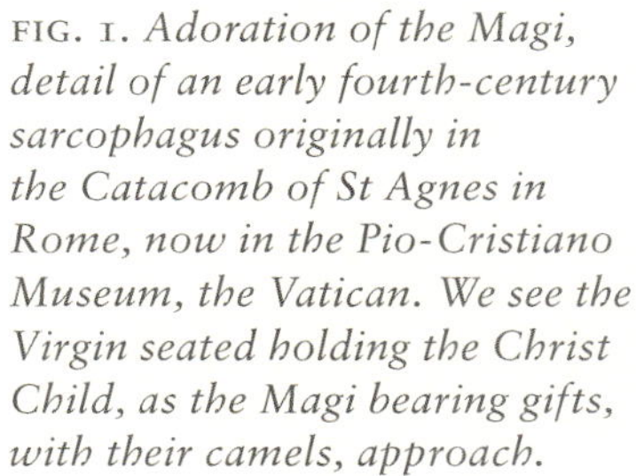

FIG. 1. *Adoration of the Magi, detail of an early fourth-century sarcophagus originally in the Catacomb of St Agnes in Rome, now in the Pio-Cristiano Museum, the Vatican. We see the Virgin seated holding the Christ Child, as the Magi bearing gifts, with their camels, approach.*

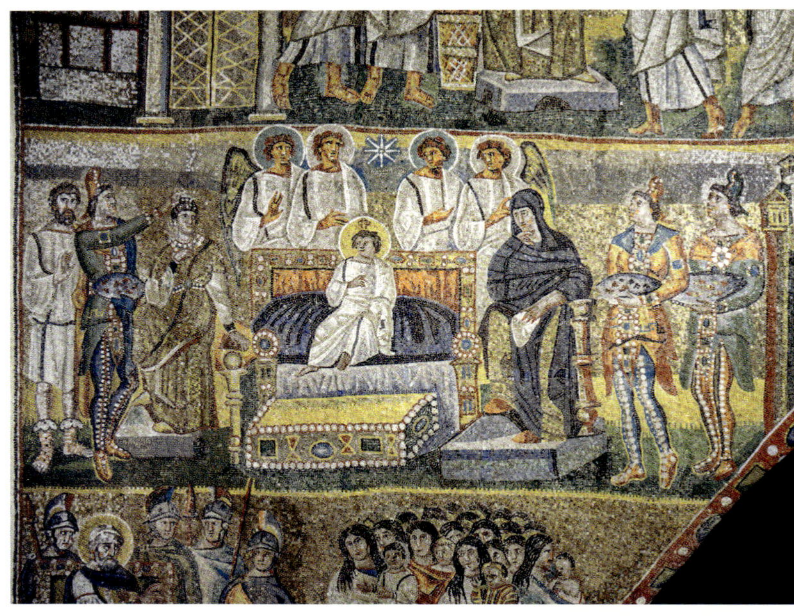

FIG. 2. *Mosaic of the Nativity on the triumphal arch in Santa Maria Maggiore, Rome, c. 432. We see the Magi with the Christ Child, seated on a jewelled throne; Mary* theotokos – *God-bearing – stands on His right, dressed in grand Byzantine robes. Joseph is at the far left. On Christ's left is a woman probably representing the Synagogue.*

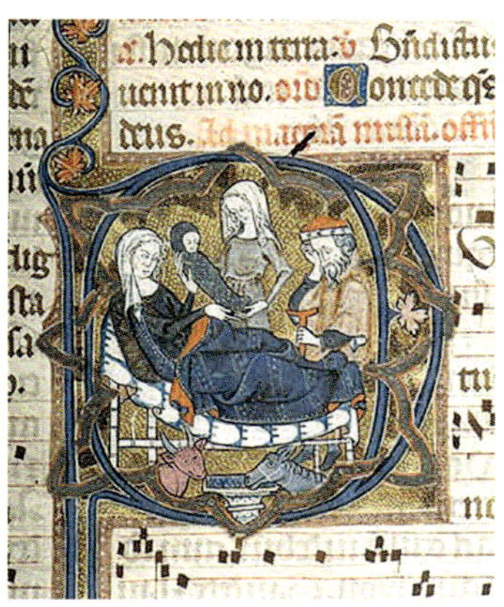

FIG. 3. *Nativity scene in the Sarum Missal, c. 1320, Pierpont Morgan Library, New York, MS M.107. Mary is shown reclining after giving birth; she reaches out to hold the swaddled Child (even His head is covered) from the midwife.*

on sarcophagi is not a newborn infant so much as a child several months old. The Gospels do not tell us how long after Christ's birth the Magi arrived at Bethlehem to worship the newly born King of the Jews, but Herod's command to massacre all infant boys up to the age of two (Matthew 2:16–18) may well suggest that Christ was no longer a tiny baby.

In the great fifth-century mosaic cycle on the triumphal arch in Santa Maria Maggiore in Rome we again witness Mary in a Nativity image with the Magi [FIG. 2]. The mosaics were created to celebrate the famous Council of Ephesus of 431, which declared the Virgin Mary *theotokos*, God-bearing.[ii] The proclamation of this definition of Mary as Mother of God made man gave rise to an intense surge of interest in Mary, the hitherto unknown young woman called to immense responsibility. Santa Maria Maggiore was the first church in Rome to be dedicated to Mary. In this image, she is richly adorned with luxurious robes and jewels, dressed in the role of a Byzantine princess or perhaps empress (even more conspicuously so in the Annunciation scene in the same cycle, where she sits enthroned). Here the Christ Child, not a newborn infant, is seated on a jewelled throne; behind him are protective angels and the star that led the Magi (two on one side, one on the other). Mary, representing both

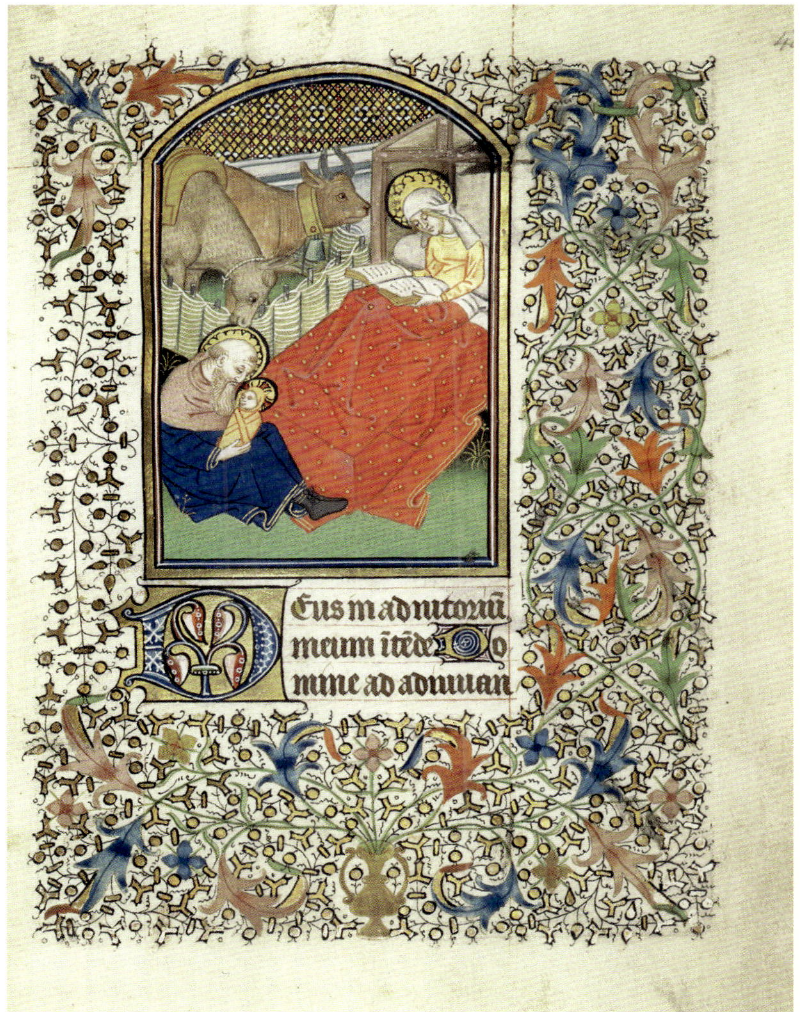

FIG. 4. *Nativity scene in the Besançon Book of Hours, fifteenth century, Fitzwilliam Museum, Cambridge, MS 69. The Virgin is seen reading in bed, while Joseph cradles the newborn Infant (a cross is visible in His halo), overseen by the donkey, breathing warmth.*

the Church and Eve, stands at her divine Son's right. On Christ's other side we see a mysterious female figure somberly clad in a dark blue *maphorion* (headcloth), generally interpreted as a representation of the Synagogue.

From this time on Mary's role was firmly established as the Mother of God in the liturgy, in art and in religious feeling. The cult of Mary developed rapidly all over Christendom, spreading far and wide.[iii] In the ensuing centuries numerous prayers, rites and feast days were introduced.[iv]

Nativity icons of the Orthodox Church traditionally depict the Virgin reclining, lying back on a kind of couch generally shown in front of the cave that she guards.[v] In the Latin West Mary's recumbent pose is also popular in painting and sculpture. On one level it expresses an indication of the exhaustion a woman experiences after childbirth, drawing attention to the human aspect of Christ's nature. Fatigued by the drama of giving birth, Mary often appears reverently and silently pondering.

Christ's human nature is visible in those Nativity scenes where we see Him gazing at His mother, or reaching towards her. Books of Hours, often used by women in their private devotions, expressed this intimacy poignantly, no doubt allowing mothers to meditate on their own role. In a missal we are shown the Virgin lying in a curved bed, reaching out to receive the Child (even His head is swaddled in a blue cloth) from the attendant midwife [FIG. 3]. Occasionally and incongruously we even find the Virgin reading in bed [FIG. 4]. This charming, if whimsical, scene is a reminder that Mary was taken as a model for encouraging women to read and, in this instance, perhaps also to rest.

We sense Mary's concern for her Son in countless ways, whether she is shown reclining, kneeling or sitting. She is watchful and silent, by day and by night [FIG. 5]. Inspired by Birgitta's vision of the Nativity, we witness Mary kneeling in adoration of the Child [FIG. 6], a pose that continued to be explored over the centuries – another way to express the mysterious meaning of the Nativity, depicting Christ's human and Divine nature, His tiny, naked, fragile body lying on her mantle on the earth, and His human mother, the Virgin Mary, *theotokos*, kneeling in prayer and awe.

In a fifteenth-century panel by Pisanello (his only signed painting, 'Pisanus') the Virgin and Child appear in a vision to St Anthony Abbot and St George, whose dragon is snarling at Anthony's boar [FIG. 7]. In the depiction of the vision, clearly an event from another, higher world, bathed in light, Mary and the Christ Child face each other with warmth and wonder, designed to draw us in: Christ's humanity and his Divinity are both present. Dirk Bouts' panel of the Virgin and Child [FIG. 8] – a subject he repeatedly returned to – expresses tangible intimacy as Mary offers the Child her breast. The fragile Child is perched on the sill of a window in a contemporary Flemish setting, his cushion tipping over the edge; the opulent honorific cloth of gold reminds the viewer that Mary is Queen of Heaven.

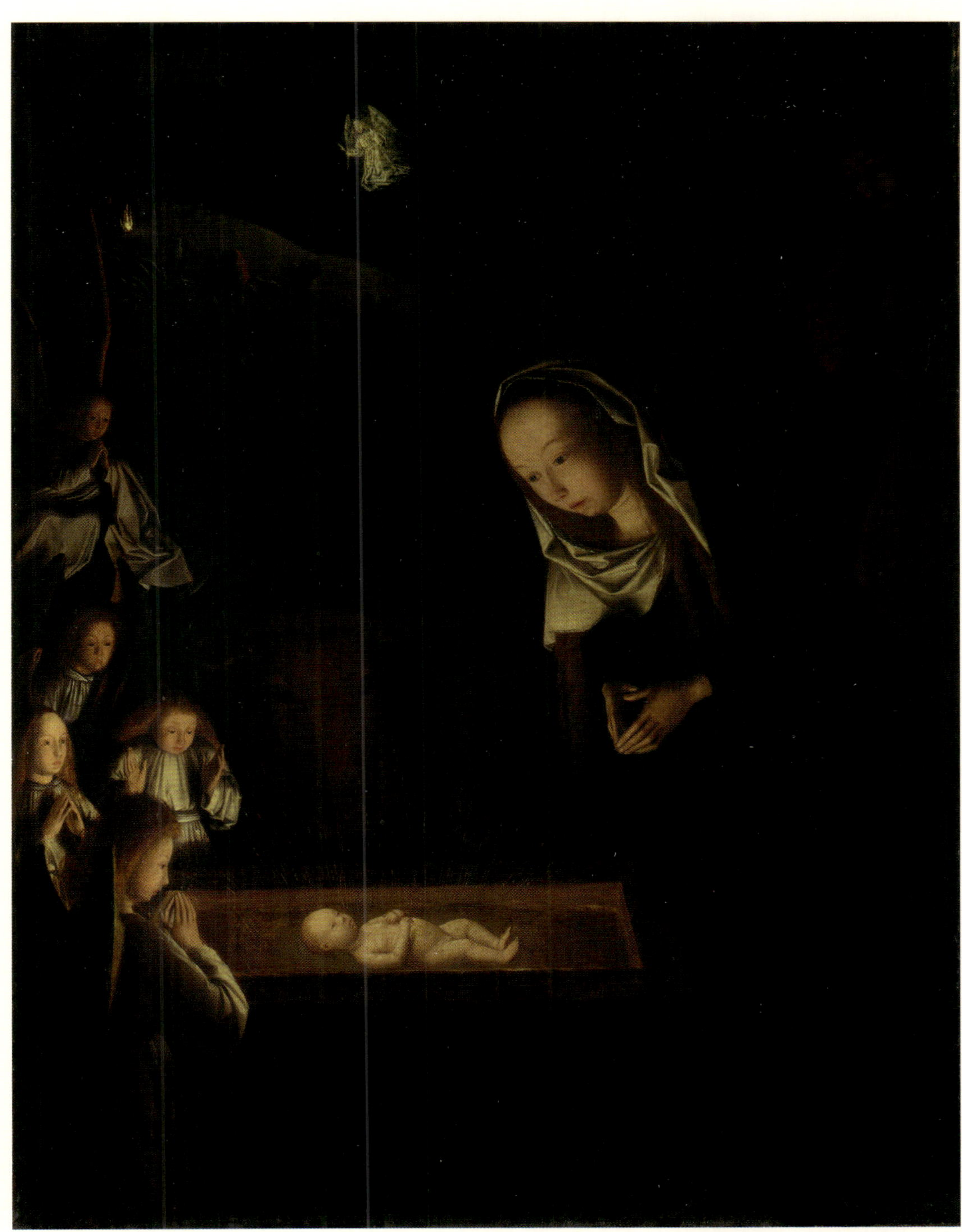

FIG. 6. *Nativity, in a Book of Hours commissioned by Charles, Count of Angoulême, father of François I, 1480, Bibliothèque nationale de France, Paris, MS lat. 1173. Inspired by Birgitta's vision, a very young Mary kneels in reverence beside her Child who lies on her mantle.*

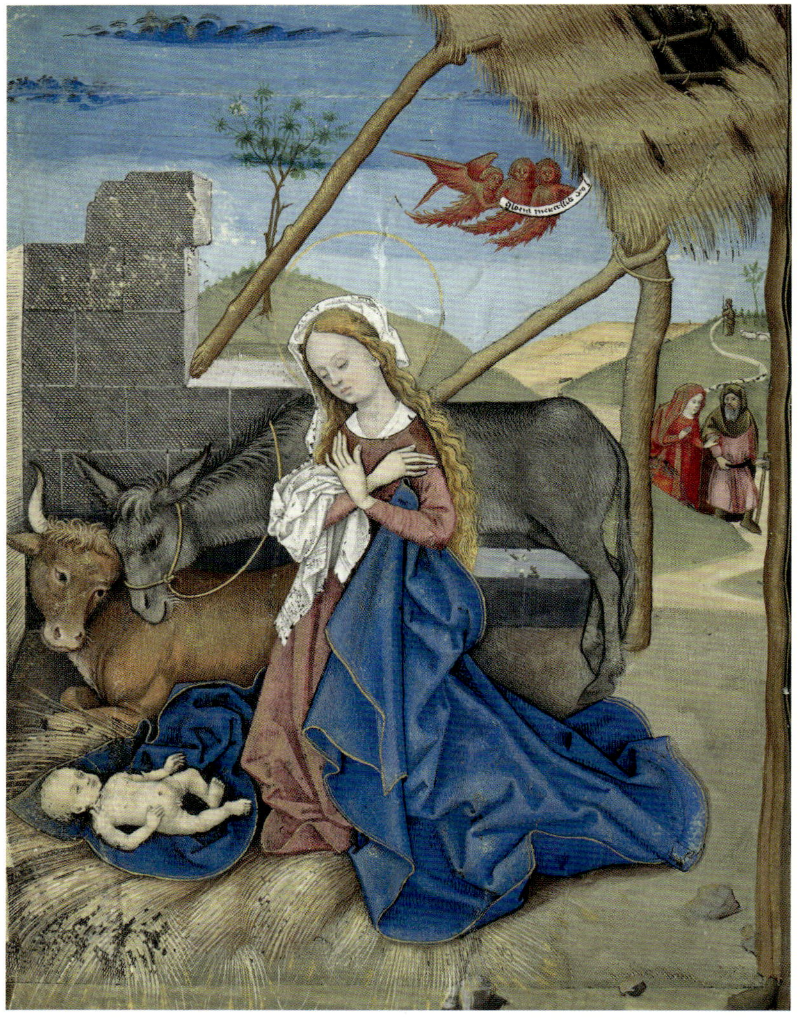

Mary's tenderness towards the Christ Child is supremely expressed by Giotto in one of his three Nativity scenes in the Arena Chapel at Padua, painted *c.* 1305 [FIG. 9]. Here we see the reclining Virgin leaning towards the swaddled newborn Christ Child, placed in the manger by the Virgin's attendant (perhaps the midwife), watched over by the ox and the ass. Time and neglect have failed to diminish the beauty of the work; its power and its luminosity remain, though the azurite – made from lapis lazuli, the most precious and expensive of all pigments – used for the Virgin's cloak and the night sky has suffered through the lime present in the stonework. We see Giotto grappling to master realism and perspective and we see his emphasis on the human aspect of Christ's nature. Above the stable, perched precariously on the mountainside, the angels rejoice and sing in glory. The shepherds learn of the birth, their sheep (a reminder that Giotto himself was once a shepherd) lie at their feet. Joseph sits facing the viewer pensively, patiently, a solid presence.

Such subtle sensitive renderings vibrate in this period with the recently founded Franciscan and Dominican Orders – not attached to monasteries, but mendicant friars who preached out of doors, in piazzas and markets, specifically to the lay population and the urban poor. Simplicity and poverty were lauded, obedience to God's laws and the love of one's fellow beings. Such emphasis on Christ's human nature encouraged and inspired individual lay piety and personal devotion.

The mid-fourteenth-century *Meditationes Vitae Christi* include a description of Mary giving birth 'standing by the pillar':

> When the hour of birth came, the Virgin rose and stood erect against a column that was there. But Joseph remained seated, downcast perhaps because he could not prepare what was necessary. Then he rose and taking some hay from the manger, placed it at the Lady's feet and turned away. Then the Son of the eternal God came out of the womb of the mother without a murmur or lesion, in a moment … The ox and the ass knelt with their mouths above the manger and breathed on the Infant as though they possessed reason and knew that the Child was so poorly wrapped that He needed to be warmed …

A fourteenth-century copy of this vastly popular text, translated into Italian and illustrated, shows Mary standing in front of a pillar, the Christ Child on the ground.[vi] It seems likely that St Birgitta of Sweden was familiar with the text of *Meditationes Vitae Christi*, as we learn from her vision, witnessing Mary standing to give birth though she does not specify the pillar (see Chapter VII). The element of the column is rare in Nativity images, though Rogier van der Weyden includes it in the Bladelin Altarpiece, his only painting of the Nativity [see Chapter VII, FIG. 9]. Is the pillar

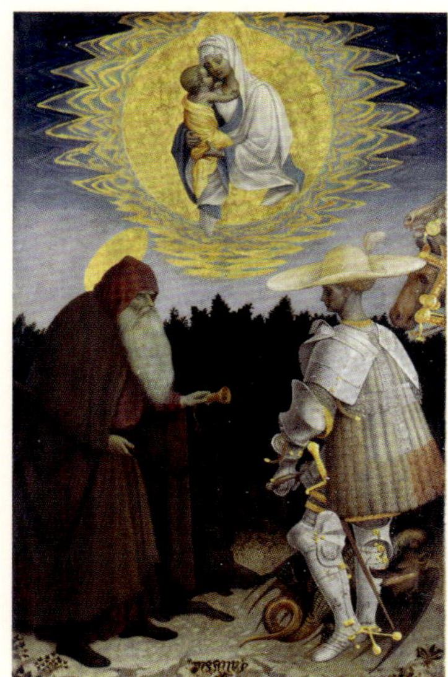

FIG. 7. *Pisanello*, The Virgin and Child with St Anthony Abbot and St George, *c. 1435–41, egg tempera on poplar, 46.5 x 29 cm, National Gallery, London. St George wears a French-style straw hat and contemporary armour. Above the saints is a vision of the Madonna and Child; very unusually, Mary and the Christ Child face each other, both with a look of deep love.*

FIG. 8. *Dirk Bouts*, The Virgin and Child, *c. 1465, oil with egg tempera on oak, 37.1 x 27.6 cm, National Gallery, London. The Virgin offers the Child her breast, an intimate expression of the Christ Child's human nature. The scene is set in a contemporary room, with a cloth of gold behind in honour of the Queen of Heaven, and an open window on to the world without – a devotional image full of love and details for private contemplation.*

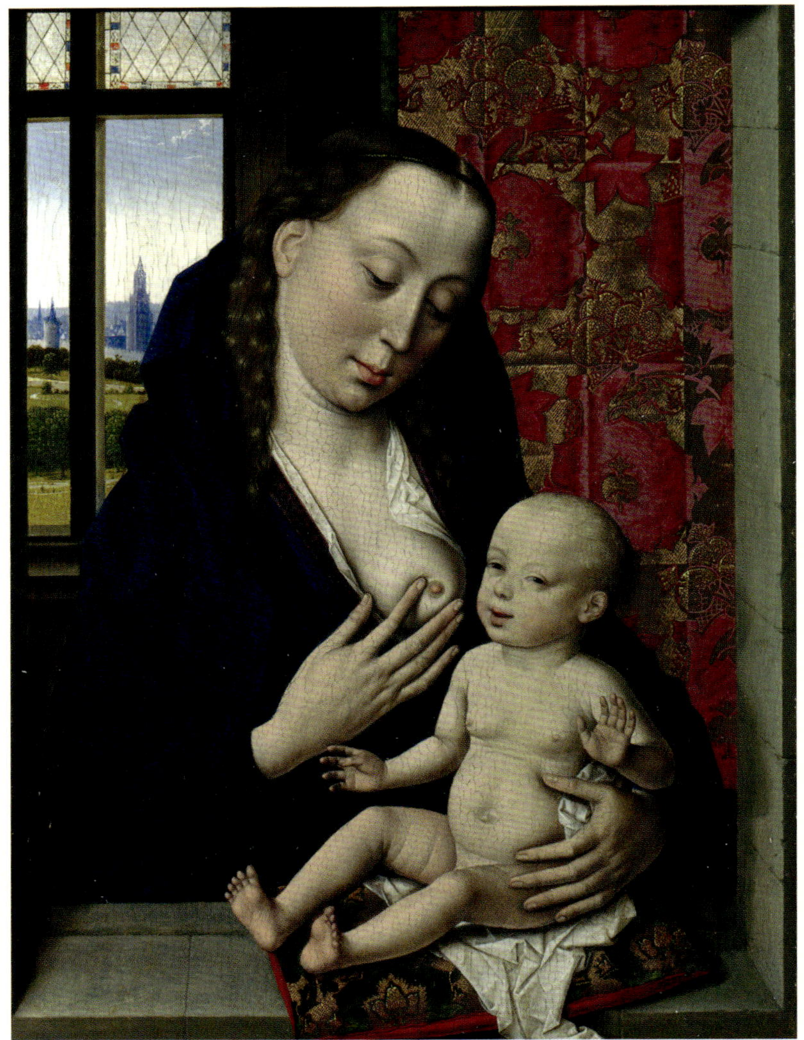

an allusion to Christ's Passion, and the Scourging at the Pillar?[vii] Or was there a cult – long since forgotten – of a relic connected with the tradition of the Nativity story contained in a particular pillar? The setting in Nativity scenes often includes a combination of Classical arches and stonework: elements of Classical architecture offer sharp contrast to the humble and impoverished wooden stable, barn, or hut where the Divine Birth takes place. Perhaps this is an invitation to witness that the pagan world is ended. The Virgin herself is an

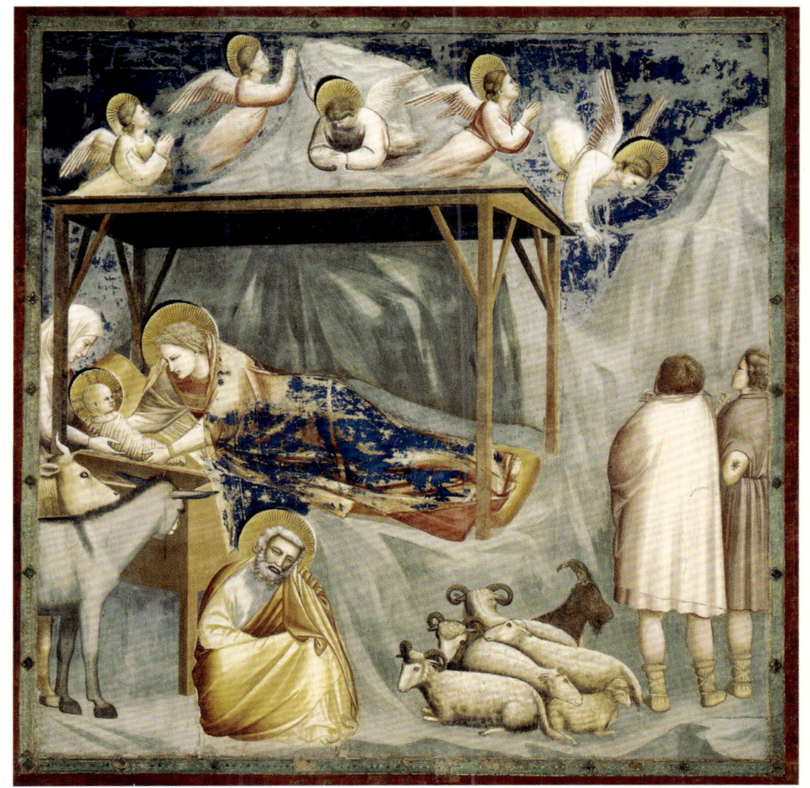

allegory for the Church; now is a new time, the dawning of a new world, the beginning of another age.

A remarkable panel is from a Bohemian altarpiece of *c.* 1350, one of several scenes made for a Cistercian monastery [FIG. 10]. The patron, Peter I of Rosenberg, Supreme Chamberlain of the Bohemian Kingdom, is included at the bottom right of the painting, offering the Abbey of Vyšši Brod to the Saviour. The Virgin, half-lying, half-sitting in bed, holds the curiously muscular Christ Child. His swaddling is draped untidily. The figures of mother and Son are disturbingly reminiscent of paintings of the Lamentation after the Descent from the Cross. This combination of tenderness and care, of supreme obedience in her role as the mother of Christ, the Redeemer and Saviour, is revealed.

In images of the Nativity Mary is exalted to the cosmic level, and at the same time she acts as an example of human love and

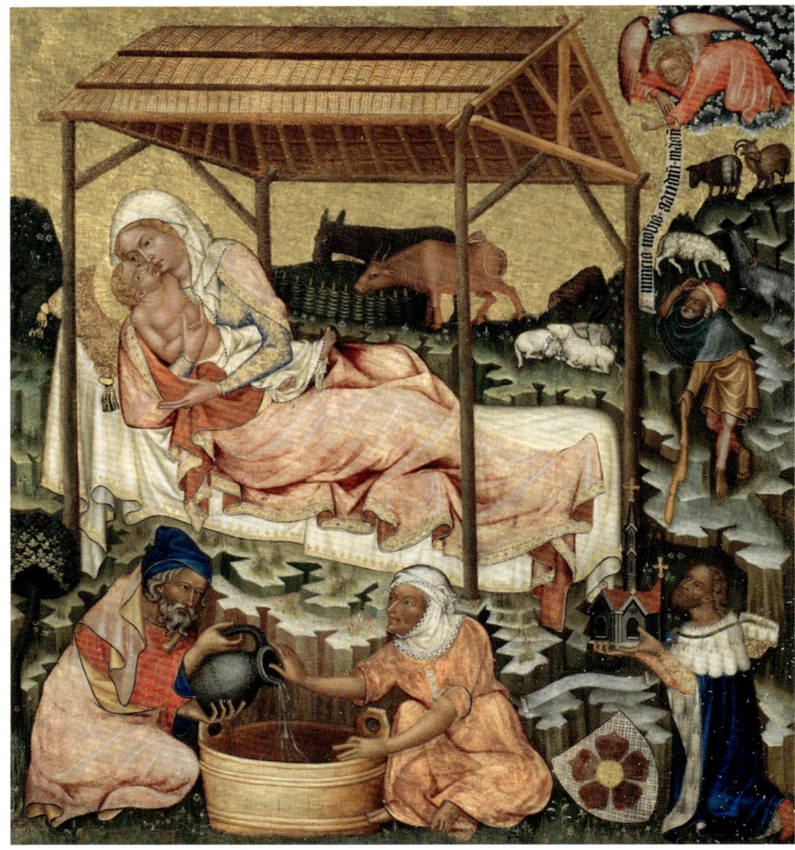

FIG. 10. *Master of Hohenfurth, Nativity, c. 1350, in the Vyšší Brod Altarpiece, tempera on wood, 99 x 92 cm, Narodni Gallery, Prague. In the bed, sheltered by the stable roof, Mary holds the muscular Christ Child in tattered swaddling, a pose reminiscent of scenes showing the Lamentation. In the foreground Joseph assists the midwife preparing the bath. Bottom right, the patron is depicted offering the Cistercian Abbey of Vyšší Brod to the Saviour.*

vulnerability. Sensitive to the meaning of motherhood and childhood – the fundamentals of human existence – she embodies spiritual force. Silently guarding and attending, she is awake to the mystery of the Incarnation, totally concerned with protecting this precious new Life.

VIII THE VIRGIN MARY: FOOTNOTES

i Sometimes known as the *Throne of Solomon*. See Ilene H. Forsyth, The Throne of Wisdom (Princeton, NJ: Princeton University Press, 2019).

ii The Council of Ephesus in 431 condemned the Nestorian heresy, which claimed the Virgin Mary could not be the mother of Christ, both human and Divine, and declared Mary *theotokos*.

iii Gathering pace in the ninth century and escalating again in twelfth century. The cult of Mary as the Virgin Mother of God had emanated from Egypt (Isis), Syria and Palestine.

iv See Hilda Graef, *Mary – A History of Doctrine and Devotion* (London and New York: Sheed and Ward, 1963); also Yrjö Hirn, *The Sacred Shrine. A Study of the Poetry and Art of the Catholic Church* (London: Faber & Faber, 1958).

v Symbolic and allegory of her heart, her innermost being (see Chapter III).

vi See P. Saenger, 'Books of Hours and the Reading Habits of the Later Middle Ages' in R. Chartier, ed., *The Culture of Print: Power and Uses of Print in Early Modern Europe* (Cambridge: Polity Press, 1989); and M.J. Clanchy, 'The Church and the Book', in *Papers and Studies in Church History*, ed. R.N. Swanson (Woodbridge: Boydell Press for the Ecclesiastical History Society, 2000).

vii This is one of four illustrations of the Nativity in the manuscript (Bibliothèque nationale de France, Paris, MS ital. 115). Isa Ragusa and Rosalie B. Green, transl. and ed., *Meditations on the Life of Christ: An Illustrated Manuscript of the Fourteenth Century* (Princeton, NJ: Princeton University Press, 1961).

viii See Shirley Nielsen Blum, *Early Netherlandish Triptychs* (Oakland, CA: University of California Press, 1969), pp. 17–27.

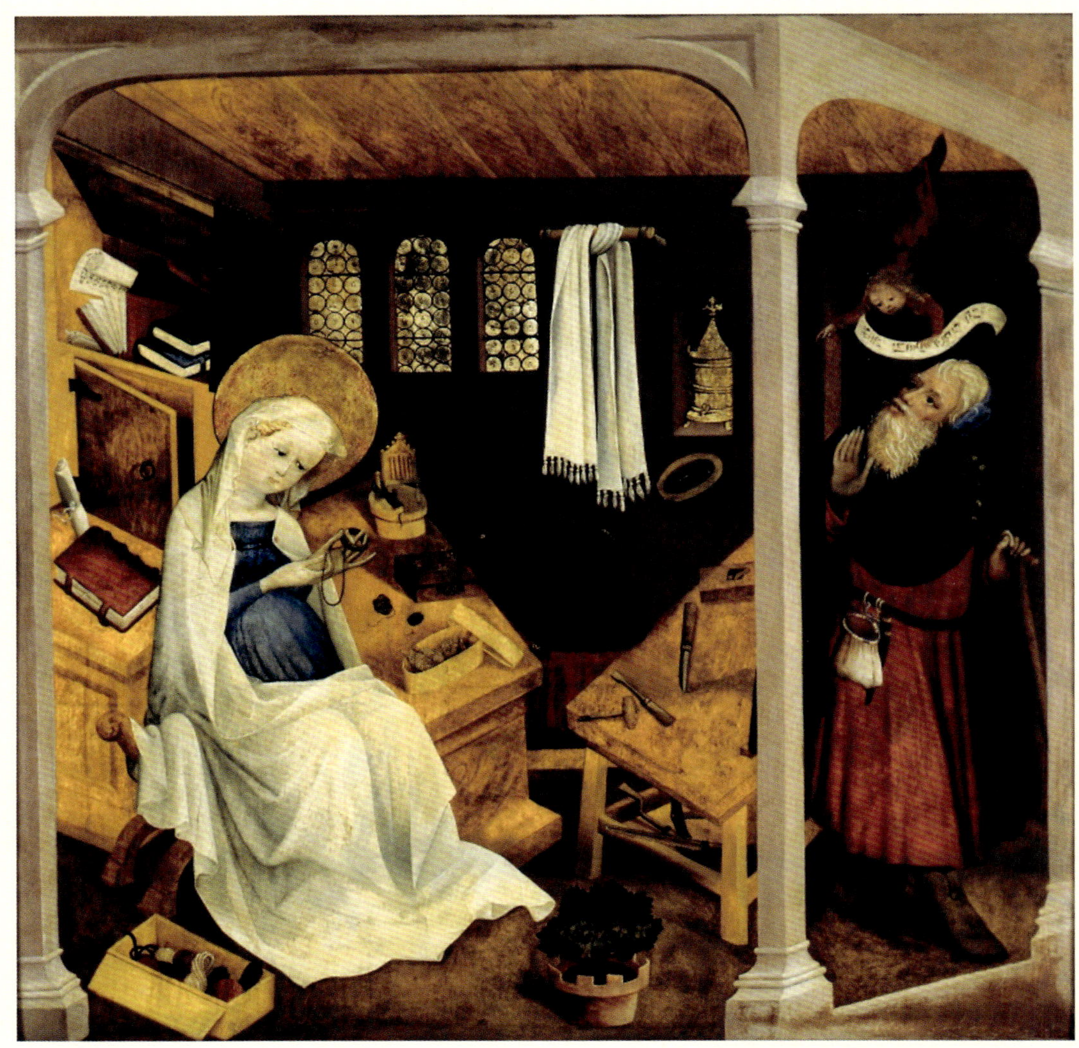

FIG. 1. *Upper Rhenish Master*, Joseph's Doubt, *c. 1410–20, oil on wood, 114 x 114 cm, formerly in the Hospice St-Marc and now in the Musée de l'Oeuvre Notre-Dame, Strasbourg. The pregnant Mary attends to her sewing, divided by a post from the aged Joseph, leaning on a crutch, standing beside his work table. The angel holds a scroll on which the words reveal the Divine source of Jesus's conception.*

IX JOSEPH

JOSEPH'S ROLE IS FRAUGHT WITH DIFFICULTIES and ambiguities from the start, as we have seen (Chapter I). Even the canonical Gospels are at variance over his lineage. His doubts concerning Mary are dispelled in a dream, during a vision of an angel, as we witness in a panel painted *c.* 1410–20 by an Upper Rhenish Master [FIG. 1]. The pregnant Mary sits with her needlework; Joseph stands by his work table, suddenly visited by an angel who instructs him in the Mystery. Small wonder that he is often shown at the Nativity as seemingly lost, perhaps even asleep [FIG. 2], looking away, puzzled or disturbed [FIG. 3]. He is repeatedly represented as an isolated figure.

According to the second-century *Protoevangelium Jacobi* Joseph was chosen as Mary's espoused husband when she was no longer young enough to continue working at the Temple. She must leave and she must marry. Joseph was among the group of eligible, elderly, men summoned to the Temple, each given a rod to determine 'by lot' which of them would take Mary. When Joseph's rod burst into flower, it was a sure sign that he was the one chosen for the role. Although the Latin West abandoned the stories told in the *Protoevangelium* and other apocryphal gospels describing the childhood of Mary and the infancy of Christ, the incidents were later retold and embellished in the much loved and widely disseminated Legenda aurea and *Meditationes Vitae Christi*. The flowering of Joseph's rod and his marriage to the Virgin were painted and sculpted throughout the Middle Ages and the Renaissance. We witness the events, for instance, in paintings by Giotto, Perugino and Raphael.[i] In Lincoln Cathedral the flowering of Joseph's rod is depicted in a thirteenth-century stained-glass window.

In St Helena's basilica in Bethlehem, dedicated in 339, an oratory was allegedly dedicated to Joseph; the earliest known church dedicated to St Joseph in the Latin West, in the year 1129, is in Bologna.[ii] His feast day, 19 March, has been celebrated in Western Christendom since at least the tenth century; in the Eastern Orthodox tradition Joseph's feast falls on the first Sunday following the Nativity. In the early Middle Ages Joseph was referred to as *Nutritor Domini* – that is, the guardian or educator of the Lord. Early on he was designated

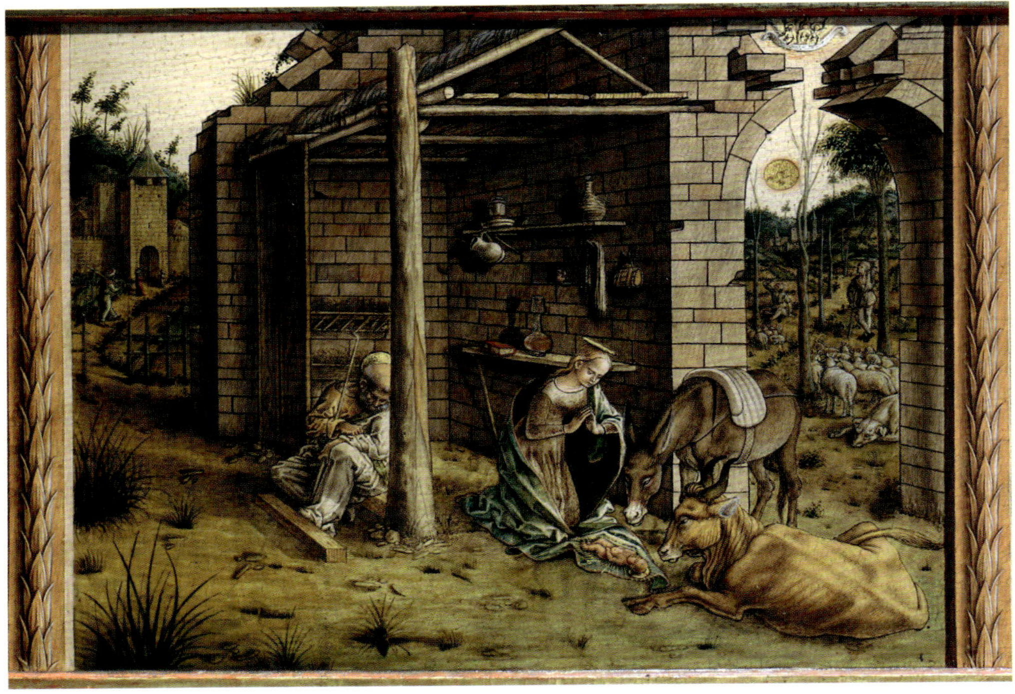

FIG. 2. *Carlo Crivelli, Nativity scene in the predella of the* Madonna della Rondine Altarpiece, *1491, oil and egg on poplar, 29.5 x 36.8 cm, National Gallery, London. Joseph is asleep. The Virgin kneels in prayer by the Christ Child who lies on the ground, warmed by the breath of ox and ass; on the right is the Annunciation to the Shepherds. We see the neat corner of the ruined building, symbolic of the old law which Christ replaces. The altarpiece was commissioned by the Ottoni family for their chapel in the church of San Francesco di Zoccolanti at Matelica, in the Marche.*

as the patron saint of workers. In Sicily Joseph is greatly revered (and unofficially regarded as patron saint), especially honoured for having prevented the people dying of famine during the Middle Ages. Here Joseph's feast day is marked by special dishes, such as *maccu*, a soup prepared from dried fava beans, and cakes whose ingredients include breadcrumbs, in order to recall sawdust, and so to Joseph's calling as a carpenter.

Bernard of Clairvaux in the twelfth century examined the nature and implications of Joseph's role, and emphasised above all else his responsibility to shelter the mystery of the Incarnation to protect Mary's reputation. He stresses the difficulties for Mary if she had no husband, observing that God in all His works maintains the law of things and time. Bernard calls Joseph the 'prudent and faithful servant … whom the Lord places beside Mary to be her protector'.[iii] He discourses at length on Joseph's virtues – his justice, his humility and his chastity. The cult of St Joseph increased and developed over subsequent centuries. Thomas Aquinas (*c*. 1224–1274), Bernardino of Siena (1380–1444), Jean Gerson, Pierre d'Ailly and others delivered homilies and sermons. They wrote influential treatises inspired by Joseph, examining and extolling his example as provider and protector, a man of humility who accepted his position, patiently submitting himself to play his retiring supportive part.

Painters and the faithful responded with admiration and devotion. In the Latin West Joseph appears in Nativity scenes as keenly attentive, both to the Child and to Mary, in marked contrast to those images that illustrate Joseph as a solitary figure. In wild flights of fancy, artists used their vivid powers of inventiveness (notably in illuminated manuscripts) to portray Joseph making himself useful: he brings a candle [FIG. 4], he brings water [FIG. 5], he warms the Christ Child, he tends to the animals, he cooks [FIG. 6] and attends to the fire. He appears as a thoroughly domestic man, caring, busy, solid and kindly.

At some point during the fourteenth century the Cathedral at Aachen acquired several important relics including the shirt of the Virgin, the cloth that received Christ's body taken from the Cross – and Joseph's stockings (*Hosen* in German). A legend of unknown origin describes Joseph removing his stockings following Christ's birth, in order to cover the Child and keep Him warm [FIG. 7].[iv] The story appealed to popular imagination and was referred to in poems and tales, songs and the visual arts for two centuries in the Netherlands and the Rhineland. Joseph's Hosen were displayed every seven years in Aachen Cathedral (the practice has recently been reinstated), a hugely popular focus for pilgrims.[v] The use of Joseph's stockings as makeshift swaddling both exemplifies Joseph's role as guardian of the Christ Child and acts as a visual metaphor of Christ's humanity and humility.

And yet, so often the figure of Joseph is shown set apart. In a small twelfth-century enamel plaque [FIG. 8] he sits upright, holding a book, his gaze directed towards the viewer, his name written above his halo. Repeatedly Joseph is a lonely figure, his head bowed in a gesture of puzzlement. Duccio, Giotto, Giovanni d Milano all depict Joseph as isolated, and we see through his slumped body, his hand

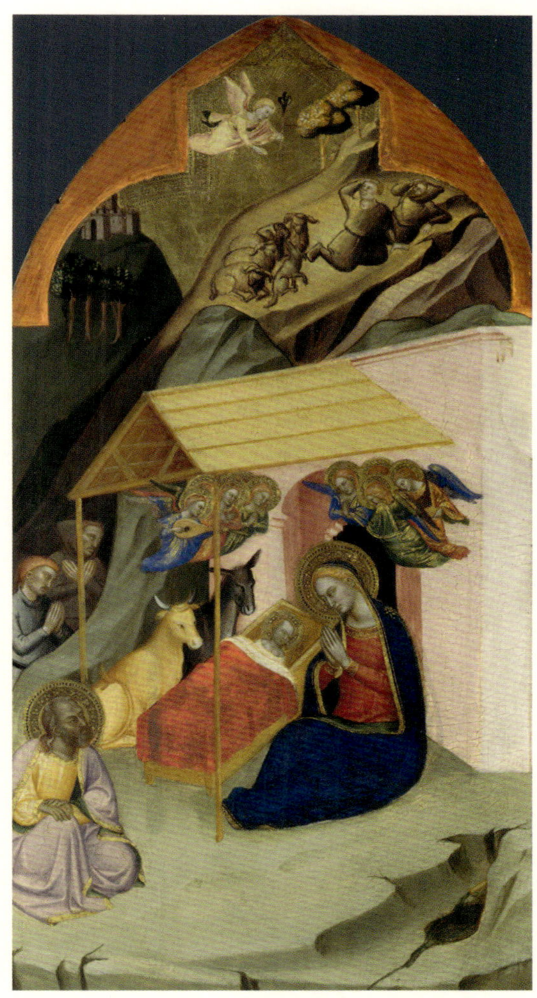

FIG. 3. *Jacopo di Cione and workshop, Nativity scene with the Annunciation to the Shepherds in the* San Pier Maggiore Altarpiece, *1370–71, egg tempera on wood, 95.5 x 49.4 cm, National Gallery, London. Joseph sits apart, nimbed, puzzling over the Mystery.*

held to forehead or cheek or chest, that he is deeply troubled [FIG. 9]. We are shown the Christ Child, born of Mary, the Mother of God, conceived through the Holy Spirit: we witness the bond between Mary and her divine Son, and we see Joseph as an isolated figure, pondering deeply.

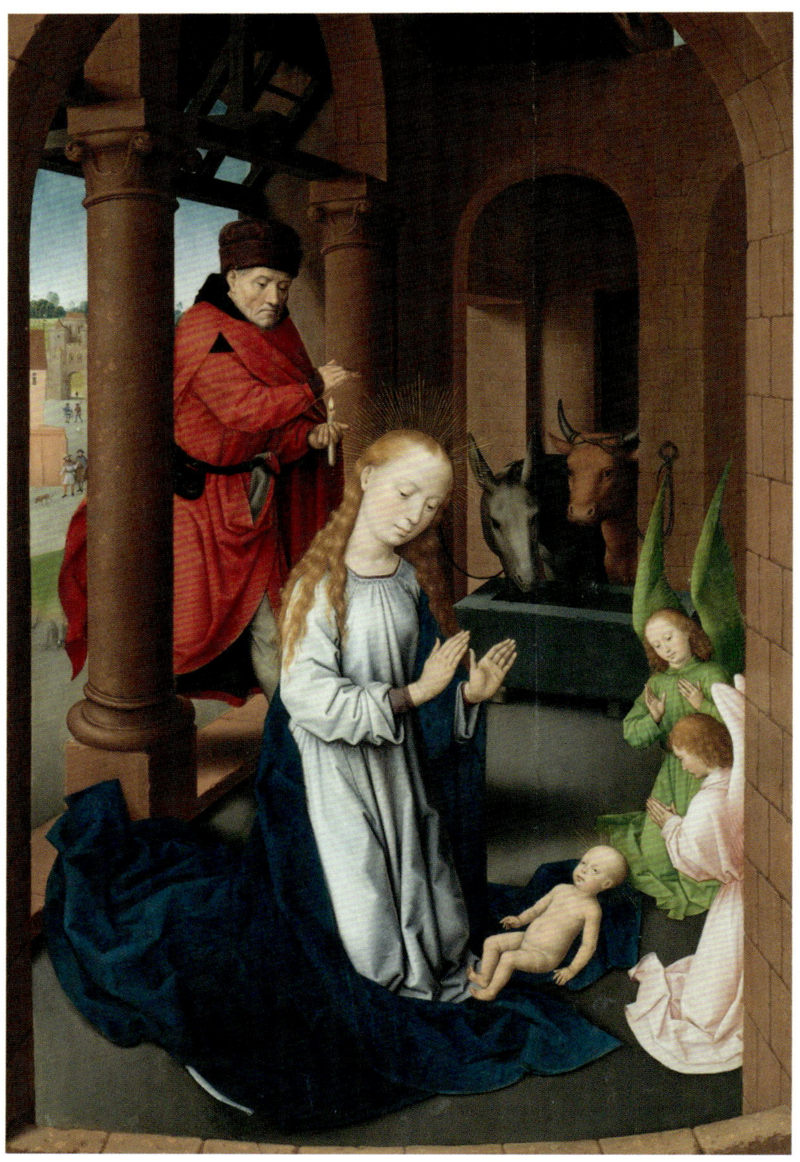

FIG. 4. *Hans Memling,* Nativity scene, left wing of the Adoration of the Magi Altarpiece, *1470–72, once the property of the Holy Roman Emperor Charles V, oil on canvas, 58.5 x 50 cm, Prado, Madrid. Joseph, wearing the heavy robe and hat of a burgher of the artist's own day, brings a candle.*

In icons of the Orthodox tradition Joseph is always depicted apart, sitting in a pose that indicates thoughtfulness, mistrust, incertitude, doubt [FIG. 10]. His body is bent over as he muses on his sorrows and difficulties; he carries the weight of insecurity and anxiety. He is shown on a lower level, in the foreground of the icon, on the

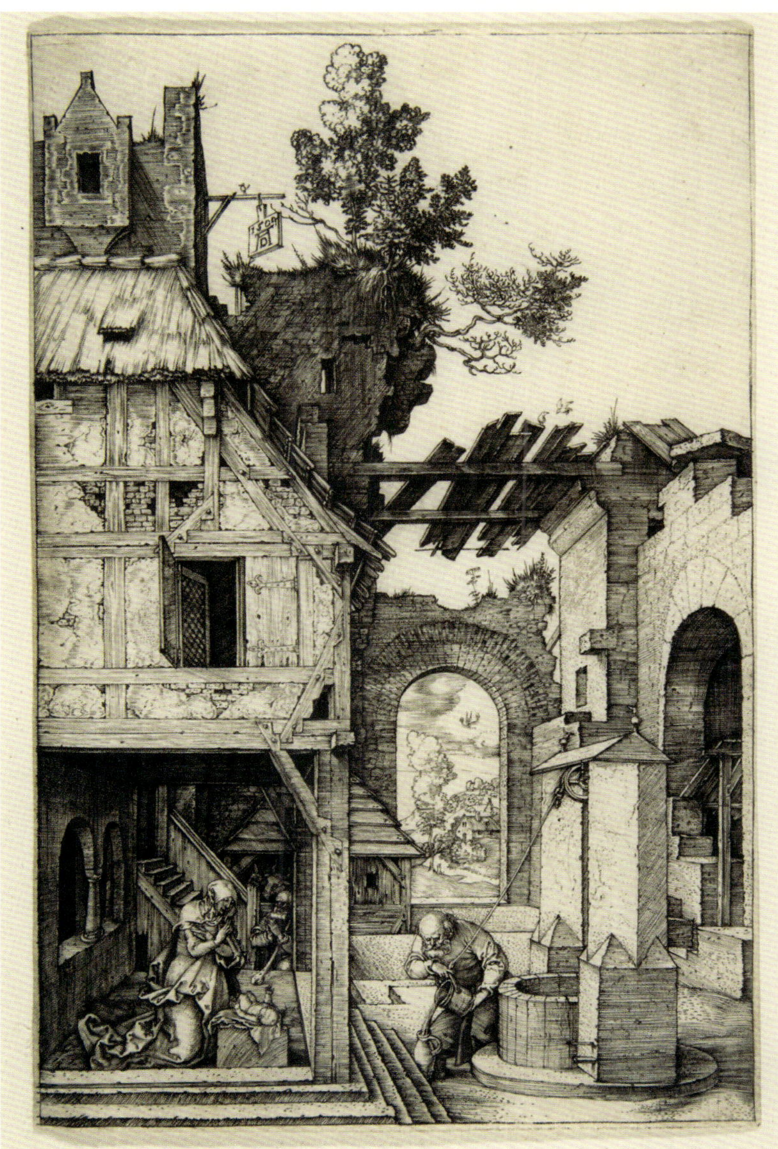

FIG. 5. *Albrecht Dürer,* Nativity, *1504, engraving, 18 x 12 cm, Metropolitan Museum of Art, New York. The figures are almost incidental to the architecture: Mary kneels in adoration near the manger in a tumbled-down house, where the figure of a shepherd leans forward to get a better view. In the centre Joseph kneels at the foot of the steps, drawing water from the well.*

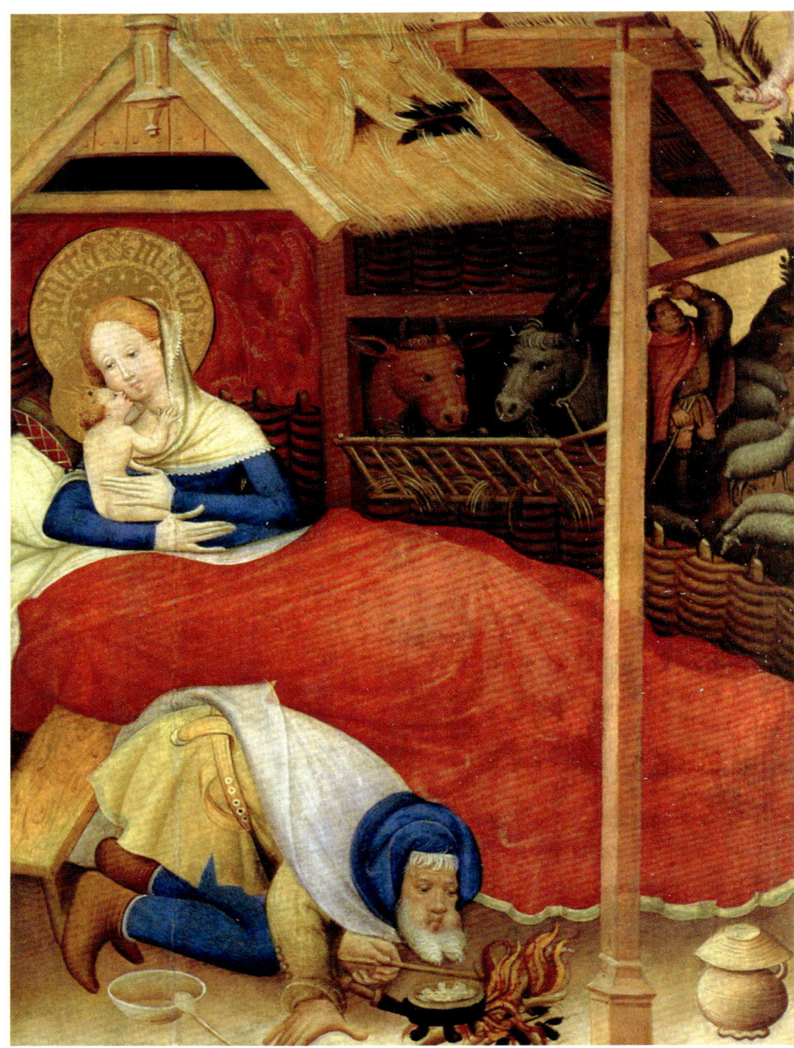

FIG. 6. *Conrad von Soest,* Nativity, *a panel in the left wing of the Niederwildungen Altarpiece in St Nikolaus, Bad-Wildungen, 1403, mixed media on wood, 73 x 56 cm. Joseph cooks, bending over a little fire, kneeling in front of the bed where the Virgin Mary tends the Christ Child, overseen by the beasts, beneath the holed roof.*

earth. Mary and the Child are in the centre of the image, where the Christ Child lies midway between heaven and earth. Joseph appears burdened by thoughts and complex feelings. Sometimes (as in this example) he is faced by a figure thickly covered with fur or wool. Is this the wolf in sheep's clothing, Satan in disguise? Traditionally interpreted as the tempter, the voice of persistent whining, nagging doubt and indecisive questioning is familiar to us all. It saps vitality and clarity in a closed circle of repetitious conflict, dragging in its

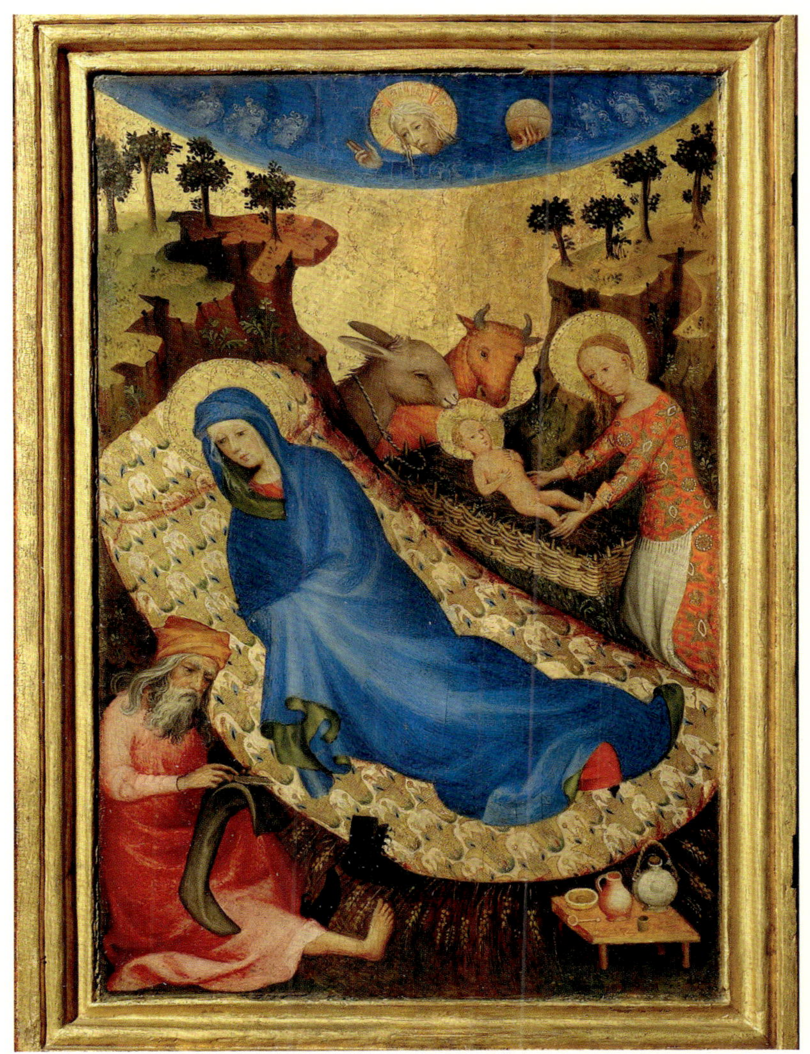

FIG. 7. *Melchior Broederlam,*
Nativity, *c. 1400, tempera on
oak, 37.6 x 26.2 cm, Museum
Meyer van den Bergh, Antwerp.
Joseph is cutting up his stocking
to be used as covering for the
naked Christ Child, held by the
midwife, warmed by the breath
of the ox and ass.*

wake isolation, confusion and meaninglessness.

In the New Testament Gospels Joseph is last mentioned at the
Finding in the Temple, the event movingly depicted by Simone
Martini [FIG. 11], who paints the distress of Mary and Joseph.
Joseph's anxiety, his sense of responsibility and care in his role as
protector, are expressed with intense sensitivity. 'And seeing Him
they wondered. And His mother said to Him, "Behold, thy father
and I have sought thee sorrowing." And He said to them "How is

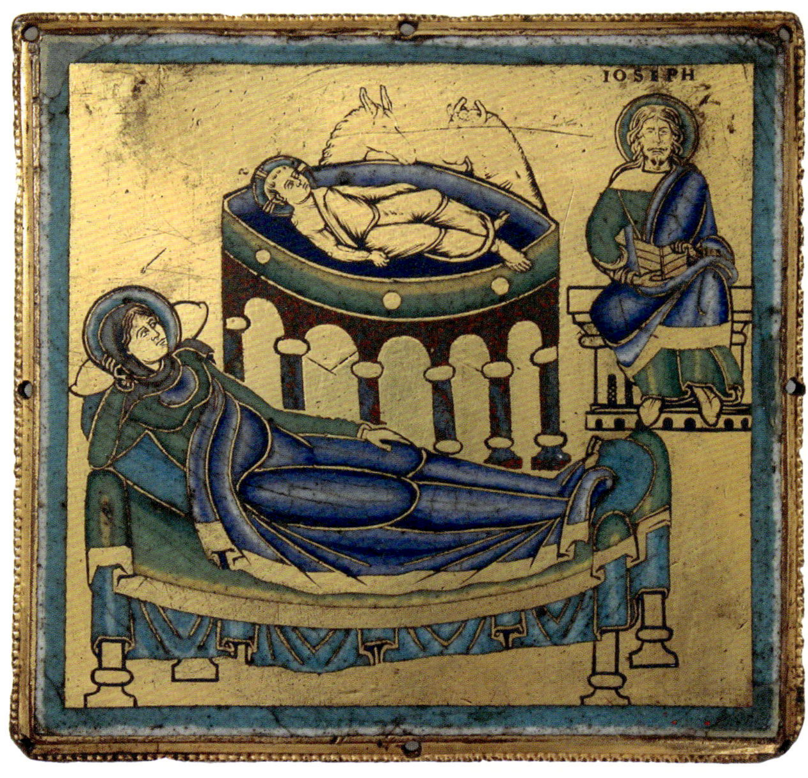

FIG. 8. *South Netherlandish plaque with the Nativity, c. 1165, champlevé enamel on copper, 11 x 11 cm, Metropolitan Museum of Art, New York. The Christ Child lies on an oval manger-altar; traces of the ox and ass are just visible. Mary reclines. Joseph, his name written above him, is nimbed; he holds a book and sits apart.*

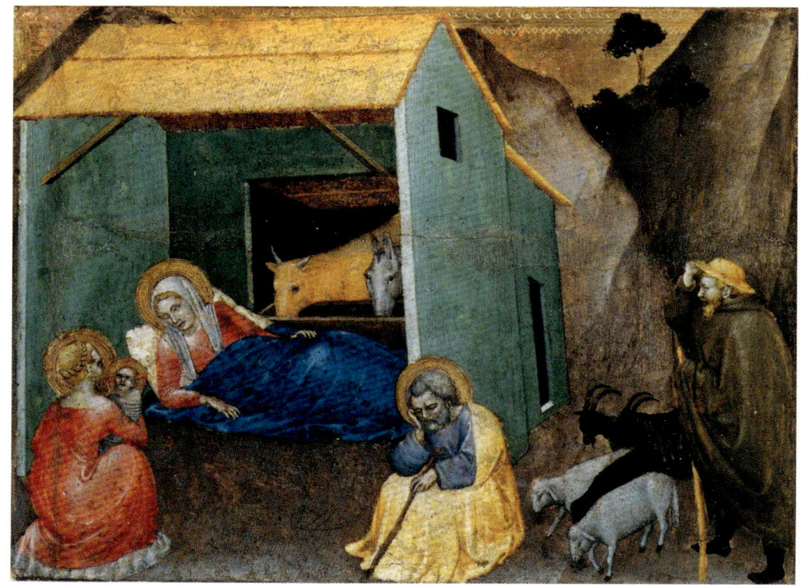

FIG. 9. *Giovanni da Milano,* Nativity, *a panel in the* Polyptych of Prato, *c. 1355, gold and tempera on wood, 21.5 x 28.5 cm, originally in the Spedale della Misericordia, now in the Museo Civico, Prato. Here once again Joseph sits pensively apart, while the midwife holds the Christ Child and Mary fondly watches. A shepherd, doffing his hat, is on the point of arriving.*

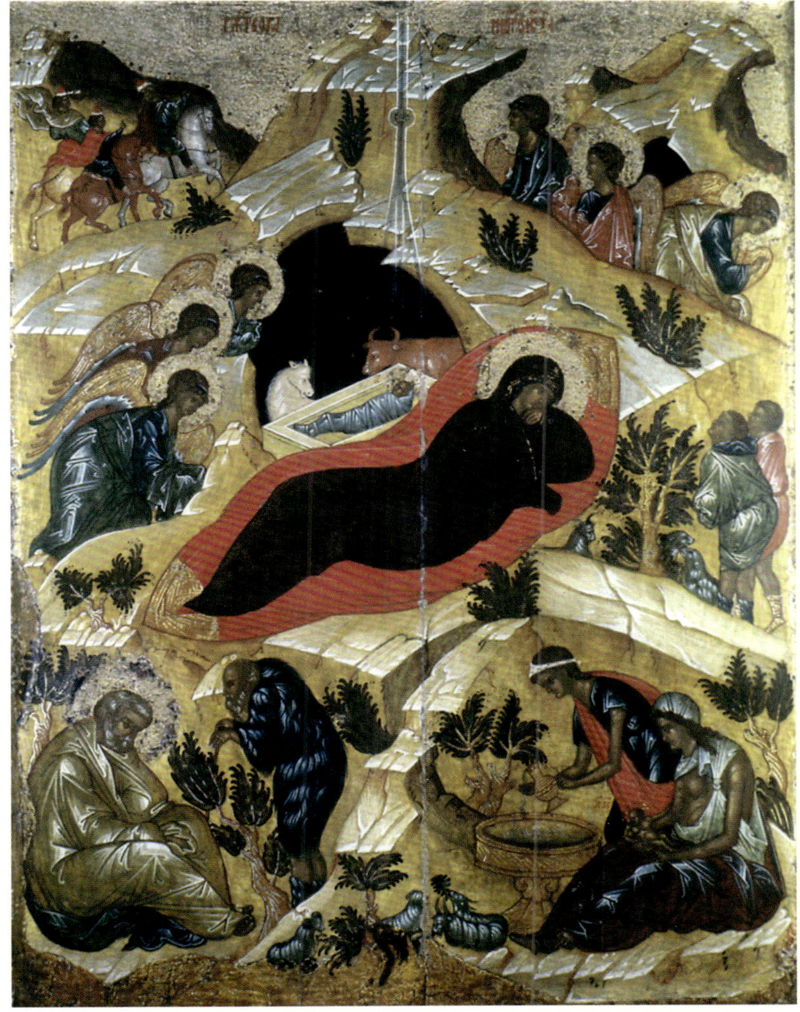

FIG. 10. *Icon of the Nativity traditionally attributed to Andrei Rublev, 1410–30, tempera on wood, 71 x 53 cm, State Tretyakov Gallery, Moscow. Joseph, sitting at the lower left of the image, is confronted by an elderly man covered with thick fur, variously interpreted as the tempter or the devil. We witness Joseph face to face with his difficulties, his disbelief, his doubts.*

it that you sought me? Did you not know that I must be about my Father's business?"' (Luke 2:48–49).

We can feel compassion and sympathy for this old man. We see that he represents humanity. In his troubled anxiety we are reminded of ourselves – mankind unveiled as confused and lost, unsure of our own place. Joseph's role is ambivalent. He is Everyman, tormented by doubts, yet trying to understand, trying to make the best of the situation, trying to accept.

FIG. 11. *Simone Martini,* Christ discovered in the Temple, *1342, tempera and gold leaf on panel, 49.5 x 35.1 cm, Walker Art Gallery, Liverpool. Joseph's concern, as he embraces the Child, that Christ should recognise His mother is poignantly paramount in this panel, possibly made as a portable altar.*

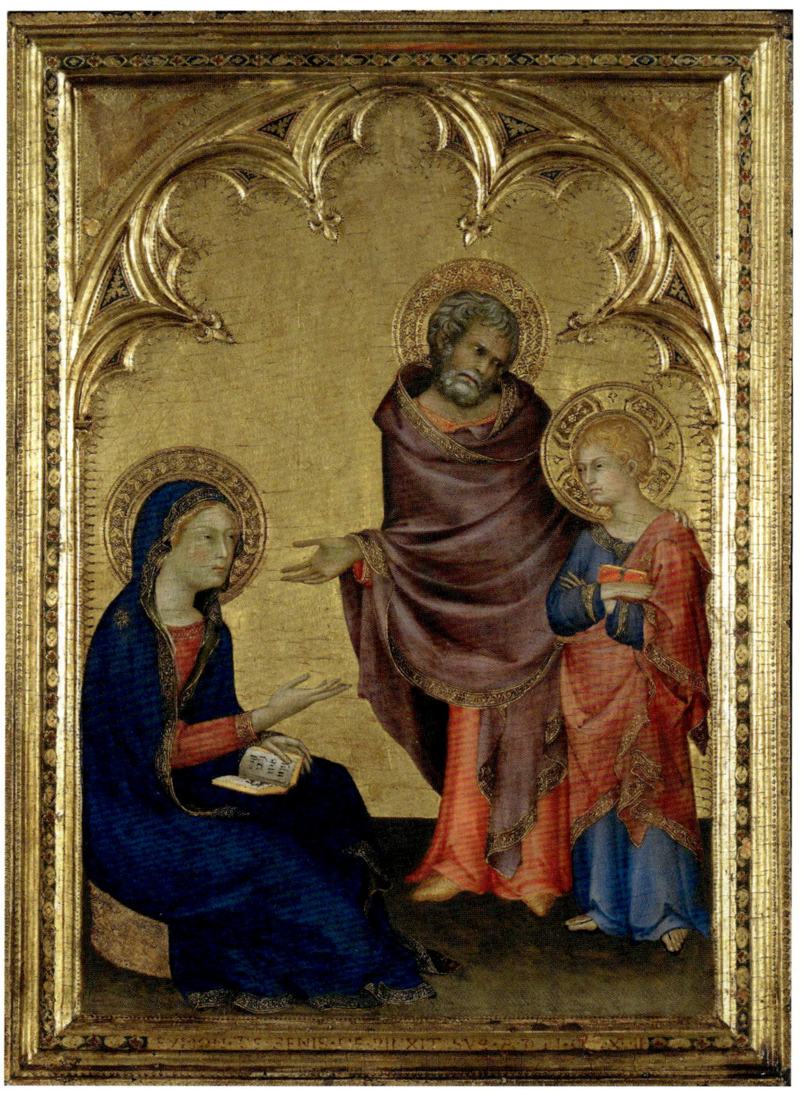

IX JOSEPH: FOOTNOTES

i Giotto (in the Arena Chapel, Padua), Perugino (Musée des Beaux-Arts, Caen), and Raphael (Pinacoteca di Brera, Milan, formerly in San Francesco in Città di Castello).

ii Built under Pope Sixtus IV. See *Oxford Dictionary of the Christian Church*, ed. E.A. Cross and E.A. Livingstone (Oxford: Oxford University Press, 2005).

iii See Brian Patrick McGuire, 'Becoming a Father and a Husband: St Joseph in Bernard of Clairvaux and Jean Gerson' in *Joseph of Nazareth through the Centuries*, ed. Joseph F. Chorpenning (Philadelphia, PA: St Joseph's University Press, 2011), pp. 49–62. And see also *The History of Joseph the Carpenter*, the apocryphal gospel putatively written in Egypt in the fourth or fifth century.

iv See Josef de Coo, 'In Josephs Hosen Jhesus ghewonden wer', in *Aachener Kunstblätter*, no. 30 (1965), pp. 144–84. Moses removed his shoes out of reverence when God appeared to him at the Burning Bush.

v It was reported that 142,000 pilgrims from all over Europe visited the site in 1496. See M.B. Foster, *The Iconography of St Joseph in Netherlandish Art 1400–1550* (PhD, University of Kansas, Ann Arbor, MI, 1981).

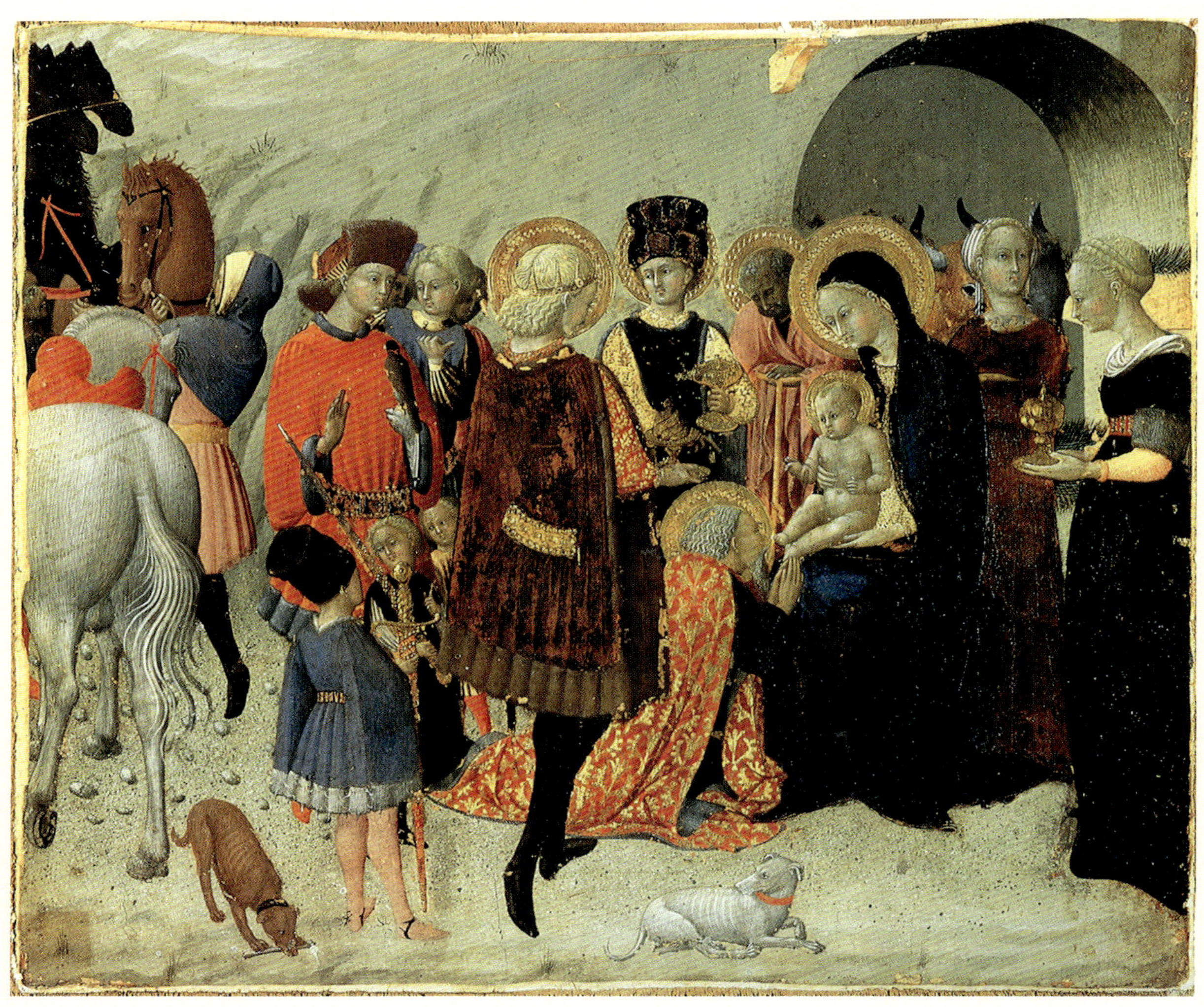

FIG. 12. *Sassetta (Stefano di Giovanni)*, The Adoration of the Magi,
*c. 1433–35, tempera and gold on poplar, 31.8 x 38.3 cm, Chigi-Saracini
Collection, Siena. This panel was originally in the same altarpiece as the
Journey of the Magi in* FIG. 1, *directly below it. The Magi (with halos),
richly costumed, arrive with some of their retinue, including pages and
dogs. The oldest Magus kneels to kiss the Christ Child's foot.*

X THE MAGI

T HE ADORATION OF THE MAGI is one of most popular subjects in all Christian art. It provides us with the opportunity to become immersed in the sumptuously lavish exoticism of the 'wise men from the east' who 'came to adore Him who was born King of the Jews' (Matthew 2:1–2). Their magnificent retinues [FIG. I] – servants, camels, gifts – dazzle and seduce the onlooker with glorious details of rich textures, strong colours, exuberant poses – in shocking contrast to the humble stable that protects the Christ Child with Mary and Joseph, the ox and the ass.

The word *magus* derives from the Persian and denotes the priestly caste who were famed astrologers. In the sixth-century Syrian legend *The Cave of Treasure* the Magi are described as Persian priest-kings. (The word then comes to us via the Greek and Latin, with the plural *magi*, and is the root of our word 'magic'.) Centres of learning and practice for magi were spread widely across Anatolia, Cappadocia, Persia and Mesopotamia, linked with the teachings and traditions of Zoroaster and with Mithras.[i] In the invisible language of allegory, might the Magi's search for Truth and Knowledge, assisted by a guide from a higher level, represent an aspect of humanity, our own yearning for Truth?

The earliest known image of the Magi, from the third century, is a wall painting in the Catacomb of Priscilla, outside Rome: it depicts three figures striding, their legs stretched out, cloaks streaming, as they hasten towards the seated Mary and Child [FIG. 2]. On sarcophagi of the fourth century we see the Magi kneeling to pay homage and adore the Saviour, who sits upright (no longer a tiny baby), enthroned on the Virgin's knee [see Chapter VIII, FIG. I]. We are reminded that in the Gospel narrative the Wise Men arrive to adore Christ after the Presentation in the Temple. Time has passed. We learn that Herod orders the killing of all boys 'from two years old and under' in the area around Bethlehem (Matthew 2:16).

In the Eastern Church all the surrounding events concerning shepherds and Magi and midwives are included, timelessly present, in Nativity icons. However, in the West individual episodes of the Magi's

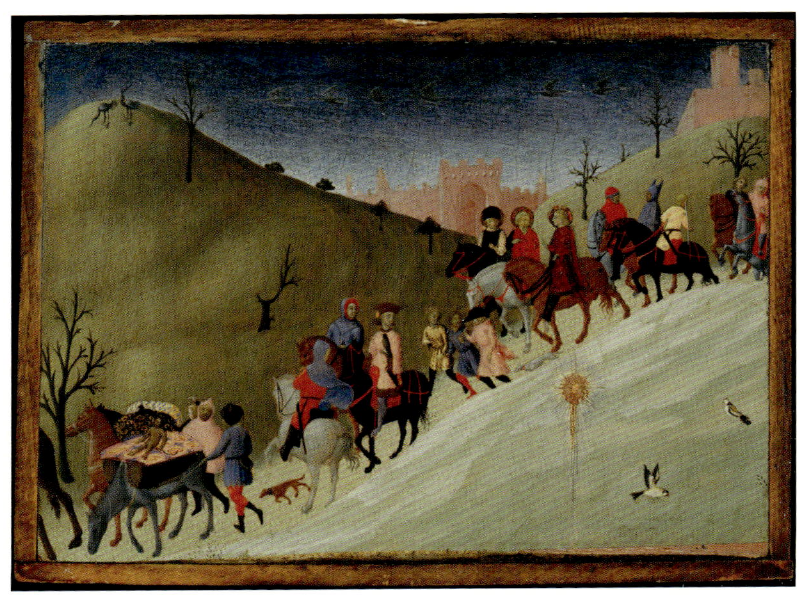

FIG. 1. *Sassetta (Stefano di Giovanni)*, The Journey of the Magi, *c. 1433–35, tempera and gold on poplar, 21.3 x 29 cm, Metropolitan Museum of Art, New York. This panel was originally in the same altarpiece as the* Adoration of the Magi *in* FIG. 12, *directly above it. The hat worn by the Magus robed in pink was probably inspired by the hat worn by King Sigismund of Hungary on his visit to Siena in 1435.*

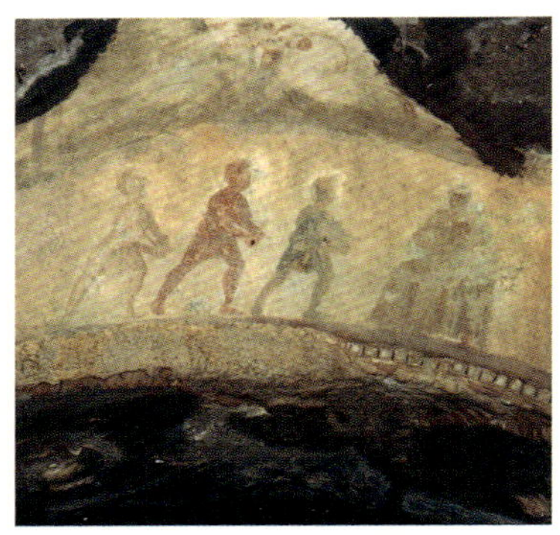

FIG. 2. *Wall painting of the Adoration of the Magi, in the main chamber for funeral banquets in the Capella Greca in the Catacomb of Priscilla outside Rome, beginning of the third century. The Magi are shown holding gifts as they stride towards the seated Virgin and Child.*

story are taken up by artists: following the appearance of the star, the Magi journey to Jerusalem to enquire of King Herod 'Where is he that is born King of the Jews?' [FIGS 3, 4].[ii] The three Magi set off together and follow the star to Bethlehem, where they find the newborn Saviour King in a stable. They offer gifts and worship Him. Then, warned of danger in a dream [FIG. 5], they 'departed into their own country another way' (Matthew 2:12) [FIG. 6].

In early images we see the Magi clad in short tucked-up tunics, leggings and shoes; they wear the Phrygian cap (rising high above the forehead) and a cloak (chlamys) often flowing behind them as they hasten on their journey[iii] – as shown in the catacomb painting [FIG. 2] and in glittering detail in the famous mosaics in Ravenna [FIG. 7]. Representing both heathens and Gentiles in their recognition of the Saviour of the world, they pay homage to the Christ Child, the King of the Jews. From the third century onwards and perhaps earlier the Magi were also referred to as Kings,[iv] an appellation derived from the Psalms (72:11) inserted into the liturgy for the feast day: 'May all kings fall down before him.' Other verses in the Psalms (68:29) and Isaiah (60:1–6) were also interpreted as identifying the Magi as kings. From at least the tenth century onwards the Magi are shown wearing crowns (large or small). In Western images they

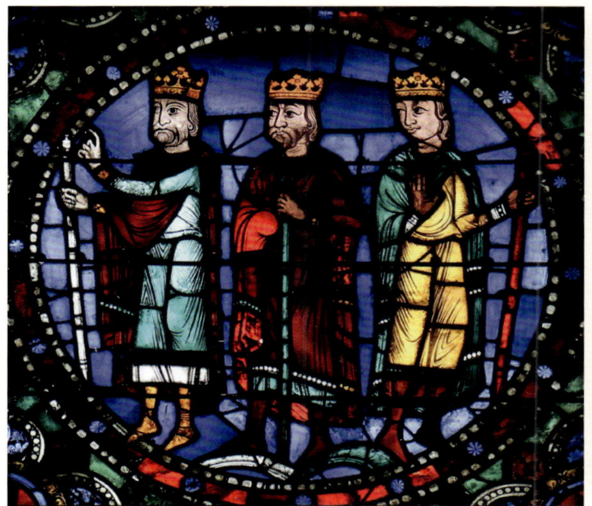

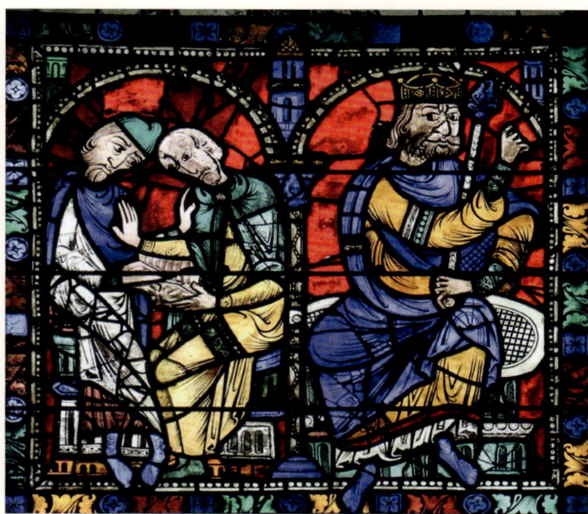

cease to wear Persian dress, and appear in robes and cloaks – often magnificent – and kingly crowns. The pre-Christian prototype for the Magi bearing gifts and paying homage to the Christ Child, now so familiar, in fact derives from a Late Antique composition showing vanquished barbarians bringing golden wreaths to a victorious emperor and generals. We see the kneeling Magus remove his crown, bareheaded in homage, sometimes barefoot, occasionally nimbed.

The Magi's search and journey is a favourite subject for artists. We witness the Magi pointing at a star in numerous images [FIGS 8, 9]. The rising of a star at the birth of a ruler was familiar in Antiquity, and in Roman art a star shown over an emperor's head indicates his divinity. In the second and third centuries the star discovered by the Magi was associated with the star of Jacob prophesied by Balaam (Numbers 24:17), and the Magi named as descendants of Balaam.[v] The feast of the Epiphany has always been a celebration of light. Liturgical readings for the feast day include Isaiah (60:1–4): 'Arise, shine; for thy light is come, and the glory of the Lord is risen upon thee', and prophecies that 'the gentiles shall come to thy light, and kings to the brightness of thy rising', enabled Church Fathers to link this passage with the Adoration of the Magi. The journeying Magi are sometimes guided by an angel. The angel is also shown as the personification of a star, a reminder of the ancient idea that angels and stars are interchangeable, creatures of light inhabiting the sky.[vi] Nicola

FIG. 3. *(above left) Stained glass in the west window of Chartres Cathedral, c. 1200: the Magi are setting off to Jerusalem. The direction of their feet, heads and gestures expresses their uncertainty as they search.*

FIG. 4. *(above right) Stained glass in the west window of Chartres Cathedral, c. 1200: the troubled Herod consults the chief priests and scribes concerning the news of the birth of the King of the Jews.*

FIG. 5. *The dream of the Magi, on a capital by the great sculptor Gislebertus from the cathedral of St-Lazare, Autun, 1120–30, now in the Musée Rolin, Autun. Two of the crowned Magi are still asleep; the third is gently awakened by the angel, who warns them of danger.*

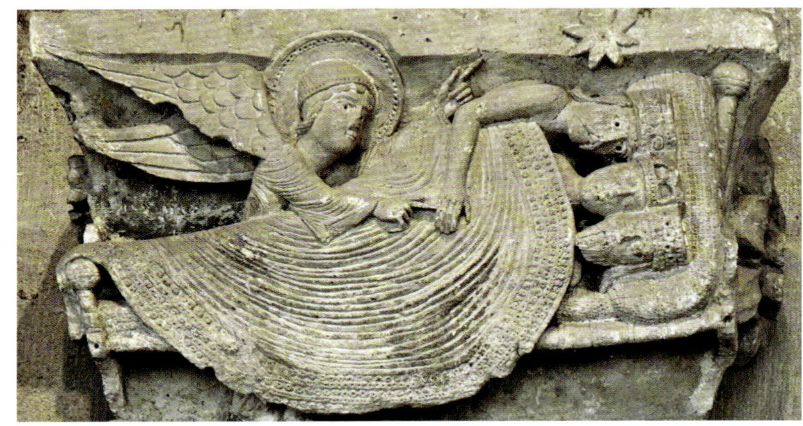

FIG. 6. *Two scenes in a manuscript of the Gospels commissioned by Conrad von Danne, Bishop of Speyer, for Neuhausen near Worms, c. 1197, 31.5 x 25.5 cm, Badische Landesbibliothek, Karlsruhe, Cod. Bruchsal 1. Above, the angel brings the warning to the sleeping Magi; below, they are returning 'another way' – in this instance by sea.*

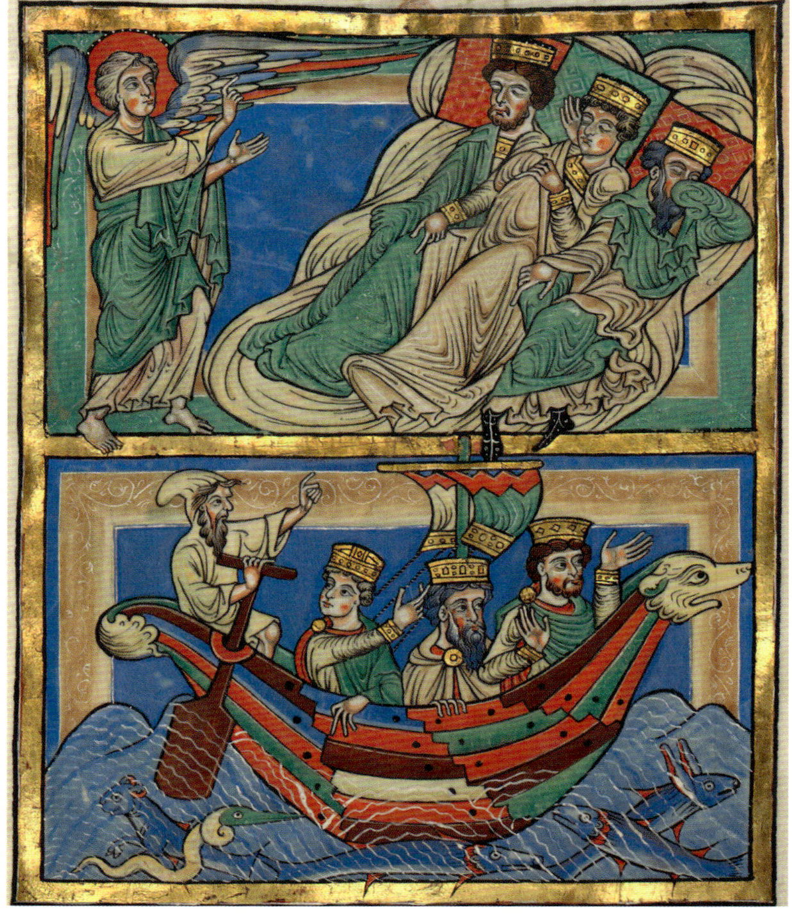

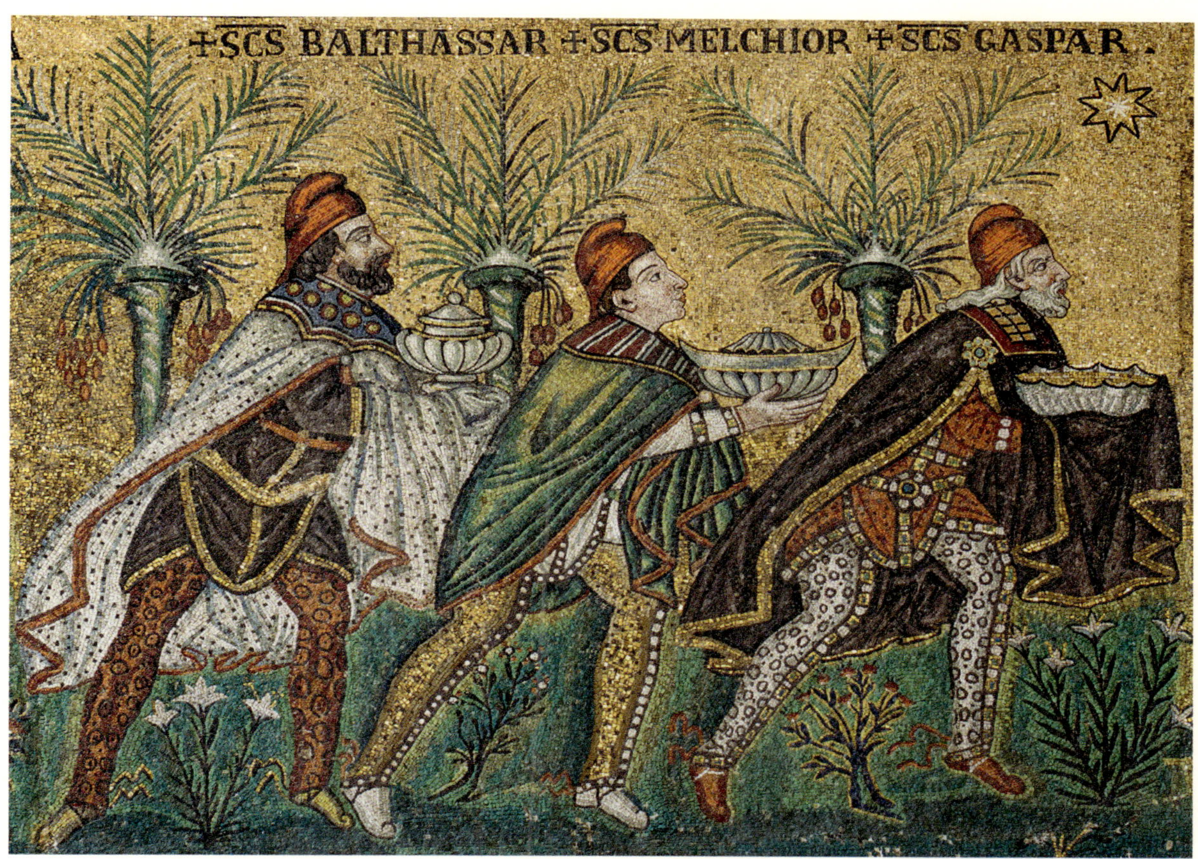

Pisano's pulpit for the Baptistery of Pisa, made about 1260, shows an angel's face in the centre of the Magi's star.

In the Middle Ages, following in the footsteps of an ancient tradition, the Wise Men were considered to represent the three known continents, Europe, Asia and Africa; one of them was sometimes shown as a Moor. Often their ages were differentiated, the oldest bearded or balding. However, according to other legends and traditions there were nine or twelve Magi searching for the newborn King of the Jews. Twelve are found in an Arian legend (based on an earlier Syrian story), and occasionally twelve are found painted on the walls of the tenth- to fourteenth-century cave-cell churches at Göreme in Turkey. At the Church of the Mother of God at Hah, in the Tur Abdin region (also in Turkey), where there was a Zoroastrian monastery, legend has it that each of the twelve Magi laid a stone

FIG. 7. *The Magi in mosaic, in the basilica of Sant'Apollinare Nuovo, Ravenna, 565. Led by the star, their names inscribed above, they are bearing gifts, and dressed in Persian clothing – breeches, capes and Phrygian caps.*

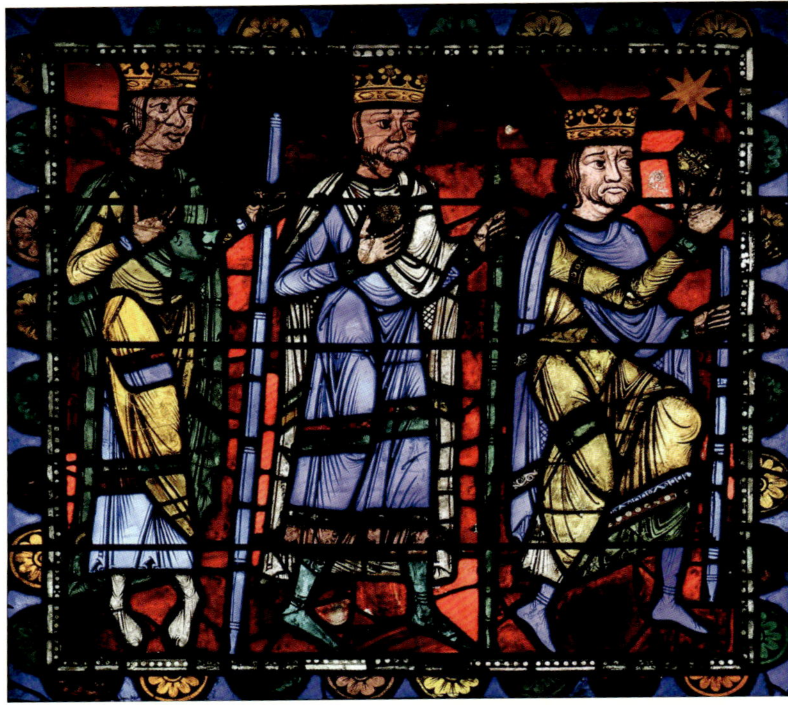

FIG. 8. *Stained glass in the west window of Chartres Cathedral, c. 1200: the Magi on their journey, firm-footed and confident, follow the star.*

surrounding the entrance to the place of worship.

Perhaps it was Matthew's listing of the three gifts (2:11) – gold, frankincense and myrrh – that established the number of the Magi at three. The names Balthasar, Melchior, Gaspar – with a wide variety of spellings – gradually became established, though even today the names differ considerably in various parts of Christendom.[vii] Traditionally Melchior was considered King of Persia, Gaspar King of India, and Balthasar King of Arabia (sometimes Ethiopia). Jacobus de Voragine used those names in the *Legenda aurea*, and associated their gifts as gold for Christ the King, frankincense for God, and myrrh for mankind. From ancient times gold has been symbolically associated with kingship; frankincense, a potently fragrant resin (derived from the Boswellia tree), symbolic of divinity, is often shown in devotional images by plumes of smoke from a candle rising heavenwards, evoking the invisible presence of God; myrrh, well known for its medicinal properties and its use in burial rituals, is associated with mortality. In Nativity images the gifts might be set on flat dishes or in horns, offered by hands that are reverentially draped in cloth, perhaps an allusion to the anointing oil indicating kingship. The receptacles containing the gifts are sometimes shown modelled on liturgical vessels – the pyxis, monstrance, and ciborium.

The relics of the Magi became the focus of intense devotion from the end of the twelfth century when they were placed in Cologne Cathedral. The history of the relics, swathed in legend, is intriguing and complex. According to Eustorgius (Greek born, Bishop of Milan 343–49), Helena, mother of Constantine, brought the bodies of the Magi to Constantinople (putatively from the Holy Land or from Ind – India) and placed them in the newly built magnificent Hagia Sophia *c.* 330. In 344 the relics were entrusted by Constantine to Eustorgius, who had them taken to Milan,[viii] to a church now called the Basilica of Sant'Eustorgio, soon an important stage on the journey for pilgrims en route to Rome or Jerusalem.[ix] In the twelfth century Milan was brought under the direct authority of the Holy Roman Empire by military force, greatly aided by Rainald von Dassel, Chancellor to Emperor Frederick I Barbarossa. When Rainald became Archbishop of Cologne he was rewarded by Barbarossa in 1164 with the relics of the Magi. Rainald commissioned the outstanding goldsmith of the day, Nicholas of Verdun, to create a sumptuous shrine to house the precious relics. Rainald also aggrandized the Cathedral.[x] The vast and magnificent jewel-encrusted shrine, designed to resemble a basilica, stands splendidly behind and above the high altar. The lower section houses the bones of the Magi, and the upper part contains relics of the martyrs Nabor and Felix.[xi] The reliquary rapidly became a magnet for pilgrims.[xii] As they walked around the shrine the pilgrims saw Old Testament figures (Moses, Aaron, David), then on one end the Adoration figures, the Virgin and Child depicted regally in a central niche, and the Baptism of Christ (the second liturgical theme of the Epiphany). The history of the relics was later recounted – perhaps not very reliably – by a Carmelite friar, John of Hildesheim (*c.* 1315–75), in his *Historia Trium Regum* (History of the Three Kings).[xiii]

Interest, excitement and enthusiasm for the story of the Three Kings gave rise to a continuous proliferation of images of the Magi in paintings, sculpture, stained glass and illuminated manuscripts. Epiphany images appear in apses of churches from the mid-twelfth century, and we find Adoration scenes sculpted in portals. We see hieratic images, which emphasise God the Son's Incarnation and His revelation to the world, for instance in the Cathedral of Verona.

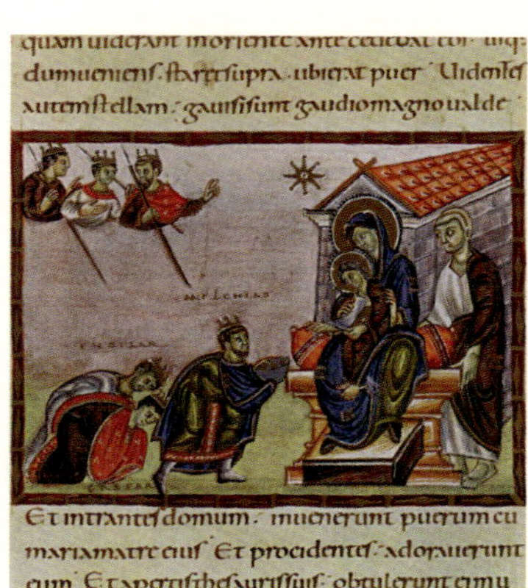

FIG. 9. *The Magi in manuscript, in the* Codex Egberti, *c. 980, Stadtbibliothek, Trier. Above, the crowned Magi carry their pilgrim staffs on their way following the star; below, they present their gifts to the Christ Child.*

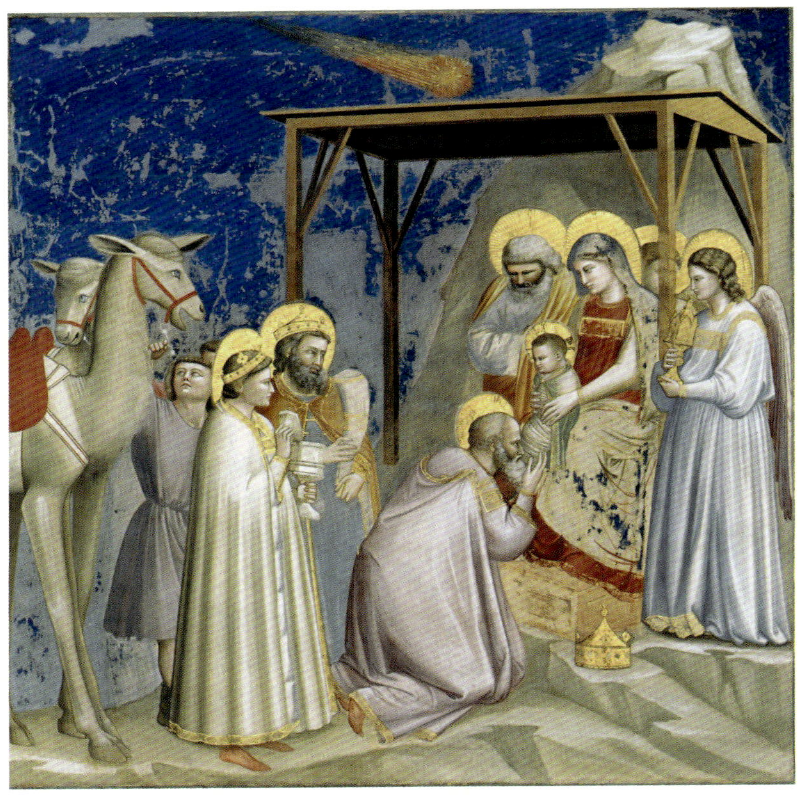

FIG. 10. *Giotto, fresco of the Adoration of the Magi in the Arena Chapel, Padua, c. 1305. Two Magi wear crowns, all are nimbed. The kneeling Magus (whose crown is on the ground) is kissing the Christ Child's feet. The shining comet-like star (Halley's Comet had appeared in 1301) is poised above the stable. An angel stands beside Mary and the Child. Dromedaries follow the Magi, held by servants.*

Here the Virgin sits frontally, a cult figure; her enthroned Son faces the eldest Magus who, kneeling, points to the star.

The powerful influence of the Mendicant Orders founded by St Francis and St Dominic at the beginning of the thirteenth century inspired a mood of devotion. Friars and their followers preached Christ's message to the urban poor, to men and women, often illiterate countrymen, who could immediately and instinctively relate to the human dimension of Christianity. We witness an intimately personal relationship between the worshipping Kings and Christ [FIGS 10, 11], as a Magus kisses the Infant's foot, and the Child, sometimes half naked, blesses the Wise Men.

But all this changes.

'Those three kings arrived with a great crowd and a noble retinue before the hut in which the Lord Jesus had been born. The Lady hears the commotion and takes the boy to them.' This description

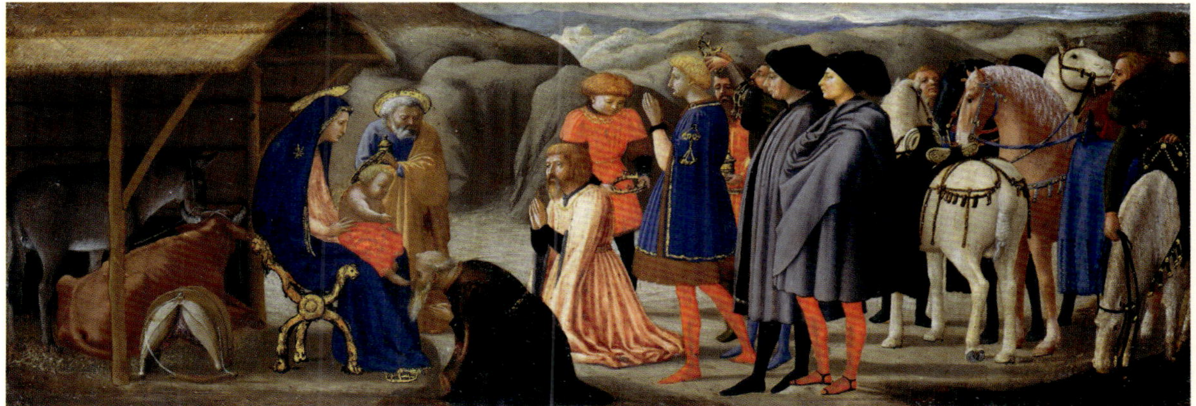

of the Magi's arrival at the scene of the Nativity comes from the mid-fourteenth-century *Meditationes Vitae Christi*. From now on the 'noble retinue' curls sinuously and magnificently into receding landscapes – with exotic beasts, sumptuous costumes, aristocratic standards flying in the breeze, servants leading horses, others with dogs [FIG. 12, see page 112]. Conspicuous consumption peaks in the fifteenth century on the walls around three sides of the little chapel in the Medici Palace in Florence, with portraits of prominent contemporaries, including John VIII Palaeologus, Emperor of Constantinople, and Piero de' Medici, in the vast entourage of the Kings, where Lorenzo de' Medici (the future Magnificent) represents the young Caspar; the artist, Benozzo Gozzoli, included himself in the crowd [FIG. 13].[xiv] Heading such stupendous retinues, idealised representations, perhaps, of the 'communion of saints' – the heathens, the Gentiles, the Church, the whole world – we witness the Three Wise Men, most luxuriously robed of all in the procession, submitting in the act of Adoration. The text of *Meditationes* continues: 'They enter the little house, kneel and reverently adore the boy Jesus.'

We admire the lavish textiles, the turbans, the bedecked horses, the charming pages, the graceful dogs – and we are dazzled, seduced. Amidst such alluringly fascinating attractions, the mystery of the central event – the birth of Christ the Saviour in a manger, 'because there was no room for them at the inn' – is almost in danger of being hidden and forgotten. Might the symbolic image of the Magi, these learned beings, searching and journeying, assisted by help from God, enable us to recall our own yearning for Divine Love?

FIG. 11. *Masaccio*, The Adoration of the Magi, 1426, *tempera on poplar, 21 x 61 cm, Gemäldegalerie, Staatliche Museen, Berlin. The Magi are shown kissing the Christ Child's feet in this, the central scene of the predella of the Pisa Altarpiece, commissioned by Giuliano di Colino, who is seen with his nephew in contemporary dress standing behind the Magi.*

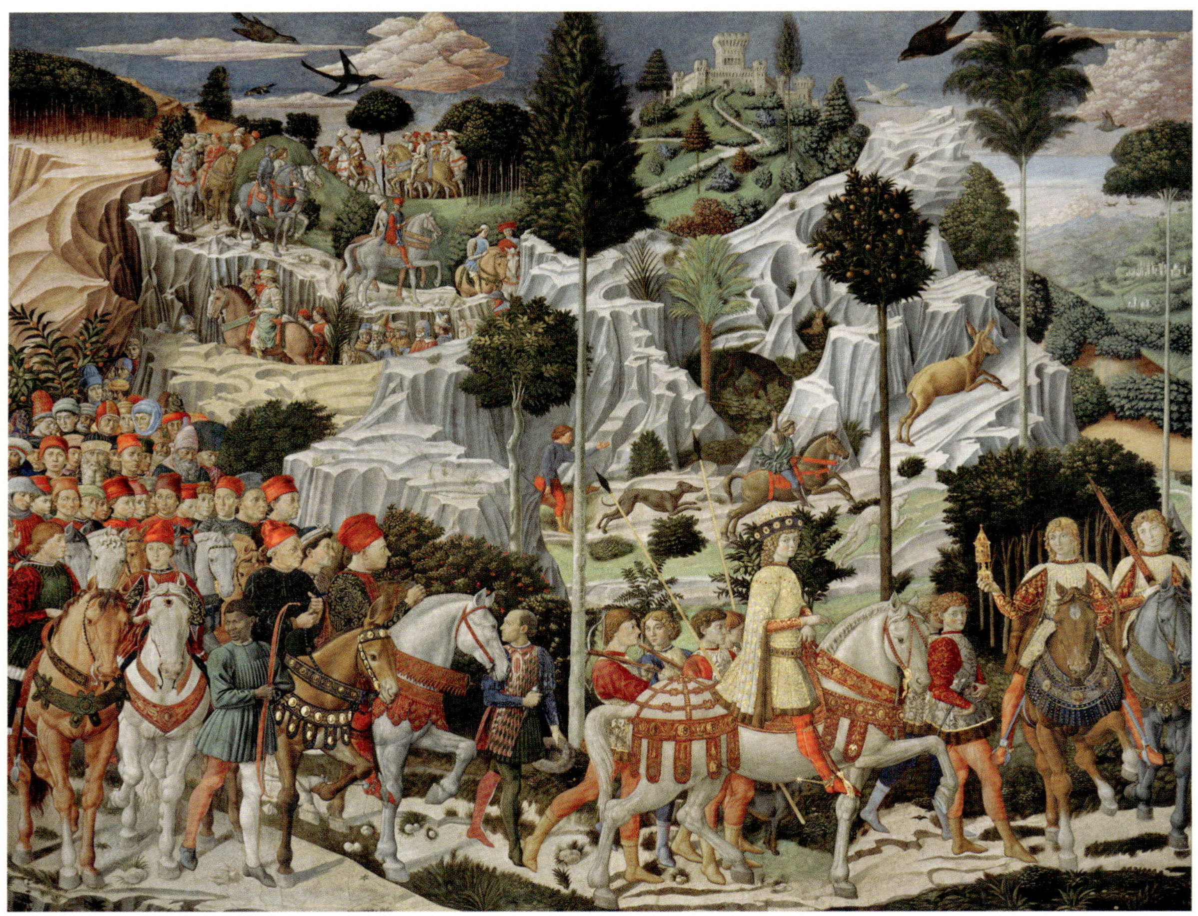

FIG. 13. *Benozzo Gozzoli, fresco of the Journey to Bethlehem in the Chapel of the Magi in the Palazzo Medici Riccardi, Florence, c. 1459. Part of the magnificent procession of the Magi includes portraits of members of the Medici family and their entourage: astride the white horse is thought to be Lorenzo (later the Magnificent), representing the youngest Magus, Caspar; mounted behind him is his father, Piero di Cosimo ('the Gouty'); and on a mule is Piero de' Medici, patriarch of the family. Benozzo Gozzoli shows himself further back in the crowded scene, between two bearded figures; he wears a red cap, on which his name is partially visible.*

X THE MAGI: FOOTNOTES

i Herodotus (*c.* 484–*c.* 425 BC) wrote that the Magi were Zoroastrian Persian priests. See Albert de Jong, 'Herodotus and the Magi' in *Traditions of the Magi: Zoroastrianism in Greek and Latin Literature* (Leiden and New York: Brill, 1997).

ii According to one legend, the three Magi came from different directions, met in 'Ind', and then set off together to Jerusalem to make enquiries.

iii This fluttering tunic and the cap are familiar from depictions of Mithras.

iv John Calvin was violently against this notion of kingship.

v In some early images Balaam stands at one end of the manger, or behind Mary.

vi The *Arabian Gospel of the Childhood of Christ*, derived from Syrian sources, speaks of the 'angel in the star'.

vii Names include Bithisarea, Melichior and Gatharapa.

viii According to different legends, the relics were carried by carts drawn by oxen, or taken by sea – possibly the origin of the Christmas carol 'I saw three ships go sailing by'.

ix Fragments of the relics of the Magi were returned to Sant'Eustorgio in the early twentieth century. A celebratory procession, in medieval dress, starting at the Cathedral and ending at the Basilica of Sant'Eustorgio, is held in Milan every year on 6 January, an almost unbroken tradition since 1336.

x Work was eventually completed in 1880.

xi Roman soldier martyrs, persecuted and killed in Milan in the early fourth century.

xii Cologne Cathedral also contained relics of Joseph's *Hosen*, with which he had warmed the Holy Child (Chapter IX). Pilgrimage was enormously important at this period (the Holy Land, Santiago de Compostela and Rome were the chief destinations), and a source of considerable income for establishments housing relics. See Jonathan Sumption, *Pilgrimage, An Image of Mediaeval Religion* (London: Faber & Faber, 2002).

xiii John's account includes some fanciful aspects: the Kings of Ind, Chaldea and Persia set off from different starting points and meet up in Ind.

xiv Palaeologus had been in Florence in 1439 to attend the Council of Churches, whose aim was to unite the Greek and Roman Churches. The emperor's headdress was of immense interest to artists, who often included it in their work.

BIBLIOGRAPHY

Anonymous — *The Cloud of Unknowing and Other Works* (translated into modern English by Clifton Wolters). London (Penguin) 1978

Michele Bacci — *The Mystic Cave: A History of the Nativity* (Brno and Rome: Masaryk University-Viella, 2017)

Sister Wendy Beckett — *Encounters with God* (London: Continuum, 2009)

John Beckwith — *Early Christian and Byzantine Art* (New Haven, CT and London: Yale University Press, 2018)

St Benedict — *The Rule of Saint Benedict in Latin and English with Notes,* ed. Timothy Fry (Collegeville, MN: Liturgical Press, 1981)

Shirley Nielsen Blum — *Early Netherlandish Triptychs* (Oakland, CA: University of California Press, 1969)

Mary Boyce — *Zoroastrians: their Religious Beliefs and Practices* (2nd edn, London: Routledge, 2001)

C.N. Brooke — *The Twelfth-Century Renaissance* (London: Thames & Hudson, 1969)

Peter Brown — *The Rise of Western Christendom* (2nd edn, Oxford: Blackwell, 2003)

David R. Cartlidge and J. Keith Elliott — *Art and the Christian Apocrypha* (London and New York: Routledge, 2001)

Mary Carruthers, ed. — *Rhetoric Beyond Words: Delight and Persuasion in the Arts of the Middle Ages* (Cambridge: Cambridge University Press, 2010)

C. Cecchelli — *I mosaici della basilica di S. Maria Maggiore* (Turin: ILTE, 1956)

M.J. Clanchy — 'The Church and the Book', in *Papers and Studies in Church History*, ed. R. N. Swanson (Woodbridge: Boydell Press for the Ecclesiastical History Society, 2000)

Josef de Coo — 'In Josephs Hosen Jhesus ghewonden wer', in *Aachener Kunstblätter*, no. 30 (1965), pp. 144–84

John Drury — *Painting the Word: Christian Practices and their Meanings* (New Haven, CT and London: Yale University Press, 1999)

Egeria — *Egeria's Travels*, transl. and ed. by John Wilkinson (3rd edn, Warminster: Aris and Phillips, 2006)

Jaś Elsner — *Imperial Rome and Christian Triumph: Art and the Rise of World Religions* (Oxford: Oxford University Press, 1998)

Jaś Elsner — *Imagining the Divine* (Oxford: Ashmolean Museum, exhibition catalogue, 2017)

Ilene H. Forsyth — *The Throne of Wisdom* (Princeton, NJ: Princeton University Press, 2019)

M.B. Foster — *The Iconography of St Joseph in Netherlandish Art 1400–1550*, PhD (University of Kansas, Ann Arbor, MI, 1981)

Ross Fuller — *The Brotherhood of the Common Life* (New York: State University of New York Press, 1995)

André Grabar — *The Beginnings of Christian Art 200–395*, transl. Stuart Gilbert and James Emmons (London: Thames and Hudson, 1967)

Hilda Graef — *Mary – A History of Doctrine and Devotion* (London and New York: Sheed and Ward, 1963)

René Guénon — 'The Heart and the Cave', in *Studies in Comparative Religion*, vol. 5, no. 1 (Winter 1971)

René Guénon — 'The Mountain and the Cave', in *Studies in Comparative Religion*, vol. 5, no. 2 (Spring 1971)

M. Hassett — 'History of the Christian Altar', in *The New Catholic Encyclopedia* (New York: Robert Appleton & Co., 1967)

Christine Heck — *L'Échelle céleste dans l'art du moyen age* (Paris: Flammarion, 1999)

Cecily Hennessy — *Early Christian and Medieval Rome* (London: Cecily Hennessy Publications, 2017)

S.E. Hijmans — *Sol: The Sun in the Art and Religions of Rome* (Groningen: University Library, 2009)

Yrjö Hirn — *The Sacred Shrine. A Study of the Poetry and Art of the Catholic Church* (London: Faber & Faber, 1958; first published in Swedish in 1909)

W. Hood — *Fra Angelico at San Marco* (New Haven, CT and London: Yale University Press, 1993)

E.D. Hunt — *Holy Land Pilgrimage in the Later Roman Empire AD 312–460* (Oxford: Clarendon Press, 1982)

M.R. James — *The Apocryphal New Testament* (Oxford: Clarendon Press, 1924)

Robin M. Jensen — *Living Water, Images, Symbols and Settings of Early Christian Baptism* (Leiden and Boston, MA: Brill, 2011)

Robin M. Jensen — *Understanding Early Christian Art* (London: Routledge, 2000)

Robin M. Jensen and Mark D. Ellison, eds — *The Routledge Handbook of Early Christian Art* (London and New York: Routledge, 2018)

Albert de Jong — *Herodotus and the Magi in Zoroastrianism in Greek and Latin Literature* (Leiden and New York: Brill, 1997)

Dale Kent — *Cosimo de' Medici and the Florentine Renaissance* (New Haven, CT and London: Yale University Press, 2000)

Robin Lane Fox — *Pagans and Christians* (London: Penguin, 1986)

Robin Lane Fox — *The Unauthorized Version* (London: Penguin, 1991)

Andrew Louth, transl. and intro. — *St John of Damascus – Three Treatises on Divine Images* (Crestwood, NY: St Vladimir's Seminary Press, 2003)

David Lowenthal — *The Heritage Crusades and the Spoils of History* (Cambridge: Cambridge University Press, 1998)

Walter Lowrie — *Art in the Early Church* (New York: Pantheon, 1947)

Bernard McGinn — *The Mystical Thought of Meister Eckhart (The Man from Whom God Hid Nothing)* (New York: The Crossroad Publishing Company, 2001)

Brian Patrick McGuire — 'Becoming a Father and a Husband: St Joseph in Bernard of Clairvaux and Jean Gerson' in *Joseph of Nazareth through the Centuries*, ed. Joseph F. Chorpenning (Philadelphia, PA: St Joseph's University Press, 2011)

Sarah McNamer — 'The Debate on the Origins of the Meditationes Vitae Christi', in *Archivium Franciscanum Historicum*, vol. 111, nos 1–2 (June 2018), pp. 65–112

Aaron Milavec — *The Didache: Faith, Hope and Love of the Earliest Christians* (Slough: Pauline Press, 2003)

Stephen Mitchell — *A History of the Later Roman Empire AD 284–641: The Transformation of the Antique World* (2nd edn, Oxford: Blackwell, 2014)

Matthew Mollier — 'Not so secular Sweden', in *First Things* (June 2014)

Bridget Morris — 'St Birgitta of Sweden', in Studies in *Medieval Mysticism*, vol. I (Woodbridge: Boydell Press, 1999)

Peter and Linda Murray — *The Oxford Companion to Christian Art and Architecture* (Oxford: Oxford University Press, 1996)

Maurice Nicoll — *The New Man* (London: Vincent Stuart and Richards, 1950)

Maurice Nicoll — *The Mark* (London: Vincent Stuart, 1952)

Ursula Nilgen — 'The Epiphany and the Eucharist: On the Interpretation of Eucharistic Motifs in Medieval Epiphany Scenes', in *Art Bulletin*, vol. 49, no. 4 (1967), pp. 311–20

Isa Ragusa and Rosalie B. Green, transl. and ed. — *Meditations on the Life of Christ: An Illustrated Manuscript of the Fourteenth Century* (Princeton, N.J.: Princeton University Press, 1961)

Gertrud Schiller — *Iconography of Christian Art* (London: Lund Humphries, 1971)

P. Saenger — 'Books of Hours and the Reading Habits of the Later Middle Ages', in R. Chartier, ed., *The Culture of Print: Power and Uses of Print in Early Modern Europe* (Cambridge: Polity Press, 1989)

R.W. Southern — *The Making of the Middle Ages* (London: Pimlico, 1993)

Jonathan Sumption — *Pilgrimage, An Image of Mediaeval Religion* (London: Faber & Faber, 2002)

Edward Syndicus — *Early Christian Art* (London: Burns and Oates, 1962)

Richard Temple — *Icons and the Mystical Origins of Christianity* (Shaftesbury: Element, 1990)

R.C. Trexler — *The Journey of the Magi: Meanings in History of a Christian Story* (Princeton, NJ: Princeton University Press, 1997)

Jacobus de Voragine — *The Golden Legend: Readings on the Saints*, transl. W.G. Ryan (Princeton, NJ: Princeton University Press, 2012)

Geoffrey Wainwright, Tucker Westfield and Karen Beth, eds. — *The Oxford History of Christian Worship (Oxford: Oxford University Press, 2008)*

Kurt Weizmann — *The Icon: Holy Images, Sixth to Fourteenth Century* (London: Chatto & Windus, 1978)

Kurt Weizmann — *The Age of Spirituality: Late Antique and Early Christian Art, Third to Seventh Century* (New York: Metropolitan Museum of Art, Exhibition catalogue, 1979)

K. Wessel — *Coptic Art* (London: Thames and Hudson, 1965)

Karl Young — *The Drama of the Medieval Church* (Oxford: Clarendon Press, 1933)

ONLINE

http://orthodoxartsjournal.org/the-recovery-of-the-arts-
pt.3-memory-of-the-heart

REFERENCE BOOKS

The Grove Encyclopedia of Medieval Art and Architecture,
ed. Colum P. Hourihane (Oxford: Oxford University Press,
2012)

The New Catholic Encyclopedia (New York: Robert
Appleton & Co.,1967)

Oxford Dictionary of the Christian Church, ed. E.A. Cross
and E.A. Livingstone (Oxford: Oxford University Press,
2005)

INDEX

ACKNOWLEDGEMENTS

Huge thanks to the most wonderful friends and to my family who have
helped all through the birth to this book. Their generous guidance,
inspiration, encouragement, support and promptings have sustained
my efforts and enriched the outcome.

Over many decades I have explored and researched images concerning the
Nativity of Christ. I am blessed with rich memories of travels in Europe and
the UK, visiting churches, galleries, museums and libraries, looking at statues,
carvings, paintings, metalwork, frescoes and manuscripts in pursuit of
works concerned with this inexhaustibly mysterious subject.

Then lockdown brought the unexpected benefit of time and relative isolation
in which to write, to read and to ponder. It provided intense nourishment
and allowed the opportunity to escape from the constraints and to
open to another world.

I am especially indebted to Serena Barrow, Rozzie Barda, Alice and Robin
Berkeley, Emily Lane (my brilliantly beady editor), Harriet Bridgeman,
Frances Butlin, Dom Edward Courbauld (who read the manuscript with the
knowledge of a theologian), Kit and Lyn Constable-Maxwell, Hettie Elgood,
Pat Feltham, Honora Furstenberg, Diana Johnson (whose enthusiasm and
eye for clarity and presentation were particularly helpful), Philippa Murphy,
Louise Mollo, Lydia and Peter Schmitt, my erudite mentor Neil Stratford,
Carl Strehlke, Dick Temple and Philadelphia Whittaker. Special thanks to
my son, Henry Wood, whose interest and unflagging patience, questions,
advice and suggestions throughout the process have been invaluable.

I am immensely grateful to Ian Strathcarron, Lucy Duckworth,
Anna Hopwood and Ramona Lamport at the Unicorn Publishing Group
for their expertise at every stage of publishing this book.